Practitioner Series

W0055416

Springer

London
Berlin
Heidelberg
New York
Barcelona
Budapest
Hong Kong
Milan
Paris
Santa Clara
Singapore
Tokyo

Other titles in this series:

Inji Wijegunaratne and George Fernandez

Distributed Applications Engineering

Building New Applications and Managing Legacy Applications with Distributed Technologies

Springer

Indrajit Wijegunaratne, BSc, MEng, MSc, PhD
inji@alphalink.com.au

George Fernandez, MSc
gfernandez@rmit.edu.au
Distributed Computing Research Group, PO Box 71, Royal Melbourne
Institute of Technology - Bundoora East Campus, Bundoora, Victoria 3083,
Australia

ISBN-13:978-3-540-76210-2

British Library Cataloguing in Publication Data
Wijegunaratne, Inji
    Distributed Applications Engineering : Building New Applications and
    Managing Legacy Application with Distributed Technologies -
    (Practitioner Series)
    1. Computer Engineering 2. Computer Architecture 3. Electronic Data
    Processing - Distributed Processing
    I. Title II. Fernandez , George
    621.3'9
    ISBN-13:978-3-540-76210-2   e-ISBN-13:978-1-4471-1550-2
    DOI: 10.1007/978-1-4471-1550-2

    Library of Congress Cataloging-in-Publication Data
    Wijegunaratne, Inji, 1952 -
        Distributed Applications Engineering : Building New Applications and
        Managing Legacy Applications with Distributed Technologies / Inji Wijegunaratne
        and George Fernandez.
        p.   cm. -- (Practitioner series)
        Includes bibliographical references.
        ISBN-13:978-3-540-76210-2 (pbk. : alk. paper)
        1. Electronic Data Processing - Distributed processing. 2. Application Software -
        Development. I. Fernandez, George, 1947- . II. Title. III. Series: Practitioner
        Series (Springer-Verlag)
    QA76.9.D5W55 1998   98-28535
    004'.36--dc21

Typesetting: Elaine Bingham, 30 Wentworth Road, Dronfield, UK.

34/3830-543210 Printed on acid-free paper

Contents

Part 3 – *Coupling and Dependency*

Part 4 – Distributed Computing and the Enterprise

Acknowledgements

We owe a large debt of gratitude to our colleagues who contributed to this endeavour. Our colleagues at "the Bank", senior technical managers at the Bank's IT division, were instrumental in developing Chapter 10, "Experiences in a Financial Institution". They were part of the driving force behind the initiative described in that chapter. We respect their wish to remain anonymous in the interests of maintaining the Bank's confidentiality. The material in that chapter lends a good deal of authority to what we say in this book, and we are sorry that we cannot acknowledge their contribution by name. Thanks also to Paul Taylor, who contributed Chapter 4, "The Three-Tier Architecture: An Object-Oriented Perspective". Paul's object-oriented perspective complements and enhances the three-tier architectural approach advocated in Chapter 3. We are very grateful to Springer-Verlag and Rebecca Moore of Springer-Verlag, for their interest and support for this endeavour.

I wish to thank Dilani, Niroshan and Arjuna, for their patience and support, and for generally putting up with a grumpy husband and father especially during the last few months of the book-writing process.

Inji Wijegunaratne

I wish to thank my students at the Royal Melbourne Institute of Technology, especially Maria Luz Munoz, for their help. Also a big thanks to my family, Maria, Lucia and Ramiro, for their patience and for sharing my computer with me.

George Fernandez

Authors and Contributors

Authors

Inji Wijegunaratne

Inji Wijegunaratne has over 17 years' experience in the IT industry, in technical, management, and consulting roles. Since 1990 he has specialized in client/server systems and distributed computing. He has consulted to several clients on distributed application architecture and has acted in consulting and technical management capacities in several client/server projects. Inji has published a number of papers and has organized and presented public seminars in client/server and distributed computing. He holds a Bachelor's degree in Electronic Engineering plus Masters and Doctoral degrees in Information Systems.

George Fernandez

George Fernandez holds a MSc from the University of Buenos Aires, Argentina. He has more than 20 years' IT experience in academic institutions, industry and government agencies, both in Argentina and Australia. George is currently a senior lecturer at the Royal Melbourne Institute of Technology, Australia, where he co-ordinates the Distributed Computing Research Group. He is active in the executive of the Australian Computer Society, and is the Australian director of the ACS and ACM university programming championships. His current interests in teaching and research are distributed systems engineering and information systems security.

Contributors

Paul Taylor

Paul has specialized in object-oriented software development for ten years, covering all aspects of the object-oriented development life cycle for a range of systems and applications. He has project managed the development of corporate software products, led a number of development teams, and delivered training courses on many aspects of object-oriented software technology. Paul holds a BSc (Hons) in Computer Science, a Graduate Diploma in Digital Communications, and a Master of Computing degree. He serves on the program committee of the TOOLS Pacific conferences and is Chairman of the Australian Computer Society's Object-Oriented Special Interest Group (OOSIG).

List of Abbreviations

ADI	Application Data Interchange
AIX	IBM's Implementation of UNIX
ANSI	American National Standards Institute
API	Application Programming Interface
AR	accounts receivable
ARPANET	Advanced Research Projects Agency Network
ATM	Asynchronous Transfer Mode
BPR	Business Process Re-engineering
BSD UNIX	Implementation of UNIX by University of California, Berkeley
CASE	Computer Aided Software Engineering
CCITT	Consultative Committee for International Telegraphy and Telephony
CICS	Customer Information and Control System
CLRR	Connectionless Request/Reply
COM	Component Object Model
CORBA	Common Object Request Broker Architecture
CS	Composite Services
DAS	Data Access Servers
DB	database
DBMS	database management system
DCE	Distributed Computing Environment
DDE	Dynamic Data Exchange
DLL	Dynamic Link Library
DTP	Distributed Transaction Processing
EBCDC	extended binary-coded decimal
EDA	Enterprise Data Access
EFTPOS	Electronic Funds Transfer Point of Sale
E-R modelling	Entity-Relationship modelling
ESQL	Embedded Structured Query Language
FAAR	Federated Application Architecture
FDDI	Fiber Distributed Data Interface
FTP	File Transfer Protocol
GI	General Insurance
GUI	Graphical User Interface
H/O	Head Office
HTML/CGI	Hypertext Markup Language

HP	Hewlett Packard
HP/UX	Hewlett Packard's Implementation of UNIX
IDL	Interface Definition Language
IG	Intelligent Gateways
IPX/SPX	Internet Packet Exchange/Sequenced Packet Exchange
ISO	International Standards Organization
IT	Information Technology
JDBC	Java Database Connectivity
L&P	Life and Pensions
LAN	Local Area Network
MIS	Management Information System
MOM	Message-Oriented Middleware
MQI	Message Queue Interface
MQSeries	IBM's Message-Oriented Middleware product
MVS	Multiple Virtual System
NFS	Network File System
NOS	Network Operating System
ODBC	Open Database Connectivity
OLE	Object Linking and Embedding
ORB	Object Request Broker
OSF	Open Software Foundation
OSI	Open Systems Interconnection
PARC	Palo Alto Research Centre (Xerox)
PL/SQL	Oracle's Implementation of SQL
POD	proof of delivery
QOH	quantity on hand
RAD	Rapid Application Development
RPC	Remote Procedure Call
SBAC	Systems Balancing and Control
SNA	System Network Architecture
SQL	Structured Query Language
TCP/IP	Terminal Control Protocol/Internet Protocol
UI	User Interface
UML	Unified Modelling Language
WAN	Wide Area Network

Part 1

Introduction and Background

1. *Introduction*

Over the past decade or so, distributed computing technologies and their applicability to information systems have evoked a great deal of interest. A confusing proliferation of products and capabilities – two-tier and three-tier client/server, middleware, remote procedure calls, request brokers, Web-browsers, applets, network computers, etc. – are available, technologies that position distributed computing as a major IT direction for the near and medium term.

It is generally agreed that information systems support the work of human beings achieving some purpose, in some organizational environment. If we acknowledge this view of systems – comprising of people, organizational context, purposeful action, and technology – then what is the role of technology? Especially in the realm of information technology, there is a factor, which can be termed "technology hand-waving". There is a ready, almost eager, embrace of technology as the solution – the new technology on the block is the answer to all problems. We have seen this phenomenon over and over in the history of the industry. 3GLs, 4GLs, databases, relational databases, RAD, CASE tools, two-tier client/server, three-tier client server, have all had their day as the silver bullet. This tendency, as common sense tells us and IT history bears out, is misguided: technology represents potential, and as capabilities of the technology changes so too does the potential it represents – opening new doors, closing existing doors and so on. However, the realization of this potential depends upon purposive actions of the human actors in the organizational context, in using the technology wisely, *in an informed fashion.*

This tendency in the industry is compounded by the lag between the appearance of a technology (or an allied set of technologies) in the IT marketplace and the emergence of principles and techniques for putting the technology to good use. Perhaps the only instance where the latter preceded the former was in the domain of relational databases, where Codd's theory of normalization made its way into the public domain before relational databases made their presence felt in the IT marketplace. The era to the late 1980s – the period that may be called the mainframe era – lasted for over thirty years or so. In this period, while technology underwent many changes so as to make the late 1980s information technologies virtually unrecognizable to a person in a 1950s time warp, techniques for application of technology made haste very slowly. Over this period, milestones were few: for example, structured programming, structured analysis and design, E-R modelling and normalization, object-oriented design and programming.

In this era though, what we might call the architectural paradigm for applications did not change in a revolutionary fashion. As we will observe in the "background" chapter (Chapter 2), mainframe-centric applications experienced a relatively evolutionary progression of capability during this period.

Beginning with the late 1980s, a new class of distributed computing products emerged and gained popularity and momentum. Some of these can be found in the area of the various forms of GUI client/server computing; some others such as middleware of different types (Remote Procedure Calls, Object Request Brokers, Messaging Middleware) provide services to the application. Technologies and infrastructure for supporting Web-based applications, Web Browsers and servers, applets, etc., is another area. Java and its ramifications both for Web-based and conventional computing is another interesting prospect. The 10 years since the late 1980s has seen a virtual flood of these technologies, and these technologies have played havoc with the trusted mainframe-centric architectural paradigm for applications. To complicate matters further, these capabilities have not pointed us to a single style to which we can turn as a replacement – rather, they have opened the door to several competing forms of application structure and behaviour, and of interaction between applications and application components. These forms can be loosely categorized into:

- the "traditional" two-tier and three-tier client/server – both the distributed object and the non object-oriented forms;
- Web-based application forms;
- the use of middleware to construct new structures for interaction between (legacy as well as modern) applications.

As we argued at the outset, technology represents opportunity. We should examine if, through these forms, applications constructed with these newer technologies have the capability to address important questions for the industry. For example:

- Responding rapidly to changing organizational requirements. Coping with change has been a major issue, hitherto not successfully resolved, in software engineering. Response to change typically has been slow and expensive. Do systems built with these new technologies offer potential in this important area?
- Typically in an organization there are a number of business processes with possibly a geographic distribution of activities, several foci of power, and user groups who value their autonomy. Computer-based systems that support them do not readily reflect the needs that spring from this kind of organizational reality. One of the factors that has contributed to the neglect of these wider organizational needs has been the standardization inherent in mainframe systems. With distributed computing technologies, it ought to be possible to include aspects of work organization and distribution in the design of the computer system, and to design applications exhibiting a model of interaction closely mirroring the behaviour of the enterprise.
- "Opportunity" is a double-edged sword. Together with new opportunities, technologies may bring with them the seeds of destruction for the unwary.

Recent evidence is beginning to show glimpses of the second edge of distributed computing technologies. Based on empirical studies and experience, the consensus among most leading industry analysts is that, in distributed computing environments, while the costs of the infrastructure is likely to go down, the costs of system management and support are likely to increase. Typically, in distributed environments, the cost of hardware represents a small part of the overall cost (typically in the region of 20 per cent). The other 80 per cent represents maintenance, integration, upgrade, support, training etc. Therefore, in comparing centralized (mainframe) versus distributed client/server computing, the costs break down differently; but there appears to be no overall cost advantage in the latter. Indeed, some studies have suggested that there could well be higher overall costs associated with systems employing these technologies. According to a recent Gartner Group analysis, over a five-year period client/server computing costs 70 per cent more than the mainframe equivalent (Duchessi *et al.*, 1998). Therefore, "good" applications constructed with these technologies should not only enhance the positives, but also restrict the negatives. Good applications should not leave the management of this predicted trend of ballooning systems management costs solely to better systems management products – they should be designed to resist this trend.

These then are some of the objectives for "good" applications in this new world. But what of principles and techniques for good applications?

Consistent with our experience of IT history, these principles lag the technology. The typical focus in the industry literature – capabilities of client/server and distributed computing development and infrastructure products, networking and connectivity issues – are all important and necessary, but *not sufficient* in themselves to bring about desired outcomes for the enterprise. It is the quality of the application, of course built upon an appropriate infrastructure, that makes the difference. We can use some of the strictures of modularity and abstraction etc. at system level, and structured programming at intra-module level; we may be able to extend or adapt (as will be seen later in this book) some of the principles from the mainframe era. But crucially, we need to recognize that systems need not (and often cannot) be implemented as a hierarchical set of interconnected software modules controlled by a mainframe-based central or root module. Different images, different understandings of the application software more appropriate to a distributed infrastructure need to emerge: for example, on what basis should we partition requirements into different modules of distributed application software? On what basis should we partition requirements between client and server components? How should we design the type of interactions between applications so that it optimally matches what is required by the business? How should we make the application structure best support the way that processes and work are distributed in the enterprise?

In this book, we make an effort to explore this territory, to develop and present generic application software structures that enable the realization of the opportunities of these technologies.

1.1   Aims and Objectives of this Book

To summarize, our primary concern in this book is to explore the different forms of application structure and behaviour that today's technology can sustain, and to determine criteria for designing and constructing "good" applications that occupy these forms.

We employ an architectural approach, a perspective that:

- describes systems at the highest level of software structure;
- describes generic forms or styles with which individual applications can comply.

We employ a dual focus in exploring the nature of "good" applications:

- the traditional software engineering stance, where we examine issues such as reuse, flexible deployment, modularity, containing "ripple" effects as well as component proliferation, and addressing some of the problems with mainframe systems;
- the perspective of the enterprise, where we analyze the role that distributed computing technology can play in the organization, map properties of application structure and behaviour to characteristics of the enterprise, and attempt to make the application structure best support the way that processes and work are distributed in the enterprise.

Our territory of interest covers two strata: the stratum of the individual application or group of related applications, where we focus on the three-tier client/server application architecture; the stratum of groups of applications supporting the processes of the enterprise, where we examine ways in which we can improve the interactions between applications – be they legacy applications or client/server applications – to better serve the enterprise.

1.2   Organization of Material

Following this introductory chapter, Chapter 2 contains topics that set the context for the main game. Under the context banner, we sketch the evolution of distributed computing to the form that we know and understand today, then discuss the definitional aspects of client/server and distributed computing, advance some concepts about the nature of an architectural approach to software, briefly survey the technology (briefly since this is primarily a book about software engineering principles) and finally, sketch some models of the enterprise. Chapter 3 is devoted to the three-tier client/server application architecture, where we introduce guidelines for partitioning application components, and consider issues of design and deployment. Chapter 4 discusses ways of designing three-tier compliant applications in an object-oriented environment. In Chapter 5, we extend the concepts of coupling to a distributed environment, and introduce the allied notion of dependency in Chapter 6. The focus of Chapter 7 is the analysis of different application architectures for a hypothetical business, and in Chapter 8 we introduce a new architectural form, the Federation, as a way in which groups of applications supporting an enterprise, or groups of applications representing a collaborating network of enterprises, can interact co-operatively. Chapter 9 describes an implementation of certain aspects of the Federation. The experience of a large financial institution with closely coupled systems, and their approach to a (Federation-like) solution is detailed in Chapter 10. Chapter 11 concludes this book.

1.3 Intended Readership

This book should be of interest to senior technical staff such as systems architects and technical managers, those employed or consulting at large companies. They should find the material on enterprise architecture particularly relevant.

In addition, in enterprises either contemplating or have already embarked upon a client/server or distributed computing direction, this book will be of interest to senior technical staff, who will find the material on three-tier architecture and design relevant. The subject matter will also appeal to project managers and software engineers involved with client/server projects, to whom the architecture and design principles will be relevant.

The book is not focused on a particular industry (manufacturing, finance, etc.) but on the proper use of distributed and client/server technologies in general, across industries.

The material here will also be relevant to academic staff in universities engaged in applied research and teaching, for example in Computer Science, Information Systems and Software Engineering Departments, and for upper undergraduate and postgraduate students.

2. Background and Context

This chapter aims to provide the reader with background and context information for the rest of the book. The chapter is organized into the following topic areas:

- the evolution of distributed computing;
- definitions of client/server and distributed computing;
- elements of an architectural approach;
- survey of client/server technologies;
- models of the enterprise.

Readers may, at a first reading, omit certain segments depending on their expertise and interests. A reader reasonably familiar with client/server computing technologies may omit at a first reading the segments on the evolution and definitions of client/server technologies. In the same vein, a reader whose main focus is the software architecture and design, and as a consequence not primarily interested in wider organizational issues, may omit the segment on models of the enterprise (apart from the definition of a task).

We recommend that the following segments should be read by all at a first reading, since they contain proposals/interpretations that we put forward that are drawn upon later in the book:

- elements of an architectural approach;
- definitions of client/server and distributed computing;
- models of the enterprise (the definition of a task).

2.1 Evolution of Distributed Computing

Evolution of Key Technologies up to the mid 1990s

1955–1970
In this era computing was an expensive resource – specifically when compared with humans – a resource needed to be carefully managed and optimized. Also, hardware was expensive compared to software. Economies of scale clearly supported centralization and optimization of computing resources, and work organized in batches was most efficient. The IT industry was very capital intensive and difficult to gain entry to because of the high capital requirements.

Large central facilities were the norm, such as UNIVAC, UNIVAC II and III, IBM 705 and 705 III, and IBM S/360, with large complements of physical maintenance administrations and operational staff, and specialized programmers developing applications in low level languages. Advances in technology such as increases in memory size and speed, on line disk storage, multiprogramming, seemed to reinforce economies of scale and centralization. The centralized installation with batched workloads was the dominant mode of organization.

1970–1980
This era is characterized by a number of trends:

- Development of on-line access. The development of on-line access in the commercial computing arena resulted in the development of transaction processing systems. Interactive time sharing systems gradually became a more economic proposition and therefore more popular. As computing became cheaper, on-line processing could be justified for transactions of increasingly lower economic value.
- Development of efficient and capable mid-sized computers. Smaller (mid-range) machines (DEC, Data General, Hewlett-Packard) became cheaper and found important niches, specifically using the advancements in communications technology (see below) to advocate interconnected machines as an alternative to the centralized model. By the end of this era, mid-sized machines, excellent for supporting clusters of around 16 to 32 simultaneous users, were growing in popularity. The development of peripherals of mid capacity, such as printers and storage units, strengthened the mid-range segment. The computer industry itself was becoming easier to enter, and the number of players in the industry rapidly increased.
- Emergence of communications technology. In the communications area, network architectures such as IBM's SNA and DEC's DECNet were made available and work on OSI (Open Systems Interconnection) commenced. These advances laid the technological foundation for the marriage of communication with computing.

The reduction of the price of hardware and the importance that enterprises started to give to computer supported business activities resulted in an important change from previous eras: some forms of human work, especially software development, became more expensive than computing time.

During this period, a number of research developments that had a profound influence on distributed computing occurred at Xerox Palo Alto Research Center (PARC). Research that led to Ethernet, the first commercial local area network (LAN), the development of Alto, the first single-user workstation, file and print servers, as well as graphical user interfaces all occurred here.

Also, work crystallized on distributed extensions to the UNIX operating system, initially a multi-user centralized operating system. The first distributed extension to UNIX was the development (at University of California, Berkeley) in the 1970s of support for inter-process communication. In the next decade, Sun Microsystems, a workstation manufacturer, working with Berkeley BSD UNIX as a starting point, developed NFS, the popular distributed Network File System. In the academic world, a number of the research efforts on distributed operating systems used UNIX as a base; examples include Amoeba, Mach and Andrew. The Kerberos system for security in distributed computing was developed at the Massachusetts Institute of Technology.

The development of the specific communication technology that makes possible the communication linkage between application components residing at different geographic locations also has its roots in this era. The first successful experiments with a packet switching network occurred with the ARPANET in 1969. Here, a store and forward mechanism with a host-centric model was used. ARPANET has now evolved to Internet, which has its own network architecture that can be described as based on a simplified OSI model. Metcalf and Bloggs, based on research done at Xerox PARC, suggested in 1976 a very different network topology to the host-centric one (the norm of that era), where the full resources of the network were to be available to every desktop. This model became Ethernet, the first local area network to be commercially available. Token ring, the other major type of LAN topology, was introduced by IBM in the mid 1980s. Equally important to communication between geographically dispersed computer resources is a network architecture, an ordered group of protocols that facilitate such communication. The most important of this era were:

- The entrance of SNA into the commercial domain, introduced by IBM in the mid 1970s to serve as an umbrella framework accommodating many different protocols. SNA recognizes nodes and links: nodes, which are addressable, are hosts, communication controllers, and control units. Links connect SNA nodes.
- OSI, the model of the ISO (International Standards Organization) and CCITT (Consultative Committee for International Telegraphy and Telephony) of a networking architecture. OSI grew out of a need to establish a standard, non proprietary, network architecture that would be a framework to interconnect proprietary computers. The OSI effort began in the 1970s and continues to this day.

1980–Late 1980s
In this era, the cost of computing dropped rapidly, with the rate of price/ performance improvement for smaller systems being faster than that for larger systems. Mid-range machines were seen to be as capable and reliable as mainframes, so sometimes rather than expanding large machines capacity, mid-range machines were acquired. Significantly, the first microprocessors became available in the late 1970s/early 1980s but in these early days, there was some confusion as to their proper place and function.

These developments led to two main models of distribution:

- cooperating clusters of mid-range machines;
- mainframe plus satellite (departmental) mid-range machines where functions from large systems could be off-loaded to the smaller ones.

Personal computing, one of the major forces which originated in this era, came to catalyze the move towards distributed computing. There were two milestones in the popularization of the PC and the creation of a mass market for PCs, both of which occurred in this era. One was the introduction of the mouse-based Graphical User Interface (GUI) technology by Apple. The second was the advent of the IBM PC, which opened the PC to the corporate and business computing sector. Windows, Microsoft's GUI designed to run on top of its well-known DOS operating system, appearing (in the late 1980s) much later than the Apple version nevertheless became the market leader and the centrepiece for running desktop software.

Another major development, again originating out of Xerox PARC, was the development of the Remote Procedure Call (RPC), a mechanism by which a program can treat a procedure located at a different node in the network in a similar manner to a local procedure. The seminal reference to RPC is Birrell and Nelson (1984). RPC and RPC-like mechanisms are employed in most of today's distributed processing products.

The network operating system (NOS) is another significant development that emerged in this era. With the advent of the Ethernet and Token Ring LAN topologies the need arose to provide some measure of control over the sharing of resources in the network. The network operating system provided this capability, where the shared resources (a file system, a printer) are managed by *servers*, while *client* machines request services from the servers. Client and server interaction over the LAN is managed by the network operating system, which typically has a component on the client machine and another on the server machine.

Late 1980s–Mid 1990s
Products and capabilities that supported distributed computing as we know it today began to emerge in this era. There were several previous advances that underpinned the development of these products and capabilities.

- The emergence of network operating systems as accepted and popular products. The better known of LAN NOSs of this period were Novell Netware, and Banyan VINES. Microsoft Windows NT, functioning both as a server and as a LAN network operating system, was introduced in the mid 1990s.
- Development of RPC-type mechanisms and the commercial availability of products with these capabilities.
- The emergence of *de facto* and *de jure* standards that facilitate interconnection and communication between heterogeneous computing resources connected via a network (IPX/SPX, TCP/IP, DDE, DLL, OLE, ODBC) etc.
- At the application level, the emergence of SQL (Structured Query Language) as a vehicle for communication. The vendors of SQL databases, such as Oracle and Informix, invested in their products the capability to accept SQL commands from remote sources (usually PCs) transmitted across the network.

It is in this era that the terms "client" and "server" took hold. In the industry, client and server terminology originated (towards the latter part of the previous era) with networked PC systems, which share file and printing resources. The server was usually a powerful PC that managed requests for use of the resource from clients, other PCs on the network. In these configurations, networked PCs accessed PC-based file and print servers, sharing applications (contained in the shared files), data, printers etc. across the network. Today, this mode of operation is standard in the typical LAN environment.

The next class of product to use the client/server label was the database-oriented, mainly the SQL-based, client/server product. These products enabled (usually) PC-based client software to communicate with database servers using SQL commands. The database server may be housed in a high-end PC, UNIX machine, or a mainframe at some network node.

Another class of products and capabilities emerged, which at the application level is not restricted to the use of SQL commands as the means of communication between client and server. These include the standards-based Distributed Computing Environment (DCE), distributed transaction processing products such as Tuxedo, CICS in IBM environments, and Encina, and messaging products such as IBM's MQ Series. These products provide programmers with an Application Programming Interface (API) with which it is possible to establish different forms of communication, RPC-type, messaging, or transactions between different computers.

On the hardware front, the distinct three-tier structure of small, mid-range, and mainframe machines became blurred; newer, more powerful PC operating systems such as IBM OS/2 and Windows NT having multi-tasking capabilities, and with mainframes using parallel multiprocessor architectures. UNIX-based machines moved to dominate the mid-range market, but PC operating systems began to migrate to the mid-range area (notably with DEC beginning to offer Windows NT on its Alpha machines).

In networking, network technologies were made available that enabled the construction of LANs from the basic 10 Mbits/sec to (with Fiber Distributed Data Interface – FDDI) 100 Mbits/sec. Technologies such as ISDN for wide area networks enabled high speed point to point communication, and provided support for integrating voice and data. Also, Asynchronous Transfer Mode (ATM) technology began to do away with the distinction between the LAN and WAN, providing an integrated high speed voice, data and video communication channel to the desktop.

Development of Distributed Computing to the Mid 1990s

From 1955 to 1970 the exclusive processing paradigm was of centralized computing; distributed computing, even as a concept, was yet to make its mark in the IT industry. By the mid 1970s some installations showed the first signs of distributed processing, such as local editing and remote batch processing, where remote terminals or minicomputers carry out some operations independently and when necessary communicate with the mainframe in batch mode.

From the late 1970s to the early 1980s three configurations of "distributed processing" arose, based on possible interconnection structures (Breslin and Tashenberg, 1978):

1. The Star Structure: the terminals are located remotely from the central installation, and are connected to the centre via modems.
2. Hierarchical Distribution: one or more remote locations have their own minicomputers, and the relevant peripherals. These locations connect to the centre via leased telephone lines. The remote locations periodically transmit required summary data (sales, expenses, inventory balances etc.) to the centre.
3. Ring Distributed Network: a number of autonomous computers linked in a peer-to-peer fashion.

Martin's (1981) discussion of distributed computing of the day contains some useful insights. Based on this and other commentaries of the era, the significant types and features of "distributed computing" of the day are summarized below.

1. Function Distribution: where some functions are distributed, but not the capability to fully process an entire transaction. Function distribution employs intelligent terminals or intelligent controllers to carry out message editing, screen formatting, data collection, dialogue with terminal operators, some security functions, message compaction or concentration.
2. Centrally Controlled Distributed Processing: peripheral small processors, which may be able to completely process some transactions, but are subordinate to a higher level computer.
3. Integrated Systems: separate systems, but with integrated design of the data in the different systems, and possibly also of the programs.
4. Non-Integrated Systems: systems of independent design (under the control of different management, containing different application programs, data stored having no common design), which are connected by a computer network. The connection allows systems to send entire transactions to one another, or for users of one system to use programs of another.

In terms of machine relationships, horizontal distribution – peer-coupled systems – was possible. So was vertical distribution, where there is a hierarchy of processors associated with the distribution and processing. In the latter case, a transaction may enter the system at the lowest level, and may have certain functions (such as editing) attended to at subordinate levels. The highest level is likely to provide access to on-line files or a database.

Several forms of division of data were also possible:

- Hierarchical data: a simple hierarchical arrangement where an extract from a higher level machine is kept in a lower level machine, or a more complex one where the higher level machine is periodically updated with a summarized edited and composite version of data from lower level machines.
- Partitioned data: where the data structure is held in different locations (records for customers of area A in area A's machine and so on) or replicated data, where multiple copies of the same data are stored in different locations.
- Separate data: where different data structures in different locations form an integrated system; for example production, purchasing, and general accounting systems with their own data being in separate machines. There

were mechanisms for transfer of relevant data, usually as file transfers. Alternatively a user may be able to connect to any one machine.

The period of the mid to late 1980s represented a major shift in the understanding of, and the "art of the possible" with distributed processing. Lorin (1988), surveying distributed computing of that era identifies four types of structural and interconnection configurations. These resemble the beginnings of what we now understand to be the capabilities of distributed computing.

1. A mainframe connected with personal computers. Here, selected functions or applications are off loaded from the mainframe into the PCs.
   - For example implementing spreadsheets, local databases without reference to the mainframe, word processing on the PC.
   - The mainframe supports the mainframe applications, mail, provides the source of background data and a pathway for access to fast and high quality printers.
2. Personal computers connected to a mid-range machine, which in turn, is connected to the mainframe. In this scenario, the mid-range machine represents a departmental level of computing.
   - As in the previous alternative, PC users use the mid-range as the backup for data, and source of applications for departmental computing.
   - The departmental machine passes data to the mainframe, which is concerned with enterprise level processing.
   - Both forms 1 and 2 have some hierarchical character. There is a clear root of the configuration, and as one moves towards the root an increase in power, function, and possibly control is implied.
3. A connection of peers. The peers may be mainframes, mid-range machines, or personal computers. The details of their interconnection and dependency may differ dramatically, but there is no obvious central point of control.
4. A collection of peer hierarchies. The connected peers may be mainframes or mid-range machines, or PCs. In the former two, each peer exhibits a hierarchical configuration, connected to a collection of "lower level" machines. The technology to support networked PCs exists, and networked print and file server configurations are now available.

Around the late 1980s, the industry underwent a significant change in its perception of distributed computing, giving birth to what we now understand and accept as distributed computing.

Until the early 1970s the exclusive paradigm of computing was the centralized one. Distributed computing was a very limited affair; intelligent terminals performing local editing, or different systems, each relatively autonomous, periodically communicating with each other – indeed, a design feature of these systems was their ability to operate autonomously in case of a failure.

Through the following decade, more sophisticated systems along the same lines were designed. Some of the functions, but not the capability to process an entire transaction, were able to be distributed. When functions are described as distributed in a hierarchical distributed arrangement, the functions relate to those necessary to prepare and route messages through the network (not to functions at the application level), plus some editing functions. Also, while transactions could be routed from machine to machine, *a transaction was serviced at a single location*. As regards the division of data, there was a high relative autonomy of the configurations; thus, systems built around these structures of data were relatively independent, communicating with another on a periodic basis.

The use of transaction processing was at the time widespread, but a transaction, while it may be directed through different machines to its ultimate location, was served at a single node in the network.

In all these systems, there is no evidence of any overarching control, that is, some form of overall control as a practical requirement for distributed computing of the day. Towards the end of this era, instances of master/slave configurations were common, as were instances of machines operating autonomously but cooperating, for example, to transfer files.

Until the late 1980s, the industry picture of distributed computing occupied a spectrum from separate, geographically dispersed applications cooperating with each other, to a single application formed by the cooperation of geographically dispersed but relatively independent, standalone, component programs (see Figure 2.1(a)). Distributed computing progressed during this period from the former end of the spectrum in the mid 1970s to cover the whole spectrum by the late 1980s. The aim by the late 1980s was the construction of a geographically dispersed application.

(a) Distributed Computing Pre Late 1980s

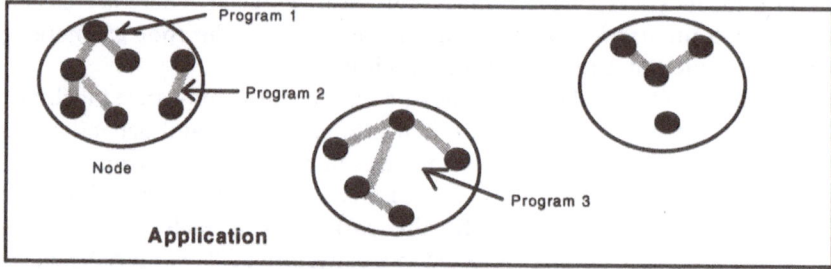

(b) Distributed (Client/Server) Computing Today

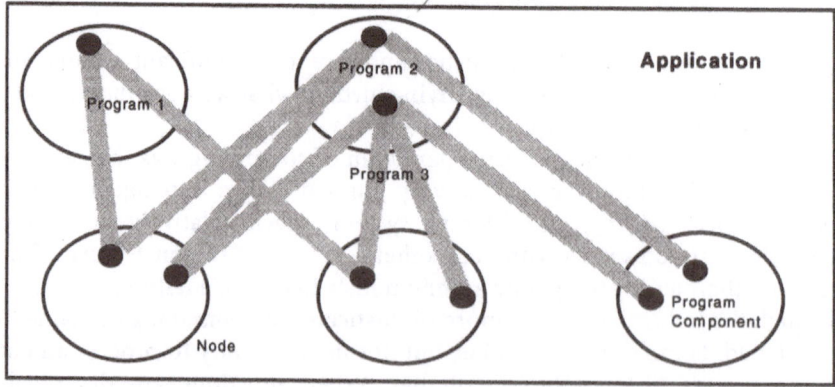

Figure 2.1: An application and its programs

Thus by the late 1980s, the capability existed to have a single application distributed across several sites or nodes; however, each site contained one or more individual programs. The seeds of the next step were evident in this era, mostly in PC networks. The file server for example was the forerunner of today's database server, where the interface between a program and its data is distributed.

Products with RPC and RPC-like capabilities found their way to the market, and capabilities such as IBM's program-to-program communication protocol (LU 6.2) were available, taking the granularity of distributed control a notch lower to have multiple control points cooperating on the sub-tasks of a fragmented task, enabling *functions of a single "program" to be distributed across the network* (see Figure 2.1(b)).

SQL-based client/server products are currently the most popular implementation of this phenomenon, with the requesting program and the database located at two different network nodes. The SQL command is transmitted across the network, translated, and processed at the database end; the results are routed back. Alternatively, with a stored procedure a message containing its identifier is transmitted across the network; on receipt at the database the procedure is invoked. In both these instances processing occurs at two nodes, with what is akin to the main procedure executing at the user's PC, and what is akin to a sub-program executing at the database end. This is extended further by products such as DCE, which makes possible to call several remote procedures residing at different network locations from a main procedure. Furthermore, the developer needs only to know that these functions are located remotely; not the actual location of each function. Distributed transaction processing systems go a step further: what is a single atomic transaction to the user can be part serviced at different network nodes. For example, debiting an account can be done at one location, and the corresponding credit at the other.

Therefore, today, the components of a program can be successfully distributed, or more correctly, processing components at different network nodes can cooperate dynamically to mimic a single program that satisfies some user need.

Figure 2.2 (based upon Enslow, 1991), presents a basis upon which to discuss this change. This figure shows five dimensions of decentralization and, over the years, the degree of distribution achieved along each.

2.2 Distributed and Client/Server Computing

Since the late 1890s, a large number of products with the "client/server" label have emerged, and the use of this term has become pervasive. However, the client/server landscape has become a complex and confusing one, characterized by products with a range of functionality and varying claims by vendors.

Client/Server Computing

In a client/server system, all shared resources (hardware components such as printers, and disks to software defined components such as files and data) are held and managed by *server processes*. *Client processes* issue requests to servers

	Mid 1970s	Late 1980s	Today		Future
Degree of decentralization of application	Multiple cooperating applications	Single application distributed across sites	Single application distributed across sites		Single application on virtual node
Degree of decentralization of programs	Individual programs at each application site	Individual programs at each application site	Single virtual 'program' distributed across sites		Single virtual 'program' on on virtual node
Degree of decentralization of data	Separate data sources	Separate data sources	Separate data sources	Single virtual data source distributed across sites	Single virtual data source on virtual node
Perception of geographic dispersion	Collection of individual nodes	Collection of individual nodes	Collection of individual nodes →		Single virtual node
Degree of decentralization of control	Fixed master/ slave Dynamic master/ slave	Replicated autonomous	Multiple control points, cooperating on sub-tasks of a task →		Multiple, fully cooperating control points

Figure 2.2: Distributed computing capability in the commercial arena

whenever they need access to a shared resource; if the request is valid, the server performs the requested action and sends back a reply. This definition of client/server computing, as server processes managing shared resources, and client processes making requests to and receiving replies from them, is a commonly agreed position.

The origins of the client/server revolution go back to file and print servers. Indeed these file and print sharing capabilities are standard in today's LAN-based environments. With these capabilities, an entire file traverses the network. Today, the term "client/server" or "client /server application" is commonly employed for capabilities where only the requested data traverses the network. In addition to the granularity, the underlying infrastructure (providing capabilities such as formatting, routing, API interfaces) enables clients and servers to cooperate dynamically to allow distributed computation, analysis and presentation.

Sinha (1992) lists the following features of a client/server system:

- a client process interacts with the user, and presents the user interface;
- multiple clients and multiple servers can exist within one client/server system;
- a client process communicates with a server process via queries or commands;
- a server provides *services* to a client; while a server *responds* to queries or commands from the client, it does not initiate a conversation with a client;

- servers may communicate with each other to provide a service to a client, but this (if it occurs) is done without the knowledge of the client.

In the execution of a single request, the requester plays the client role and the recipient or provider the server role, *for the duration of the request*. Although this interaction-based behaviour exists, the current convention, especially in commercial systems and products, is to label client and server components on their predominant behaviour over time. Examine the distributed application in a client/server environment. It contains shared resources (data sources, printers, etc.) managed by software. The application also contains software that interacts with the users of the application. *Over time*, software managing shared resources will *predominantly receive requests, attend to them, and send replies – play the server role.* This software may, on occasion (perhaps in response to a client request), issue a request to another server, but the predominant role over time is that of receiving and attending to requests. The place to locate such a software module is a shared hardware platform: a high-end PC, a UNIX machine, or mainframe. Equally, the overall support of the user's business task, including the presentation logic, needs to be vested in the software that interacts with the user. Therefore, *over time*, software interacting with the user will *predominantly send requests and receive replies – play the client role.* This software may contain the capacity to receive unsolicited replies such as broadcast messages; but the predominant role is that of sending requests and receiving replies. The obvious place to locate such a software module is the user's hardware platform: the PC or the workstation. Hence the labelling of PC-based components of the application responsible for user interaction (and allied functionality) as client components, and shared, server-based components as server components; hence also the capability for server components to interact with other servers (usually in response to a client request), without suffering an identity crisis.

Models of Client/Server Computing
In the industry, we often hear the terms two-tier and three-tier client/server. The term two-tier is perhaps the better understood. In the beginning, there was two-tier – the original client/server computing products supported the following type of configuration.

- A network, usually a LAN, connecting several PCs to a larger machine, a server.
- The entire application executes in client memory (PC). The executable is located at the PC or at the server, which in the latter case is available to the PC as a remote drive.
- The database is typically located at the server, the application makes database calls using a remote connection to the database via the LAN.

This type of configuration is now termed two-tier, or to be more precise, "two-tier fat client". This two-tier model, although fit for MIS type applications, is now regarded as being unsuitable for enterprise operational computing. Some of its main drawbacks are:

- A model that restricts all network interactions to database calls is not conducive to network efficient application design. Especially where the need arises to transcend the single LAN, for configurations encompassing LAN and WAN arrangements, the performance tends to become unacceptably slow.
- The PC platform does not provide adequate security for the requirements of most operational systems. In addition, two-tier application development environments did not provide the robustness (nor in some cases the processing sophistication) necessary for operational systems.
- The cost of administration of PCs has the potential to grow out of control as the user base grows, since individual PCs tend to be the focus of administration.

The next generation of technologies enabled the application to overcome these limitations, transcend the LAN, and provide support for an organization's main operational processes. Essentially, these products enable the partitioning of the application so that components of the application are located remote to each other. "Middleware" (and supporting services such as directory services) provide the capability for these distributed components to talk to each other.

This gives a great deal of flexibility to the application designer, to partition the application to house application software components at the most appropriate location for their function. The three-tier model provides us with the tools to potentially address the shortcomings of the two-tier model. *With good design,*

- we can now develop network-efficient applications, since we have the capability to contain data intensive network traffic to high-bandwidth areas of the network;
- security, performance, and robustness considerations can be addressed because we can house application components at appropriate locations;
- PC-based administration costs (while still needing attention and strategies for control) is much less of an issue, since we now have the capacity to make the client "thin".

Good design is key. Although the technology exists, and its potential extolled loudly in vendor literature, there is still confusion as to what the three tiers are – that is, how best to partition the application.

For example, the three tiers have been variously described as:

- user interface/business rules/database;
- client applications/application services/data services;
- presentation/application/data;
- client front ends/application servers/resource manager servers;
- graphical user interface/application business logic/data access functions;
- client/departmental server/enterprise mainframe.

Furthermore, we have observed some references to the three tiers as physical, that is, machine-based, tiers. Some other references have implied that they are logical ones. It is obvious that the touted benefits of three-tier applications cannot be realized without proper design; the questions of the scope and content of the tiers, the partitioning principles for the application, issues of appropriate deployment are crucial to success. This is the aim of Part 2, where we present principles of three-tier application architecture.

Distributed Computing

There is considerable overlap in the IT industry usage of the terms "client/server" and "distributed computing". The latter term though, tends to be used more often in discussions of infrastructure environments such as Distributed Computing Environment (DCE) and Common Object Request Broker Architecture (CORBA) providing services that enable application components to be distributed. The focus of this book is the application, and our usage depends on the context. In Part 2, we focus on the application – either the single application or related groups. Here we use terms "client/server", "distributed client/server" and "distributed computing" synonymously to refer to applications whose components can be distributed across network nodes. In Part 4, the focus shifts to the enterprise, where we concentrate on how we configure such groups of applications, draw boundaries around them, and how such groups communicate with each other.

The main attributes that an environment supporting distributed, dynamically cooperating application components should possess, as elucidated in the literature, are summarized below. These capabilities can be regarded as services that the application – and the application designer – may employ. The reader will find that these capabilities are more likely to be available with the more function-rich distributed computing environments such as DCE and CORBA-compliant ORBs. The standard client/server development product may provide some of these services; some may provide interface access to DCE, CORBA or equivalent for these services. This list of attributes is a useful yardstick to assess the distributed capabilities of a client/server development product.

Access and Security
Access, or global access, is the ability of the environment to offer the same functions to the user regardless of the user's location. From a security standpoint, security in a distributed system includes three main aspects:

- Access control – for every resource, and for every operation on that resource, identities of the allowed requesters should be known, so that every request can be checked.
- Authentication – for every request, the identity of the requester must be reliably ascertained.
- Auditing – the facility should exist to log every operation if desired.

Concurrency and Maintenance of Consistency
Concurrency is a natural occurrence in a distributed environment. At the user end, where a user can execute several requests to one or more servers at the same time, and at the server, where each server can respond to different requests from clients at the same time. Consequently, consistency issues can arise either as normal consequences of concurrency and distribution, or because of abnormal activity such as system crashes.

Fault Tolerance (Availability)
Redundancy and recovery are the two main approaches to solve this problem. An example of redundancy in the design of fault tolerant computers is the "hot standby" machine. In a distributed system, however, fault tolerance can be implemented at a finer grain, by replicating critical servers or server functions.

Heterogeneity and Transparency
A distributed system is a collection of heterogeneous components. An essential feature is transparency, the ability for the system to provide a consistent image to users to conceal from them the separation of these components. ISO's Reference Model for Open Distributed Processing defines eight forms of transparency:

1. Access – no distinction between local and remote operations.
2. Location – access to resources without knowledge of location.
3. Concurrency – concurrent use of shared resources by several users.
4. Replication – users/application programs need not have knowledge of any replication of shared resources including databases and data.
5. Failure – users completing tasks despite failure of system components.
6. Migration – movement of objects without affecting users/application programs.
7. Performance – system reconfiguration as loads vary.
8. Scaling – changes of scale in the environment does not require changes to the application structure.

It is acknowledged that meeting all these criteria is difficult. Two of the most important are access and location transparency, sometimes grouped together as *network transparency*, a feature that provides a level of anonymity for shared resources akin to that found in a centralized system.

Inter-process Communication
A distributed system contains components that are both logically and physically separate. They must communicate with each other reliably and efficiently in order to present a consistent, transparent image to the user. Communication can involve the transfer of data, as well as of synchronization intelligence. The Remote Procedure Call is a common implementation mechanism.

Naming
The shared resources of the system must be named. Unlike in a single system however, the domain of the name must be global, that is, the overall system should deal with named entities without room for ambiguity or misinterpretation. Separation of physical and logical names is useful to preserve attributes such as scalability and transparency, and it is desirable to delay the binding between the two to be as close to execution time as possible.

Openness
By its nature, a distributed environment can contain many interfaces. For the system to be open, it must be possible to find out about interface connection details, so it is important that these interfaces are *published*. While desirable, it is

not essential, however, that the interfaces follow industry standards, since official standardization is cumbersome and takes time.

Scalability

Systems often have to be scaled up as the demand for them increases. There are two basic strategies to solve the problem of demand on a shared resource: increase the capacity of the resource, or replicate the resource. In a distributed environment it is possible to replicate with better results than in a centralized one, by replicating the shared resources of the system – memory, processors, storage, printers, databases. While this replication strategy is much more viable than in a centralized system, there are certain limitations:

- As the system grows, other aspects of the system such as system management can become a constraining force.
- External rules and conditions can impose limitations on replication of components. For example, while it may be technically feasible to replicate corporate data, in practice it may not be allowed or be unwise to do so. Data entities usually have complex relationships, which the applications will need to maintain. This can make applications very difficult to write.

Resource Sharing and Management

Shared resources exist both in centralized and distributed environments. In a distributed environment, however, a shared resource must be managed by a program with a communications interface (a *resource manager)* so that the resource can be reliably accessed and manipulated.

Also, a distributed system can contain a multiplicity of shared resources (plus resource users) scattered across the network. The human systems manager managing this must be provided with the tools to monitor and regulate a large collection of geographically dispersed components of different type.

2.3 An Architectural Approach

Application Architecture

We can describe as the "architectural level", the highest level of representation of software structure. Pressman (1994) states that the architectural level defines the relationship among the major structural components of the system. Others put forward similar views: for example, the architectural level:

- pertains to the gross structure of a software system represented as a high-level organization of computational elements and interactions between those elements (Garlan and Perry, 1995);
- deals with system organization and system-level properties (Shaw, 1995);
- contains a system structure that consists of active modules, a mechanism to allow interaction among these modules, and a set of rules that govern the interaction (Boasson, 1995).

This is not a contentious or controversial perspective. Boasson (1995), for example, maintains that the definition of the architectural level as being concerned with the organization of and the interaction between high-level software modules is now generally accepted.

The term software or application architecture has a further connotation – that of an *architectural form or style*. An architectural style defines constraints on the form and structure of a family of architectural instances (Garlan and Perry, 1995; Perry and Wolf, 1992; Abwod *et al.*, 1993). In other words, an architectural style is a representation, at this highest level of description, of a *generic* structure – the software concept analogous to the Georgian architecture or the Victorian architecture. Just as the latter connote distinctive forms or styles, so would software architectural forms. Just as an architectural design of a proposed building may conform to Georgian architecture, so could a particular systems design comply with a certain software architectural form. Associated with a particular architectural form would be a set of architectural principles; principles of structure and behaviour of the software components visible at this high level, principles that define the members of the family of software instances – the individual systems compliant with the architectural style. This is the view that we take in this book. To summarize:

- the architectural level is the highest level representation of software structure;
- there is the *architectural form* or *style* on the one hand, and the *architectural instance* on the other. The architectural style defines a family of instances. The instance is a particular design (or construction) of a system that is *compliant with* the principles associated with the style.

While Shaw (1995), Boasson (1995), and Garlan and Perry's (1995) domain of interest encompasses large software systems in general, the focus of interest of this book is narrower, covering the computer-based applications of an enterprise's information system. We use the term "application architecture" or "software architecture" to refer to the macro level structure and organization of computer-based applications supporting the operations and decision processes of an enterprise.

Within this scope, a software architectural style can draw upon the following:

- While an architectural style should not be dependent on a particular product, it can nevertheless presuppose certain generic product or technology capabilities. For example, a distributed architectural style may assume certain types of infrastructure capability that make possible specific types of communication and interaction between distributed application components. For instance, for an architectural style we propose later in this book, we use Message-Oriented Middleware as a major conduit of information exchange.
- A software architecture may make certain premises about its domain of applicability. For example, a software architecture for an enterprise may need to recognize and support generic features of the enterprise – such as its structure and organization. We do not imply by this that the wider aspects of the enterprise milieu – such as manual procedures, informal groupings and

their communication (Giddens, 1984), organizational politics, power and its impact (Davenport *et al.*, 1992) – are *within* the software or application architecture; we deliberately avoid the use of the term "information systems architecture" for this reason. We merely maintain that an enterprise application architecture that recognizes and supports these facets of organizational reality is better suited to the enterprise than one that does not.

We believe that this type of architecture can render a great deal of assistance to IT professionals: first, it is consistent with the emerging trend to provide domain-specific, reusable, frameworks and component technologies (Garlan and Perry, 1995; Lewis, 1995). Secondly, it has the potential to be a clarifying force in today's IT environment, which presents to the IT professional a plethora of opportunities brought about by new technology/product capabilities. In this context, an architecture has many benefits:

- It provides a "comfort factor" – the knowledge that someone has been there before, understood the pitfalls, and cleared a path for those who follow.
- An architecture makes for cheaper entry –
  - it reduces the initial costs of investigation and feasibility, setup, training and familiarization;
  - it can provide a basis for the initial planning and organizing the project(s).
- An architectural approach reduces the costs of development and maintenance–
  - the family of compliant applications that an architectural style relates to not only should resemble the architectural form, but also should be "good" applications in some defined sense. That is, the architectural style should contain principles for developing "good" compliant applications;
  - makes for "template" or "framework" based development; each new compliant program or application typically need not be built completely from scratch. Based on an architectural style we can build a framework, an intermediate point that can serve as the superstructure for individual compliant applications.

Figure 2.3 illustrates the context of the application architecture. Ideally, the components of Figure 2.3 relate to each other in the following manner. A template or framework for the applications is predicated upon the application architecture and the available infrastructure. The individual applications then leverage off these components. The design of an individual application is compliant with the architecture and uses the superstructure that a pre-existing framework affords. The application is built upon the capabilities and interfaces that the infrastructure provides. The infrastructure capabilities are in turn selected and constructed around a technology architecture. In the same manner that an application architecture includes principles of "good" application design, a technology architecture should include principles of "good" infrastructure design.

In this book we focus upon the left side of Figure 2.3, application architecture and design; in the process, we touch briefly on frameworks. We present two application architectural styles, the three-tier client/server architecture, and the Federated enterprise architecture. The term "three-tier" is now a common one in

IT circles, but there is a lack of clarity as to what the three tiers are: we specify a three-tier structure, and develop a set of principles for partitioning application components into the three tiers. The Federated architecture is an enterprise-wide architecture, suitable for managing sets of groups or applications.

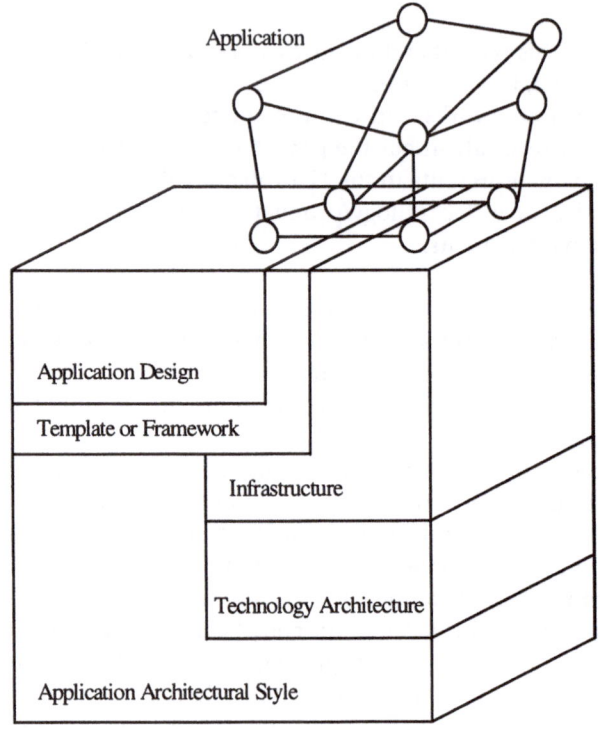

Figure 2.3: Application architecture in context

2.4   Elements of a Technology Architecture

A component of Figure 2.3 illustrating the context of the application architecture shown in that discussion was the technology architecture. The infrastructure upon which the application is built is predicated on this technology architecture. In the following pages, we survey components of a technology architecture. We do not build a technology architecture, which should include well-justified architectural forms as well as principles of design and construction – such is not the aim of this book. Rather, we use the component typology of a technology architecture to survey required capabilities, to set another aspect of the context for our main theses.

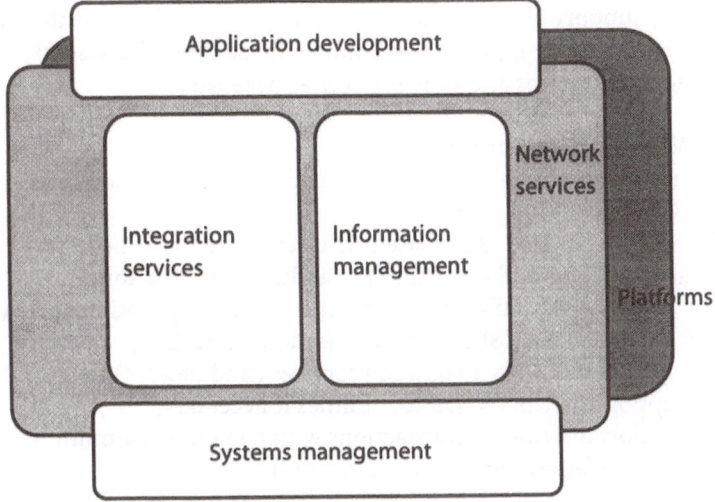

Figure 2.4: Elements of a technology architecture

Architecture Constituents

The main constituents of a technology architecture, as depicted in Figure 2.4, are:

Capabilities for Application Development
These are products enabling the building of distributed client/server applications. Some of the key characteristics sought are:

- GUI capabilities at the client; client and server environments powerful enough to support application logic;
- ability to hide complexities of underlying – integration service, O/S, network – environments from developers;
- capabilities for Rapid Application Development (RAD), prototyping, incremental development and testing, simulation of clients (server software) and servers (client software).

Integration Services
These are products that provide the infrastructure for different, possibly physically distributed, application components (and application groups) to work together; commonly termed *middleware*. Key characteristics are:

- provide a call (or message) interface to client and server application components that hides location and implementation details;
- support necessary routing and translation;
- if necessary, provide store and forward and guaranteed delivery services;
- support synchronous /asynchronous messaging as necessary;
- if necessary, support distributed transactions;

- if necessary, support global directory and naming services (so that locations and names of system components are known throughout the system);
- support security services and time services as necessary.

Information Management: Databases
Key database (DB) capabilities that support distributed applications are:

- provision of a standard SQL-based DB language – if necessary, provide procedural extensions and capability to handle DB transactions;
- ability to interoperate efficiently with the server application, providing an ANSI SQL (in practice ANSI SQL plus extensions) interface;
- ability to interoperate with integration services (middleware);
- ability to support distributed DB capabilities if necessary;
- ability to support distributed transactions with two phase commit;
- provision of replication capabilities, if necessary.

Systems Management
This cover mechanisms for managing and controlling the various physically distributed components in a distributed, possibly multi-vendor, environment. Elements to be managed are:

- computers: PCs, multi user systems, file servers, print servers;
- software: business applications, DBs, networking software, E mail, etc.;
- peripherals: printers, disk drives etc.;
- network elements: routers, bridges, etc.

It also covers capabilities to remotely configure and manage these components, and manage software distribution.

Network Services
These are the networking hardware and software that support distributed applications. Typically, there is no direct interface to the application, rather these capabilities provide interfaces to integration services, information management services and to the platforms.

Platforms
These are the machines and operating systems.

Middleware and Application Development Products

Figure 2.5 is a summary of middleware and application development products. We provide a summarized survey of products in Appendix 1. Readers seeking more detail should consult works such as Orfali *et al.* (1994), Orfali and Harkey (1995) and Butler Group (1994).

An important feature of distributed computing is the infrastructure, commonly called middleware, that enables the geographically distributed application components to interact with each other. We can conveniently

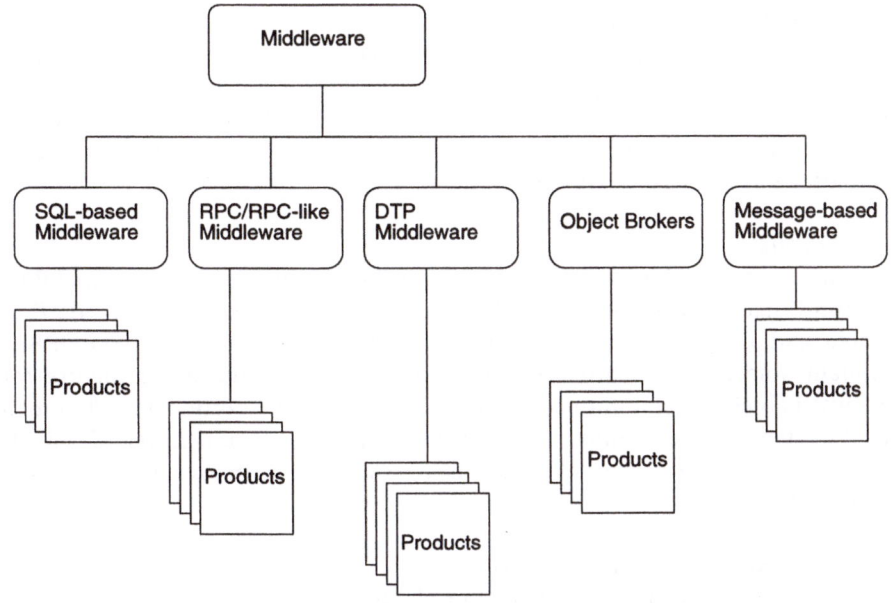

Figure 2.5: Middleware

approach the capabilities of application development environments, "coming up" from middleware. The following classification is a loose, informal classification, primarily a means to structure the discussion. A more rigorous typology is presented in Chapter 5.

SQL-based Products
In the early products, communication between PC-based clients and a LAN-based SQL database was achieved by SQL commands. This class of products has progressed in several ways: firstly, call-level interfaces such as ODBC have enabled desktop access to more than one SQL database; secondly, gateways such as EDA/SQL and Omni SQL Gateway have enabled connectivity to transcend the LAN, and consolidation of different physical databases into a single logical one; and thirdly the development of procedural capabilities in SQL has resulted in the availability of stored procedures and triggers, which enriches server capabilities as well as the modes of communication between client and server.

RPC (RPC-like Mechanism)-based Products
The RPC is an extension of the familiar procedure call, where the called procedure is physically remote from the calling procedure. RPCs are usually specified in an Interface Definition Language (IDL), and an IDL compiler produces the source code stubs for both client and server. Open Software Foundation's (OSF) Distributed Computing Environment (DCE) is the major commercially available environment in this class, offering, in addition to the RPC, a range of other distributed computing services, and currently ported to most major platforms.

Distributed Transaction Processing (DTP) Monitors
Some, such as Encina, operate on top of DCE. Others normally use mechanisms conceptually similar to a RPC. They provide the additional capability of grouping several such services (whose providers may be located at different network nodes) as a single unit of work, which is executed in an "all or nothing" fashion. Other examples are BEA's Tuxedo, IBM's CICS, and AT&T's TopEnd.

Object Brokers
These have been perceived as the next major "wave" of client/server capability. Common Object Request Broker Architecture (CORBA), is the major standard in this area, and players such as IBM, DEC and HP have recently introduced CORBA-compliant object request brokers (ORBs). ORBs provide the infrastructure for distributed objects to communicate. There is, however, an additional twist here in that the standards are moving towards compound document-based clients communicating with server objects, through an object broker (for example, JavaBeans/CORBA and ActiveX/DCOM).

Message-Oriented Middleware (MOM)
These products contrast with RPC-like products in that they offer asynchronous communication between distributed processes, usually with store and forward and guaranteed delivery capability. Examples are, IBM's MQ Series, Momentum's Message Express, TIBCO's TIB, Peerlogic's PIPES.

Middleware vendors are increasingly "bundling" different types of capabilities into their products. For example, certain MOM products (MQ Series, TIB) provide some transactional capability; some messaging products (e.g. TIB) provide asynchronous request/reply capability, while most object brokers provide transactional capability. BEA provides object broking as well as messaging capabilities in addition to their central TP capability around Tuxedo. Also, there are technologies such as DCOM, which does not easily fit into the above scheme – DCOM is positioned between RPC and object broker categories.

2.5 The Enterprise

With client/server or distributed computing technologies, we can distribute various software components of an information system among different platforms in different geographic locations. Equally, these technologies enable us to distribute the user interface (and supporting logic) throughout the enterprise. These technical capabilities provide an unprecedented opportunity for the information system to be molded to the requirements of the enterprise; requirements arising from the work of the various organizational actors (and groups of actors) performing their organizational duties. Therefore, under-standing the organization, partitioning, and flow of work within the enterprise is an important prerequisite to good client/server systems design. To this end, we briefly discuss the enterprise, as part of setting the context for the distributed application issues that follow.

Forms of Organizational Structure

"Traditional" Organizational Structure

Traditional work organization in enterprises can be traced back to sources such as Frederick Taylor's scientific management principles (Davenport and Short, 1990), the command and control model of the army (Drucker, 1988), and Adam Smith's economic principles (Hammer and Champy, 1993). The basic structural alternatives of this model are the *functional organization* and the *divisional organization* (Hill, 1984; Gerloff, 1985). In the former, jobs that share a common function are grouped together, and coordinating (managerial) responsibility is assigned to the group; that is, organizational units follow functional lines. Common functions are purchasing, marketing, finance, personnel, production, research and development. Its hierarchical structure is determined by the span of control, the number of subordinates reporting directly to a supervisor (Greiner, 1979). In the product or divisional variant, jobs associated with a specific product are grouped together. This form is popular in organizations originally structured by function, but have grown in size and number of products (Hill, 1984; Gerloff, 1985). Even in a divisional structure, the allocation of work within a division is very likely to be on functional lines. Gerloff (1985) identifies a few other structural types, one of them being geographic departmentalization; but here, too, at each geographic location, the firm is likely to follow a functional division of work. Recent opinion concedes that the functional type of structure, with divisional or geographic overlays, is still dominant (Drucker, 1988; Hammer, 1990).

Challenges to Tradition

Proponents of the newer forms of organization challenge this traditional structure, reasoning that its relatively narrowly defined tasks, separation of supervisory and work duties, and aggregation of people within a defined range of specialization to functions, is not appropriate for today's needs. One should look to other, more suitable, forms of structure. These new forms of structure can be loosely categorized into (a) the "network organization", which is not single structure, but has the general characteristics of a loose, flexible configuration, with information technology playing a strong enabling role; (b) "process orientation", which represents a specific way of organizing the firm, around its processes. Here, too, IT can play a powerful enabling role.

There is another view, which holds that this traditional view is in fact a simplification. The organization is really a much more complicated place, and one needs to account for these complexities and their consequences to form any real understanding of the enterprise.

Networked Organization

This suggests that enterprises will increasingly be organized around the free flow of information that the recent advances in IT stimulates and catalyzes. For example, Rockart and Short (1991) stated: "As more and more members of the organization do an increasing portion of their work through workstations and as these workstations become easily linked to pervasive networks, we move towards the possibility of a more flexible organization." This idea has been discussed in works such as Drucker (1988), Keen (1991), and Scott-Morton (1991). It exhibits some or all of the following, complementary, features:

- Integration across the value chain: traditional value chain (activities that transform business inputs into outputs) collapsing into three major segments: producing new products, delivering products to customers, and managing customer relations (Rockart and Short, 1991). Also, IT enabled links have been forged with suppliers and customers (Keen, 1991).
- Team-based structure: researchers such as Rockart and Short (1991) and Hammer and Mangurian (1987), suggest that the IT networks that pervade the modern enterprise enable formation of *ad hoc* teams to accomplish tasks as they arise, this structure in some instances emerging as the primary organizational form.
- A flatter organization: Drucker (1988) asserts that as the organization focuses on information, layers of middle management, whose function is to serve as information relays, can be cut.

Process Orientation

An organizational process is defined as "a set of logically related tasks performed to achieve a defined business outcome" (Davenport and Short, 1991); "a collection of activities that takes one or more kinds of input and creates an output that is of value to the customer" (Hammer and Champy, 1993). Some processes produce goods or services to external customers, some to internal customers. Examples of processes are: (a) fulfilling an order, involving all the activities from the receipt of the order to the acceptance of payment for goods received by the customer, or (b) processing an insurance claim, from the receipt of the claim to its payment.

Proponents of business process re-engineering (Hammer, 1990; Davenport and Short, 1991; Davenport, 1993; Hammer and Champy, 1993; Johansson *et al.*, 1993) are critical of the work organization in a functionally organized enterprise, arguing that processes tend to fragment, an outcome not healthy for the enterprise (e.g. Hammer and Champy, 1993). They advocate re-engineering the organization around its processes. Re-engineering in this manner has the effect of integration across the value chain described under the networked organization, but in a preferred way – around organizational processes.

The Complex Organization

There are several schools of organizational thought who reason that the types of structural configurations discussed above are a simplistic description of the enterprise. These types of explanation do not take account of other factors and forces that are in play in the organizational domain, and can perhaps lead to a misleading representation of the form, structure and behaviour of the enterprise.

The conventional view that the formal structure alone legitimately allocates roles, responsibilities and accountability is at odds with the structuration perspective (Giddens, 1984). This stance is that the informal structure within the enterprise, consisting of a network of informal and unstructured groups and alliances, is not a side-show, but the main act. The interaction of these informal groups – dialogue, negotiation, conflict – defines the organization's practice and operation. Some, such as Zand (1981) take a more orthodox view of the significance of the informal organization. He, however, asserts that managers can make use of it – indeed shape a parallel unstructured organization, the collateral organization, to supplement the existing formal organization.

Silverman (1970) and Silverman and Jones (1976) look at organizations from a social action standpoint. They criticize most organization theory for attributing thought and action to the organization, a social construct. In their view, this attribution confuses the actions of managers with the behaviour of the organization. Silverman urges that, in theorizing about organizations, one should adopt a view of the enterprise as the outcome of actions of people – the interaction of motivated people attempting to resolve their own problems and to pursue their own ends.

Conflict, according to Perrow (1973) was seen by the classical organizational theorists as a failure of leadership, control, planning and execution. Perrow, however, tends to the view that conflict should be regarded as a fact of organizational life. Some researchers view conflict as primarily occurring between formal groups (Perrow, 1973), and some regard it as set in a more amorphous and confused organizational milieu (Goldner, 1970). Cyert and March (1963) argue that even the fundamental goals of the enterprise can be multiple, and be in conflict. Therefore, corporate exhortation to pursue even these basic objectives may not necessarily reduce organizational conflict.

Politics and power (e.g. Pfeffer, 1986, Mintzberg, 1983) are closely related to conflict. This perspective asserts that those in positions of power in organizations (whether it be formally or informally endowed) act in ways to increase their power; the achievement of the "rational" organizational aims and objectives is a secondary concern. Davenport *et al.* (1992) reasons that organizational politics and power are the major causes for the network or information-based organization (discussed previously) still being largely a fantasy – despite the technological capability very clearly being available, and its merits clearly being evident: "When information is the primary unit of currency, we should not expect its owners to give it away".

The Workgroup

The group can be reasoned to be the level at which work gets done in the enterprise. One can extend the simple and complex views distilled above to the level of the group as well. According to the simple view, groups can be identified by analyzing the organizational structure. The more complex standpoint maintains that, in addition, there are others, networks of informal groups, within the organization. The simple view assumes a clear demarcation of roles and duties within the group, and cooperation among groups, to achieve organizational objectives. The complex outlook suggests that roles may not be clearly demarcated, the purpose of the group may not be clear or there may be multiple objectives, and that there is a dimension of conflict in the way group members behave towards each other and towards other groups.

In the following section, we present a model for the organization, a model that provides a useful point of reference for the application architectures we develop later.

An Organizational Model

In most enterprises, the dominant theme for organizing work is likely to be the function. In the typical modern enterprise however, overlaying this is likely to be secondary themes of organization. These overlays may be of varying degrees of strength. For example, in a functionally organized enterprise, *ad hoc* workgroups have formed to expedite certain processes; a functionally organized firm, as a result of BPR is experimenting with an additional reporting structure based on its processes; a functionally organized firm has a divisional overlay; a firm that has taken the network paradigm to heart has organized workgroups spanning value chain activities. Furthermore, enterprises may be actively attempting to introduce new forms of work organization, thought to be more effective for their needs. Therefore, in modelling the enterprise, one must not only be able to represent any single organizational form but one should also have the capacity to provide additional views of the enterprise to show other organizational overlays that may be present, or to provide an input to designs of other forms of organization.

The following paragraphs outline a model of an organization. It is not claimed that this offers a complete description of all facets of the organization. We know that organizations are complex entities; this model offers a partial perspective, to enable one to capture the distribution of work.

The following are taken as the major organizing constructs:

- task;
- workgroup;
- function;
- process;
- organizational unit.

Task

In an organization, individuals are assigned work; put more formally, employees in organizational roles are assigned to *tasks*. Organizational processes are accomplished by staff performing these tasks. "Process Customer Order", "Add General Insurance Policy", "Amend General Insurance Policy", "Open Cheque Account", and "Deposit into Cheque Account" are examples of tasks in different types of business. Wijegunaratne *et al.* (1994) describe the task as follows:

- a task is an element of work consisting of a set of activities, producing a deliverable that contributes to a business process; and
- a task is usually performed by a person in a single organizational role.

The characteristics of a task are shown in Figure 2.6 and examples of tasks in an order fulfilment process are given in Figure 2.7 (Wijegunaratne *et al.*, 1994).

Component	Explanation
The task performer	The individual in an assigned role who carries out a task: e.g. the bank teller opening a savings account.
The information required	The task performer needs certain information to carry out the task: the bank teller needs the customer name, address, proof of identity etc. to open the account.
The activities and procedures involved	Each task consists of activities; for some tasks these must be executed in a defined sequence.
The task deliverables and their recipients	The task produces a deliverable a customer or another task performer will receive or act upon: after opening account, the teller provides the customer with the account number and a passbook. Also, a new computer based record is created with account details.

Figure 2.6: Task characteristics

Task	Performed by	Organizational Unit (Function)
Enter order	Order entry clerk	Sales (Marketing and Sales)
Allocate orders to stock in hand	Order allocation clerk	Finished goods distribution (Distribution)
Allocate back orders	Order allocation clerk	Finished goods distribution (Distribution)
Enter manufacturing request (goods not in stock)	Order allocation clerk	Finished goods distribution (Distribution)
Schedule manufacturing run	Manufacturing scheduler	Manufacturing planning (Manufacturing)
Manufacture goods	Operator	Manufacturing operations (Manufacturing)
Dispatch finished goods to warehouse	Finished goods dispatch clerk	Manufacturing operations (Manufacturing)
Receive finished goods	Warehouse clerk	Warehouse (Distribution)
Schedule vehicles	Vehicle supervisor	Logistics (Distribution)
Consign allocated orders to vehicles	Warehouse clerk	Warehouse (Distribution)
Pick and load consignments	Storeman	Warehouse (Distribution)
Deliver goods	Driver	Logistics (Distribution)
Produce invoice	Accounts receivable clerk	Accounts receivable (Finance)
Accept payment	Accounts receivable clerk	Accounts receivable (Finance)

Figure 2.7: Tasks in an order fulfilment process

How are individuals performing tasks organized into larger groups? It is the different ways in which this can occur that provide diversity to enterprises: for example, along functional lines, or (somewhat rarer) along process lines. There may also be formal or informal workgroups that cross the primary organizational unit boundaries.

Workgroup
A workgroup – sometimes formal, sometimes informal, sometimes permanent, sometimes *ad hoc* – performs a group of tasks that aim to achieve some purpose.

Function
A function is a segment of specialized business activity that is essential to the operation of an organization – for example, manufacturing, marketing and sales, finance, or human resources. An organization usually contains several functional areas.

Functions can be classified into two major groups: primary functions such as manufacturing, distribution, and sales; and support functions responsible for supporting the primary functions such as human resources and finance. A function may be partitioned into one or more smaller functions; each of which may in turn be further sub-divided.

Process
As outlined previously, a process consists of a set of tasks which yield a tangible outcome of value to the business; that is, goods or services to external or to internal customers.

Organizational Unit
Organizational units describe the way the organization is physically arranged into divisions, departments, sections, and the like. In a functionally organized enterprise, organizational units follow functional lines. In a functionally organized firm with a formally defined process overlay, there may be organizational units following functional lines juxtaposed with those following process lines. On the other hand, a functionally organized enterprise may have informal overlays of networks: here the organizational units will only follow functional lines; the complementary overlay of informal workgroups will not be reflected in the organizational unit structure. An organizational unit usually has one manager. The managers of individual organizational units within a larger organizational unit usually report to the manager of the latter.

Finally, we must understand that a model such as this is a simplification. There will be an overlay of the elements of the complex organization – politics, conflict, interest groups, ambiguity – over this simple structure that we have described.

Requirements of the Information System

These facets of the organization are interesting, you may say, but what relevance is there to the computer-based application? Fundamentally, the application is designed and constructed to service the organization. Hence as IT managers, architects and designers, we need an understanding of the form and structure of the enterprise that applications serve. Furthermore, and most importantly, this understanding needs to be expressed in the attributes of the applications we design. Other things being equal, applications that better recognize and address this organizational reality stand a better chance of success than those that do not.

Accordingly, first we have put forward a model for the organization, which will provide a useful point of reference for the application architectures we develop later. Secondly, study of the organization yields some of the generic organizational issues that we need to recognize and take account of in our designs of systems. For example:

Changeability

Changeability has become part of organizational life, and the rapidity with which things change has increased. This has placed increasing burdens upon the information systems that support the enterprise. Therefore, the capability to respond rapidly to change is an important requirement for enterprise applications.

Formal and Informal Communication

Applications need to recognize the extent to which formal and informal communication is prevalent within the organization and facilitate these communication needs.

Variation from a Standard

The extent to which the form and structure of the task can vary: tasks can be standardized and narrowly defined, horizontally (greater task variety) or vertically (greater task authority) enlarged, or have a high or low level of structure.

We must look at the extent to which it is possible to define task boundaries. The fit between organizational roles and tasks can be relatively clear, or task boundaries can shift within a workgroup depending on organizational contingencies: for example, a bank teller's task is usually clearly defined, the individual task boundaries of a team of sales and technical staff collaborating to develop a proposal less so.

Additionally, the extent to which the roles assumed and the tasks performed by the individual can vary between simple and complex.

In their design, applications need to recognize and allow for the potential for this type of variation from a standard.

Visibility and Interoperability

The extent to which the organizational form (the structure and relationships between organizational units) is significant in the organization needs to be considered. These arrangements often have considerable undertones of politics and power, and therefore, systems and applications that do not respect these demarcations often face strong opposition. These considerations have a great deal of impact on decisions on information system and application boundaries, visibility of data and processes outside of particular organizational domains, and the extent of cooperation between applications serving different domains.

Do systems built with the newer distributed technologies have the capacity to address these issues – are they better equipped to address these issues than traditional centralized applications? Indeed, the capacity to address these issues form part of the criteria for "good" applications, or to be more precise, since these are generic issues, they form part of the criteria for "good" *application architectures*. We visit some of these issues in different parts of this book, as we analyze and develop the application architectures we propose.

Part 2

The Distributed Application

3. *The Three-Tier Application Architecture*

3.1 Partitioning the Application

Design Principles

A client/server application is characterized by the existence of more than one "place" to locate software components. Also, when compared with a centralized application, we need to partition client/server application constituents into smaller components. Because of these features, organizing and partitioning application components becomes a very important design consideration. In this endeavour, we must:

1. Contain the complexity of the solution

In client/server environments, costs break down differently to that of centralized mainframe computing. As mentioned in the Introduction, surveys on the costs of client/server computing suggest that the typical cost of hardware is about 20 per cent, while the other 80 per cent represents maintenance, integration, upgrade, support, training etc. There is also growing evidence that client/server computing could well result in higher overall costs than centralized computing. Indeed, the push for network computing as well as centrally administered systems stems from a recognition (even among the vendors!) of this phenomenon. Currently there is a debate in the industry about the relative merits of these different technology solutions. While the right technology is important, we must not neglect the application: in constructing applications, there are certain things we can do to contain the effort and cost of maintenance and support. In keeping with the theme of this book, we concentrate on these application level solutions. We can guard against the proliferation of application components and the ensuing complexity in the following ways.

- Building modular, cohesive client and server application components, with simple interfaces between them, so that ripple effects of change are contained.

- Making optimum use of reuse potential, so that application components do not proliferate. There are several forms of reuse. On a decreasing scale of the extent of reuse, reuse by:

  - sharing a software component at runtime (single development copy, single deployment copy, one or more instances of the deployment copy at runtime);
  - replicating the same component (single development copy, several deployment copies, one or more instances of each deployment copy at runtime);
  - controlled adaptation of components at development time (e.g. developing object class hierarchies);
  - independent adaptation of components at development time (adapt from a single copy, adaptations change independently thereafter); and
  - independent development (no reuse – develop afresh).

Reuse is a major weapon we should use to contain the number of components in the system and thereby to assist development and maintenance. Where possible we should realize opportunities for higher forms of reuse such as sharing a single runtime copy between two or more components that require its use.

2. Create convenient groupings of software components which may be developed, operated, administered and maintained as a single unit

3. Make the application capable of flexible deployment
A client/server application is potentially capable of being deployed in many different configurations. These configurations should be achievable without development time changes to software – if this were the case, then we would end up maintaining several different versions of the same software, one for each runtime configuration. The different deployment arrangements should be achievable by configuring the software at installation. That is, flexible deployment should be factored into the design.

4. Consider performance and efficiency
Information carried by services (between client and server components) traverse the network; its volume can have a critical impact on performance. If there is limited capacity in some part of the network, services carrying large volumes of data can easily degrade performance.

Equally, a software component must be housed at a location capable of providing adequate processing power.

5. Satisfy access and security requirements
Decoupling the application into components in different physical platforms and locations pose a new set of security and access concerns. We need to house software components at locations able to offer security adequate for their needs.

6. Preserve integrity
In partitioning data, in reading and updating data, integrity is especially important in client/server systems, where those initiating operations of data may not be at the same location as the custodians of that data. Furthermore, the distributed

nature of the system may impose dependencies between components at different physical locations. Groupings of components and mechanisms of coordination of components that preserve system integrity are needed.

7. Fulfil the immediate requirements of the particular application
While the other criteria define a "good" design in a generic sense, we must not overlook the requirements of the particular system that we are building.

Classifying Types of Application Behaviour

An application is required to exhibit several different types of *behaviour*. Each may be satisfied by a software component – either a tightly cohesive module of processing or a tightly cohesive module of processing that encapsulates some data. While there are many behaviours, they fall into a limited set of different categories. These categories are found both in traditional centralized systems as well as in client/server or distributed computing systems. As we shall see, this classification has a very important use in client/server and distributed applications. Required behaviours fall into the following categories:

1. Presenting data to the user and associated logic
This category involves responsibility for the look of the user interface of the software. Examples are: customer query results are displayed in a listbox with each line relating to a single customer; selecting between financial and non-financial information by clicking on a radiobutton; minimum increment in the exchange rate displayed (in a spin button box) is $0.01.

2. Responsible for task structure and navigation within the task
This category relates to the processing controlling the sequence or sequences (if any) in which the activities of the task are presented to the user; that is the logic governing way(s) in which the user can navigate through these activities. Examples are: "Once you do a 'Save' from screen A, the tabs for 'Screen D' and 'Screen G' become available"; "'OK' provides the default navigation path by doing a 'Save' and taking the user to the tabbed folder G"; "After the pricing actions are over, the 'Approve' tab becomes visible for all users".

3. Performing calculations or operations on corporate data relevant to the business process of which the task is a part
These may act upon either data entered by the user, results of enquiry (invoking other components) on corporate data, results of other calculation functions, or a combination of these. The results may be used for presentation to the user, to validate user input, to update corporate data, as input to another calculation, or for a combination of these. In each case, other components may be invoked. Examples are: "The minimum repayment is R per cent of the outstanding balance"; "Before accepting an order from a credit customer, check that previous balance plus this amount does not take him over the limit of $5000"; "The formula for computing the take home pay is..."; "The capital/interest proportion of a home loan repayments is calculated as follows..."; "the General Ledger account consists

of four three-character segments, the allowable codes for segment 1 are..., for segment 2 are..., for segment 3 are..., for segment 4 are...".

They do not enquire on or update corporate data in themselves; any enquiry or resulting update will be done under the ambit of one of the relevant behaviours (types 4, 5, or 6) below.

4. Responsible for maintaining relationships among data entities

There are operations that not only require the interaction with two or more entities ("entities" in the commonly accepted sense of the term – e.g. Finkelstein, 1989) but also serve to maintain a relationship between the entities concerned. A common example of this type of component is the debit and credit operation, where some amount is debited from one entity and credited to another: "Debit the order quantity from the inventory and add it as the new order line"; "When the customer transfers money from account A to account B, the amount must be debited from A and credited to B." Other examples in this category are: "When processing the premium from a policy, the agent's commission must be paid"; "Before a customer is deleted, a check should be made for outstanding orders and payments".

5. Responsible for enquiring upon (reading) corporate data

These service various queries on corporate data. For example, simple enquiries like "Get Customer Balance", and "Read Order Details", or more complex ones such as "Find all Open Invoices for Customer X within the Period 1/97 to 12/97".

6. Responsible for maintaining individual data entities and their attributes

These carry out the fundamental storage operations on a data entity. Examples are: "Create Order Header", "Create Order Line", and "Update Customer Details".

The creation or deletion of an entity, or addition or deletion of one or more attributes to an existing entity will result in changes to this category of behaviour. Note that a change to a value (e.g. the rate of interest) or even to a formula, both of which could have an impact on the components responsible for presentation and calculation, need not have a corresponding impact here. An impact will only occur if it is required to add or delete data attributes; not simply because the values of these attributes will now change.

7. Responsible for providing configuration and security information

This category of processing provides information about access and security as well as location (where application components, other system resources such as printers are located in the network). Strictly speaking this information does not belong in the application domain, but is a service provided to the application. Examples of this type are components that return the network address of data to which a user has access: "accounts receivable (AR) is handled on a departmental basis; user Throgmorton belongs to the Newcastle Department; therefore his AR data is held in the IBM AS/400 at Newcastle, at Network address..."; components that determine access rights: "function 'Change Credit Limit' can only be accessed by Ms Bean the Financial Controller, Mr Heap the Credit Control Manager".

As we see from the preceding discussion, the processing responsible for these behaviours do not stand alone; they interact with each other. For example, the user enquires on some data, browses the returned information, and then enters some data. Then he or she presses "OK" and navigates to the next screen. These operations invoke behaviours that are responsible for display of information (data entry and browse), enquiry components, components for calculation, update of corporate data, and task navigation (using the "OK" button).

Major Organizing Themes

Assignment of Work

The "distributed" tag attached to client/server computing usually refers to the distribution of data and processing across the nodes of a network. A feature of client/server systems not often emphasized is that *the user interface (and supporting processing) can also be distributed across the enterprise.* Imagine a single workgroup, with the members having different responsibilities. With a client/ server approach, it is possible to distribute the system's functionality so that each member's PC presents a different portion of the system, the one relevant to his or her responsibilities. Since the enterprise comprises many such groups, we have a significant opportunity to mould the system around the people in the enterprise and their work organization. This opportunity to apportion system functionality differently to different users constitutes a significant advance over older technologies. For this endeavour, we can draw upon the organizational model we previously discussed, where the unit of work assignment to an organizational role was the *task*. Therefore, we can mirror the manner in which work is organized and allocated in the enterprise packaging and presenting the system's functionality to the users by way of tasks. That is, that the user interface (plus some supporting processing yet to be determined) is partitioned by tasks.

Figure 2.7, reproduced from Chapter 2, gives an example of the tasks involved in an order fulfilment process.

Client Software. If we agree that the user interface (plus some supporting processing) is contained in client software, then the most effective way of partitioning client software is by way of the task: a single module of client software is designed to support a user in carrying out a single task (we use the term "module" here to describe one or more software components – "Forms", blocks of code, GUI constructs, etc. – that are treated as a single unit for operational and administrative purposes). For example, each of the tasks in Figure 2.7 will have an individual client software module.

Organization of Data

The second major partitioning theme is the organization and distribution of data.

The nature and rules of the business predicate the corporate data items and relationships between data items; the degree of distribution of business activities predicates the "best" locations to house different items of data – and hence the degree of distribution of data. In addition, there is the practical matter of existing data and their organization, which often is the most expensive aspect of a system to change. The manner in which data is organized (either designed anew or the existing organization depending on the circumstances) gives us a way of grouping the components responsible for the basic storage and enquiry operations on the data – a way of organizing some of the server components of the application.

Task	Performed by	Organizational Unit (Function)
Enter order	Order entry clerk	Sales (Marketing and Sales)
Allocate orders to stock in hand	Order allocation clerk	Finished goods distribution (Distribution)
Allocate back orders	Order allocation clerk	Finished goods distribution (Distribution)
Enter manufacturing request (goods not in stock)	Order allocation clerk	Finished goods distribution (Distribution)
Schedule manufacturing run	Manufacturing scheduler	Manufacturing planning (Manufacturing)
Manufacture goods	Operator	Manufacturing operations (Manufacturing)
Dispatch finished goods to warehouse	Finished goods dispatch clerk	Manufacturing operations (Manufacturing)
Receive finished goods	Warehouse clerk	Warehouse (Distribution)
Schedule vehicles	Vehicle supervisor	Logistics (Distribution)
Consign allocated orders to vehicles	Warehouse clerk	Warehouse (Distribution)
Pick and load consignments	Storeman	Warehouse (Distribution)
Deliver goods	Driver	Logistics (Distribution)
Produce invoice	Accounts receivable clerk	Accounts receivable (Finance)
Accept payment	Accounts receivable clerk	Accounts receivable (Finance)

Figure 2.7 (reproduced): Tasks in an order fulfilment process

Server Software. We encapsulate a group of related data plus the functions responsible for the basic storage and enquiry operations on that data as a single unit of development and administration. We name these constructs *Data Access Servers (DAS).*

The first step is to group together data of candidate Data Access Servers.

- Each group contains data that is physically related. That is, the data should reside in the same physical database, and be linked in some manner: in a relational database, by key fields, in a hierarchical database by being in the same segment, etc.
- The data in a group is related in a business sense. That is, the data entities must serve the business in a similar manner: For instance, order header and order item, or stock item and stock location, are related in a business sense.

Therefore, data currently (or to be implemented) in a single physical database should be grouped into smaller chunks of data. A group, however, cannot span physical locations. This grouping is a conceptual exercise, and need not alter the existing database design.

The processing part of a Data Access Server is broadly defined by the capability to manage the encapsulated data. How is this processing partitioned into individual *Data Access Services?* The selected group of data contains one or more entities (to use the Entity-Relationship modelling terminology), each with some number of attributes. Adding, updating and deleting each attribute of data represent the essential processing capabilities (for example, in adding, updating, deleting a customer record). Therefore, the design decisions generally revolve around what data attributes of the server to include and what to exclude in a particular enquiry, update, or processing service; and what, if any, safeguards are needed to preserve the integrity of the server's data.

Therefore, a Data Access Server can contain one or more Data Access Services. These are the means by which a Data Access Server provides services to the outside world. That is, as Figure 3.3 will show, Data Access Services encapsulate the server's data; access to the data is only possible via the public interface of a service.

The physical effect of the grouping of Data Access Servers in a single database comes into play only in determining the capabilities and distribution of the services. The services are designed so that, in a single physical database, there is a clear demarcation of the maintenance of data in any server: each service is associated with one and only one server. Therefore, no two servers can share a Data Access Service; in other words, a Data Access Service cannot span DASs.

The Third Tier

So far, we have discussed the composition of clients and Data Access Servers. These stem from the allocation of work and the distribution of data in the enterprise or the organizational area under analysis. These represent two of the three "logical" tiers of the application.

Some thought indicates that these two tiers are not sufficient, there are components of an application that do not belong to either of these two tiers. For example, a validation service (validation of a GL account or a customer code or a product code) is reusable among many different clients, and as such do not belong in the client tier; a service that debits a stock item and credits an order line (with some quantity of stock) does not belong either with the "Order" or the "Inventory" Data Access Server. We name this third tier *Composite Services (CS)*. This is also a server tier in that it will field requests from one or more clients; unlike the Data Access Server though, the CSs may in turn make requests to other CSs or DASs.

For example, in creating an order line, the responsible CS will make requests of the Order DAS and the Inventory DAS; it may also manage this exercise as a single transaction.

Figure 3.1 summarizes these organizing themes: client software mirroring the assignment of work and the business processes, and Data Access Server software following the distribution of data.

Partitioning the Components

Figure 3.2 indicates our current position. We have several types of behaviour, some design criteria, and three "locations" in which to house data and/or processing representing these behaviours. The problem at hand is to allocate these application components to default "homes" based on our design criteria. Let us take each behaviour type in turn and try to establish a default location.

Category 1: Responsible for presenting data to the user and the associated logic
As indicated in our previous discussion in "Major Organizing Themes", presentation components belong at the client. With most environments, separating presentation components from client software will result in interfaces complex to develop and difficult to maintain. Furthermore, if housed remotely from the client, they will typically involve large quantities of data flowing across the network (especially for GUI objects) being inefficient in terms of network usage, incurring response time penalties and performance problems. Therefore, these categories of components should be implemented at the client.

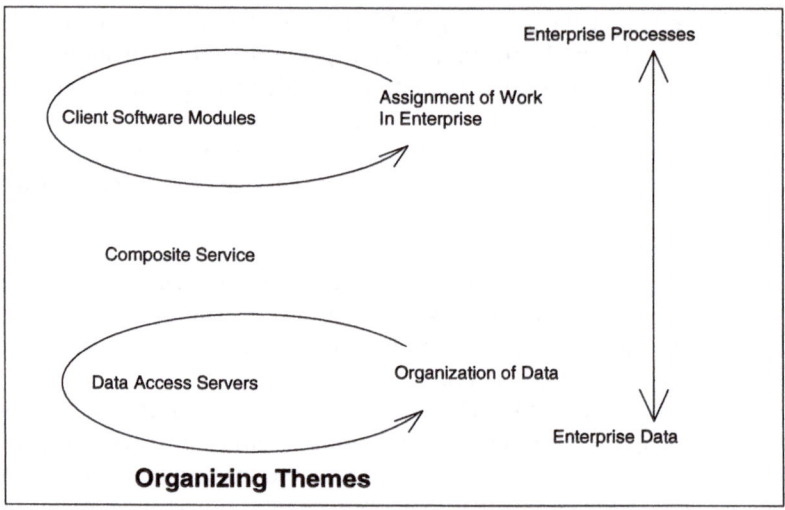

Figure 3.1: Organizing themes for client and server components

Behaviour types	Design criteria	Candidate locations
Presentation and associated logic	Contain complexity	Client
Task structure and navigation	Consider performance, efficiency	Composite Server Function
Maintaining individual data entities and attributes	Ensure access and security	Data Access Server
Maintaining relationships among data items	Preserve system integrity	
Enquire upon corporate data	Satisfy current system's requirements	
Calculate/operate on corporate data		
Responsible for providing configuration and security information		

Figure 3.2: Partitioning the components

Certain presentation components (e.g. GUI objects) are amenable to reuse between client software modules. However, for performance and network bandwidth reasons discussed above, for conventional GUI clients these objects are not normally suitable to be located at a remote server platform to be shared at runtime. For GUI objects, the more practical alternative is to reuse existing GUI objects in client software at development time (employing the replication and controlled adaptation reuse strategies outlined in "Design Principles").

Category 2: Responsible for task structure and navigation
These components too support a specific task, and determine the flow of navigation within the task. For example, the structure of the task "Apply Insurance Premium" is specific to that task, and the same goes for task "Enter Customer Order". Therefore, they are unlikely to be reused. Furthermore, in general, there is no performance issue in locating this type of component at the client. Accordingly, the client appears to be the natural home for these components. However, there are two provisos.

First, it is generally considered bad GUI design practice to design client software that is strongly procedural. The normal approach is to avoid, wherever possible, imposing procedural constraints on the user. Typically in character-based systems, screens for user interaction with the system contain procedural elements that can easily be eliminated in a GUI design providing equivalent functionality. For example, insurance policy entry may contain six screens, each of which requires the user to press "enter" and commit, before the next screen is displayed. Each screen contains a part of the policy. In a GUI system, we can bring the entire policy into client memory and display its contents on six tabbed folders in a container. The user is free to navigate between any of the tabs, enter data in any order, before he/she presses a button to commit the entire policy. Alternatively, in a GUI system recording a receipt and allocating it to outstanding (open) invoices, we enter the receipt details and then browse the invoices and select the ones in which we are interested. We then allocate the receipt among them. Finally, we commit the receipt plus the allocations. At any time before the final commit, we can navigate to any of the tables to change (a) the receipt details, (b) the invoice search, and (c) the allocation details. With this type of strategy, we minimize the task navigation logic that is required, and at the same time provide the user with a good deal of freedom in accomplishing the task. Therefore, the first point is that it is good practice to minimize the extent of task navigation logic within a client; what navigation there is may be incorporated within the client.

The second point is that certain aspects of task navigation can involve security/access rights. For example, in the customer maintenance task-based client software module, there is a customer credit tab. Only the credit control manager has permission to access this tab; for all other staff who are authorized to maintain customer information this tab is disabled. In this type of situation, the access rule that grants or denies permission to access the tab is treated separately; it is a type 7 component; as we shall see below, its default location is the CS tier. The client requests the tab permissions from the CS tier, providing as an input argument the "Who am I" information. Having received the tab permissions from the CS, the client will execute components (resident at the client) to enable/disable the tabs.

Category 6: Responsible for maintaining data entities and their attributes
As we discussed in "Major Organizing Themes" above, the Data Access Server components, shown in Figure 3.3, encapsulate functions plus the data for which they are responsible. We can further justify this encapsulation by referring to our design criteria.

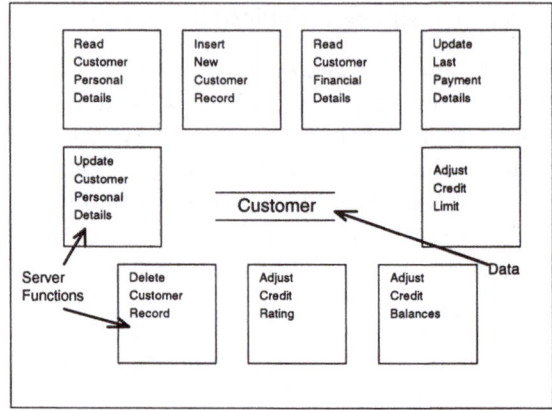

Figure 3.3: Data Access Server: Customer (adapted from Wijegunaratne *et al.*, 1994)

In general, the responsibility for adding, deleting and updating a single data entity can each be held by a different task. Hence, a single set of services shared at runtime makes most sense – indicating a shared, server, environment. In most environments, the security at the client is perceived to be much weaker than that at the server, and a server implementation may be indicated here. Furthermore, reasons of efficiency and performance indicate that these components need to be physically close to the data upon which they operate.

This physical closeness is also indicated from an integrity perspective. In a distributed environment, if we take the components carrying out the different storage operations on a single data entity and distribute in different client modules; and if this is done for all the data entities of interest, the system is likely to become a nightmare for maintenance. Server completeness (ensuring that the complete set of storage – add, update, delete – operations are designed for and are consistent) is not a trivial issue in a distributed environment, and is especially difficult where the storage functions are housed remote from the data. It is very important not only to house groups of data and their custodian functions locally to each other, but also to encapsulate them so that they may be managed as a single unit.

Therefore, we (a) group related data in a single physical database into smaller chunks of data, and (b) arrange the services carrying out the fundamental enquiry and storage operations on this data "around" it, so that access to the data is only permitted through those services – the Data Access Server and the Data Access Services.

It is very important to construct Data Access Servers so that Data Access Services are responsible for all storage operations on the server, and also that server completeness is ensured by the operations of this set of services. Therefore, from an integrity point of view, this implementation of Data Access Servers is strongly recommended.

A Data Access Server is, at minimum, object-based (El-Riwini and Hamilton, 1995). It is possible to implement a Data Access Server either with object-oriented or conventional technology.

Category 4: Responsible for maintaining relationships among data entities

Since we have encapsulated a related group of data and its basic enquiry and storage functions as a Data Access Server, any data relationships within one will be handled internally to it. This category concerns components responsible for maintaining relationships between data of two or more Data Access Servers.

It is evident that, first, these components are not normally suitable for implementation at the client: typically, two or more task-based clients will need to access them – therefore, a shared (server) tier is indicated. Equally, they cannot be part of a Data Access Server, since its functions, the Data Access Services, only operate on its own data and not on any other Data Access Server. Therefore, a second server tier is indicated. This server tier consists of components, termed *Composite Services*, which respond to client requests and (in this case) access the Data Access Services of the Data Access Server tier.

The single largest integrity concern is the possibility and the consequences of a service that invokes operations on multiple Data Access Servers failing in the middle of execution. Such a failure can occur due to a network failure or a failure at one or more of the servers, and can have potentially severe consequences where multiple write operations are managed. Apart from the type of operation, the comparative resilience of the different locations of client/server environment and their ability to recover from failure are important issues. Integrity then is another reason that militates against implementing this type of component at the client, where the infrastructure normally (without transaction support) does not offer reasonable safeguards against recovery from failure. The *distributed transaction* is the first candidate for this situation, as (a) all the necessary recovery capabilities are extended by the distributed transaction processing (DTP) environment, and (b) there is no restriction on the location of the Data Access Servers: they may be located at any network node "within reach" of the DTP monitor. If DTP capability is not available, it is still feasible to implement the capability as a Composite Service, with the proviso that all the required Data Access Servers are in the same physical location as the Composite Service. In this scenario, failure may be safeguarded against by the recovery capabilities of the server platform. If the DASs are in different physical locations and if DTP capabilities are not available, we could still implement a Composite Service; however we need to code explicitly for recovery at application level.

Therefore, this type of component should be implemented as a Composite Service, using distributed or local transaction capabilities where appropriate.

Category 5: Responsible for enquiring upon (reading) corporate data

Enquiries can be of two types: enquiries (or reads) that can lead to subsequent updates of the enquired data, and queries that are enquiry only.

Let us first regard the former. These components are likely to be invoked by more than one client; therefore, a shared (server) tier is indicated. Moreover, for integrity reasons they need to be part of the Data Access Server, because of the requirement to operate in close conjunction with the relevant update processing (the need to lock records between read and update etc.). Therefore, the Data Access Server should contain all the basic read and write processing for the encapsulated data. Secondly, these basic reads can also be invoked for read-only purposes: requested by other, more complex enquiry only components, or for display only purposes at the client tier (for example in an order entry task, the customer's credit limit will typically be display only).

For more complex queries, the Composite Service tier is indicated where there is a likelihood for the query to be invoked by more than one client module. Also, reasons of efficiency may suggest the Composite Service tier, for complex queries where performance is an issue or for queries where a large volume of data needs to be processed to yield a relatively small quantity of data as the result. In addition, where the query needs to access more than one DAS, proximity to the relevant category 4 service(s) is indicated. Also, security/access considerations point to a server tier. Since these cover most circumstances, the typical implementation tier for complex queries is the Composite Service tier.

Category 3: Responsible for performing calculations/operations on corporate data
If a component of this type is reusable, then one should consider the Composite Service tier for its implementation, so that the different clients that use this component may invoke a single, shared copy. There may be instances where security is an important issue, where the client platform is not perceived as offering sufficiently strong security. Equally, the calculations may be complex, warranting the greater processing power than is available at a client. All these factors indicate a server tier. Some of the operations may be integral to a single DAS (for example, the validation logic for a product code is part of maintaining the integrity of the product DAS) or there may be a need to manage access to more than one DAS (for example the calculation for pricing an order reads the Product DAS [for standard price and for volume-based discounts] the customer DAS [customer-based discount] the Order DAS [quantity ordered]. The calculation component – category 3 – has been combined with the multiple DAS access component – category 4 – and housed at the CSF tier). Alternatively, there can be certain processing based on user input that returns the result to the UI, a result that may or may not be saved (for example, the account manager, in developing a proposal to an existing customer, uses certain parameters [based on the volume of previous business, future potential etc.] to price the proposal. He/she typically does several "what if" scenarios before settling on a pricing structure); these components belong in the CS tier.

Accordingly, depending on the circumstances, these components may be implemented either as part of a DAS or at the CS tier.

Category 7: Responsible for providing configuration and security information
These services are typically shared by more than one client, indicating a shared server tier. There will be a directory of users and their permissions (to access

application components as well as other system resources). These components belong to this sub-system, which we can regard as providing services to the application. This administrative subsystem typically uses capabilities allied with the network operating system (such as a distributed directory) and systems management software. If, however, this part of the system were also to be designed, we can achieve this using the architectural principles we describe here. These components will typically have a CS part as well as a DAS part.

Partitioning Summary

Types	Default location
Presentation and associated logic	Client
Task structure and navigation	Client (proviso: most GUI designs contain minimal procedural constraints)
Maintaining individual data entities and attributes	Data Access Server
Maintaining relationships among data items	Composite Service
Enquire upon corporate data	DAS for simple reads
	CS for complex queries
Calculate/operate on corporate data	CS or DAS depending on type
Providing configuration and security information	Part in CS and part in DAS

Figure 3.4: Partitioning summary

We have now defined default locations for components implementing each of the behaviour types (see Figure 3.4). These are "default" locations because we are specifying an architecture, defining a class of designs. For each design, we can take this classification as a guide – as a means of simplifying the design. In the design of an application compliant with this architecture however, we need to carry out a similar analysis for the actual application components. While the majority will follow the guidelines of the architecture, a few of the software components we encounter in a design may require special treatment, perhaps requiring deviations from the default. For example, we may decide to include discounting calculations (normally a CS component) in the "Inventory" Data Access Server; for the order entry task we may choose to house task structure information in the CS, etc.

Form of the Architecture
The broad sketch of the tiers that we made at the beginning of Part 2 has taken shape now.

1. Client Software Module
The first of the generic locations encountered is the client. This tier is organized on the basis of business tasks (recall that the task is the work carried out by a single organizational role in some business process – e.g. Process Order, Register Guest); each task being supported by a corresponding module of client software. In this way, the manner in which work is partitioned and allocated in the

enterprise is mirrored in the software. The client software module fields all user interactions applicable to the task. Components relevant to the task for (a) presentation of data to the user and presentation logic, (b) any task structure and task navigation logic (categories 1 and 2), normally reside in client software. All other components relevant to the execution of the task are located at other tiers, and are invoked via services. Indeed, tasks may be regarded as the means by which these components are threaded together to make business sense.

A single task-based client software module is operated and administered as a single unit.

2. Composite Service

A Composite Service (CS) is responsible for execution in response to a service from a client or from another CS. A Composite Service can be used to:

- maintain a relationship between data in different Data Access Servers (category 4);
- provide validation, calculation or processing services where the data may come purely from the client, or by executing services to Data Access Service at one or more Data Access Servers (category 3);
- provide complex queries (category 5).

An application component may be implemented as a Composite Service for one or more of reuse, performance, security, or integrity considerations. Since this is a shared tier, once implemented (although reuse was perhaps not an initial consideration), possibility exists to share the component.

Each Composite Service is designed to be as cohesive as possible; their public interfaces are designed to minimize coupling (cohesion and coupling in the sense introduced by Yourdon and Constantine, 1979) between the various software components of the system.

3. Data Access Server

Like the Composite Service, this is also a shared tier. The Data Access Server contains a related group of data (e.g. Product, or Customer, or Proposal), plus the Data Access Services supporting all basic storage operations against the data (category 6). It also provide basic queries on the server's data (category 5), especially those used to read the data before a subsequent update.

Partitioning data in this manner need not be a physical exercise – an existing schema need not be altered for this purpose. The design and construction of the individual services of the Data Access Server simply aim to insulate the data from updates from any other source. The Data Access Server construct is a convenient grouping for design, construction and maintenance purposes. Additionally, where the infrastructure permits the capability, it can be a unit of administration.

4. Rules of operation

Figure 3.5 illustrates the possible components of the three-tiers.

A client (tier 1) may invoke one or more Composite Services or Data Access Services. A Composite Service (tier 2) may invoke one or more of its kind or Data

Access Servers. Equally, a Composite Service may be invoked by one or more clients, or one or more of the other Composite Services. A service at a Data Access Server (tier 3) may be invoked by one or more Composite Services, or one or more clients.

5. Distribution of Data

In the simplest distributed application configuration, the data is centrally located and the processing components distributed. In practice, though, for a variety of business, technical or political reasons, one may need to distribute data, or work with already distributed data. In aiming to distribute data, the smallest unit involved is the Data Access Server; one cannot distribute fractions of Data Access Servers. Data distribution is discussed further in the section "Development, Deployment and Controlling Complexity".

Nature of the Tiers

The client, Composite Service and the Data Access Server are *logical* tiers in the sense of representing logically distinct software components with certain relationships among them. If we observe these relationships in the design of an application, then we will have a "good" design in that:

- the design satisfies the major design considerations enumerated in the beginning of this chapter (controlling complexity, ensuring performance and efficiency, integrity, security, etc.);
- the design will have the potential for flexible deployment, as we shall see later in this chapter.

However, we do not mean "technology independent" by the term "logical": although the design principles are independent of individual development and implementation technologies (i.e. PowerBuilder, Java, Forte etc.), this form of the application is predicated upon certain classes of technologies, technologies we discussed in Chapter 2 (and Appendix 1). That is, we need one or more of these products to support its operation. There will be more about supporting technologies later in this chapter.

As befitting an *architectural style*, the analysis we carried out leads to a generic result. We can design an application compliant with this style by applying these scoping and partitioning principles to the design of an individual application. Since some of the principles are conditional (i.e. having different outcomes under different conditions), the design process, in common with most types of engineering design, involves trade-offs and the use of judgment.

Finally, allocating certain classes of components to certain tiers under certain conditions avoids a concentration of processing at any single tier. It also provides the flexibility in different implementations to deploy components of the same application differently, in response to possible differences in the volume, performance and geographic requirements of different implementation environments. Deployment is discussed later in this chapter.

Figures 3.5 and 3.6 illustrate this architecture.

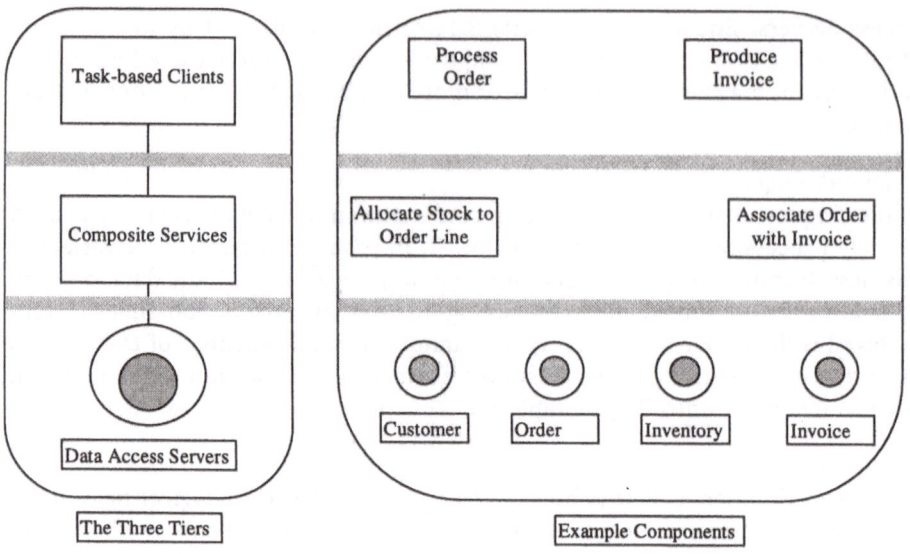

Figure 3.5: Example of the components of the three tiers

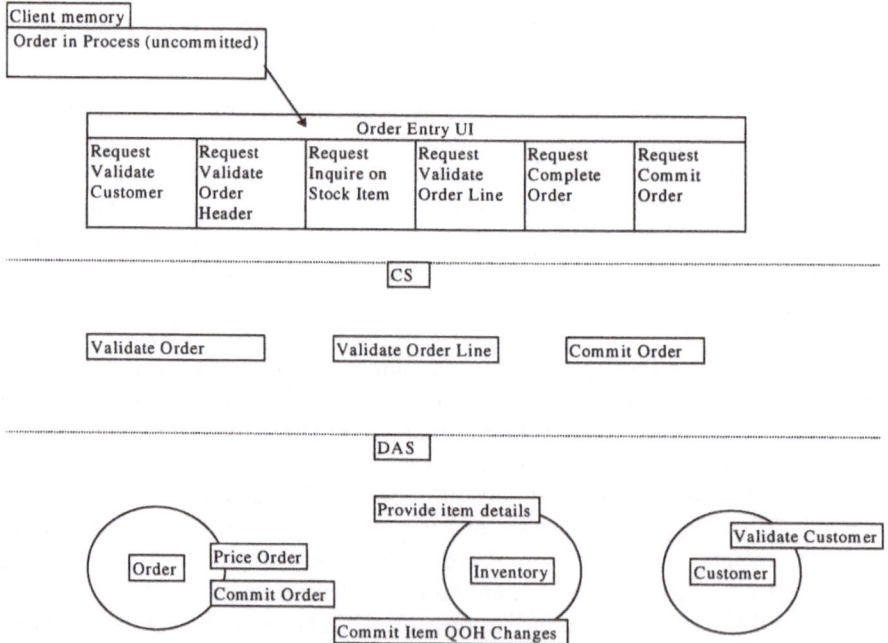

Figure 3.6: A task-based client and its interaction with the server tiers (discussed in "More Design Issues")

3.2   Development Implications

In constructing a client/server application compliant with this architecture, we will use a development language/environment for client and server application components (e.g. PowerBuilder for both client and server; Visual Basic for client and C++ for server; Java for client and server; Progress for client and server; Smalltalk for client and COBOL for server, etc.) and some middleware capability to effect communication between remote application components (SQL, CORBA, DCOM, Encina, CICS, MQ, etc.). Some development environments contain their own middleware capability (for instance Progress) or are strongly tied to one (e.g. Oracle development tools and SQL). If we choose a relatively closed development environment then the programming skill set required is narrower and we need to master a relatively small domain to proceed with design and construction. However, the system we build is not likely to be capable of interacting with systems and system components built with other products. If products and middleware with more open interfaces are selected, then the opposite is the case: we will need to master several environments as well as their interfacing/inter-operating, but the product we build will be capable of interacting with other systems and system components. Furthermore, if we follow the architecture we propose in this chapter, then the interfaces we build between components of the application are as loosely coupled as possible to minimize the ripple effects of a change to one component. Where the technology is relatively "open" we should be able to insulate each component from the implementation of another component. We can argue that the latter scenario exploits a powerful feature of the three-tier architecture: if the server components are reusable, then, in multi-environment situations, having the capability to reuse components regardless of the environment in which they were developed is a great asset; indeed, it may be possible to move to a situation where application components are traded as commodities (some of the discussion on "business objects" revolve around this theme).

Figure 3.7 contains a summary of characteristics and issues of implementing this architecture in these different physical environments:

- using a client development environment, SQL as middleware capability, and SQL stored procedures to implement the server;
- using RPC or RPC-like middleware between client, CS and DAS components;
- using an Object Broker between client, CS and DAS components;
- using a DTP monitor for communication between client, CS and DAS components;
- using message-oriented middleware between client, CS and DAS components.

3.3 Development, Deployment and Controlling Complexity

In a client/server environment, we need to give a great deal of thought and planning to controlling complexity and the attendant costs, arguably more so than in a centralized environment. We need to think about the technology infra-structure and suitable systems management products and capabilities, about

Middleware type	Client	Service	Server	Ease of component deployment	Comments
SQL-based	May be physically located on user PC or on LAN server (server location far preferable) and executed in client PC memory.	Stored procedure call; typically client language independent, not server language independent.	Many server locations possible. However separate physical locations for DAS and CS tiers not practical. Also, capability to separate these two tiers within a single physical location questionable.	In general, cannot redeploy CSs without recompilation.	21/2 tier?
RPC/RPC-like	As above.	RPC call; client and server language independent.	Many server locations possible. Generally, separation of DAS and CSs into two physical platforms possible.	Minimum condition for redeployment of CSs without recompilation: CS/DAS inter-faces need to be RPCs, with an independent directory service containing naming and location information.	
DTP Monitor	As above.	Different implementations. Some with RPC-like service with the additional ability to group together several such services into single unit of work..	As above. In contrast to above, however, possible to provide transaction integrity by participating in transactions managed by the TP monitor.	As above.	
Object-Broker	As above.	Object method (mediated via an Object Request Broker).	Many server locations possible. DASs and CSs implemented as object classes; static (as in RPCs) plus dynamic method invocation possible.	Location information needs to be maintained in a directory service. Lowest unit of "easy" deployment is the object class.	Note that the server components need to be objects, or at least appear object-like to the middleware. Client components may be compound documents.
Message-oriented middleware (MOM)	As above.	Different implementations, but essentially asynchronous messaging.	Many server locations possible. Note that asynchronous semantics require a particular approach to application program logic, applicable to client and server components – the synchronous request/reply paradigm is not appropriate.	Since MOMs do not have point-to-point semantics (unlike RPCs), possibly easiest redeployment.	The strength of message-based middleware is the very loose coupling it enables between application components. Among other benefits, can link applications not compliant with this architecture with compliant systems.

Figure 3.7: Implementing the logical architecture using different types of middleware

management and control issues, and about the application structure. In this chapter, we focus on the last of these matters. One aim of our architecture is to attack the tendency of distributed systems towards increased complexity, by the way in which the application is constructed. Consequently, the application not only fulfills current and future organizational requirements, but should also be efficient in containing life cycle costs.

Deployment is a critical issue in client/server systems. However well-designed from a functional standpoint, lack of deployment forethought may bring about the downfall of a system. Let us examine how it impacts on complexity. Imagine the following scenario: Company Widget Master Inc. has developed a new three-tier client/server system, and have deployed it in their seven branches A, B, C, P, Q, R, S, by replicating Data Access Servers and the appropriate CS components at their local servers. We look at two DASs, the Product DAS and Customer DAS. The client software is physically and individually installed at each PC. Three branches (A, B, C) have deployed the CS components at LAN servers and the DASs at the branch server. The others (P, Q, R, S) do not deploy CS components at a separate LAN server, they deploy all server components at the branch server. In the design, a local call (say from a CS component to a DAS component) has been coded differently from a remote call. Therefore, the two configurations have, in effect, resulted in two versions of the CS and DAS software components.

Branches A and P now want changes to the Customer DAS, requiring a separate bill-to address. This means a change to the Customer DAS, and a change to the customer maintenance client software. However, the other branches do not require this change. This will now result in two different modules of customer maintenance client software (in other words, two executable versions of the client software module, both of which need to be maintained). Each roll-out needs to go physically to each client PC to install the new version. In addition, we need two versions of the affected server components for each of the branch groups [A, B, C,] and [P, Q, R, S] – Customer DAS (plus affected CS components) with Bill-to-Address for A, and without for [B and C]; and a similar set for P and [Q, R, S]. Now a new "product category" field needs to be made available at the Product DAS, again, branches B and Q use this field, the others do not. This implies another divergence for client software, another divergence for the server software, and again the roll out needs to make changes in each individual PC.

This scenario is a maintenance and administration nightmare – we can see that there certainly is a trap here for the unwary. However, there are several weapons in our battle against component proliferation.

Technology Solutions

There are a number of technology solutions: certain network operating systems enable the installation of software at individual client PCs from a LAN server; most enable client software to be executed from a remote drive that is physically located at the LAN server; certain client/server products enable the latest version of client software to be automatically downloaded to the client PC from a specified central location at login time. Indeed, there are several major pushes in industry in this direction: the thin client (featuring Web-browser-based as well as non-browser based clients), zero administration (which has several strands: NetPC or Network Computer, powerful systems administration software, Winframe type of technology), and minimizing client-side administration features prominently in the arguments advanced in favour of these technologies.

- The simplest way to minimize client-side administration is never (unless absolutely essential) to install client software at the PC. Client software should typically be installed at a LAN (or branch) server, and executed in client memory. In conventional PCs, ideally the maximum that should be installed is some startup shell, with a pointer to the startup program at the remote (LAN Server) drive. The startup program, executing in client memory, should initialize the execution environment and enable the user to select the required task-based client program (which again is installed at the LAN server, and executes in client memory) from the menu.
- A second strategy is to install all software at a single central location for the enterprise, and then to distribute to the relevant target locations. Thus the interface to the development environment is this single location. From this single location, we typically need only to distribute to LAN servers (PCs instantiating client code in local [PC] memory from the server). There are many ways of distributing software from a central location to the individual LAN servers; there are, for example, products that distribute software via an Intranet or Extranet; alternatively one can simply use FTP over a TCI/IP link etc.
- A third approach in today's terms is using a "pull" approach. For example, the branch server wakes up, compares the versions of its application software with those at a central repository, and if newer versions are in the repository, copies them over.

Organizational Solutions

Distributed computing can facilitate forms of IT departmental organization other than the central DP department: for example, a central group may be responsible for developing shared server components, exporting services to the development groups in the business units who are responsible for developing, administering and maintaining the client application software. Alternatively, client software, once developed centrally, can be made the responsibility of the local developers who then customize them for local use, operate and maintain them. These types of organizational forms devolve (among other functions) administrative and operational responsibilities to a local level within the organization.

The Application Perspective

The third solution is from the application perspective, the standpoint we focus on in this book. Managing complexity was a major objective of the architecture we proposed.

Designing for Reuse

Reuse is a cornerstone of this architecture. Obviously, reuse controls the spread of components by enabling runtime sharing (or replication or controlled adaptation), so that the development environment components are minimized and controllable.

- Reuse is most visible in the design of the server tiers. These tiers are the home of reusable components, where they are shared at runtime by other application components. This is an instance of the "single development copy, single deployment copy, one or more instances of the deployment copy at runtime" type of reuse. Specifically, the partitioning principles and analysis employed in distributing components across the three-tiers ensure that *in the logical architecture, a business object or component is normally implemented only once*. This principle effectively restricts component proliferation.
- We may need to replicate Data Access Servers and Composite Services. We also need to replicate task-based client software, since different individuals in the same organizational role need access to the same task-based software module. Here we employ a different style of reuse: "*single development copy*, several deployment copies, one or more instances of each deployment copy at runtime". Need for replication brings up software deployment and propagation issues (especially of new versions) and introduces an additional measure of complexity into the equation. However, this complexity can be contained through the deployment strategies we discussed earlier.
- User interface software components (GUI objects, object templates) may be reused as well. Here we can reuse the same GUI object between different client software modules, or follow a slightly more complex alternative in having controlled variation in development copies of software, such as in object class hierarchies. We can employ this latter type of reuse in both client and server developments.

Logical Groupings of Software
Grouping of software into units of administration is another useful way of managing complexity. A unit of administration is the smallest component we administer as a whole, so that a version or a release consists of a whole number of units of administration. Partitioning client software on the basis of tasks provides a logical way of grouping and therefore managing client software; Data Access Servers provide the same potential for server software.

Designing for Flexible Deployment
One of the major design principles underpinning this architecture is to make the application capable of flexible deployment; that is to be able to achieve different configurations without changes to software. In other words, the objective is to develop *so that deployment decisions can be deferred* up to the actual deployment time. While some development environments (such as Forte) facilitate this objective, others do not extend features to support this directly. In either case though, we do need to explicitly design the application in a way that enables us to achieve this objective.

In our architecture, the smallest units of distribution of the server components are the Composite Service and the Data Access Server. Communication occurs as follows:

- client components will call either CS or DAS components;
- CS components will call either other CS components or DAS components.

Therefore, an important prerequisite for flexible deployment is to build these interfaces to be able to operate either as local or remote interfaces. In other words, we should develop the interface of each CS component or the interfaces of each DAS component to be able to field either local or remote calls. In this way, satisfying a particular deployment requirement becomes a configuration issue, rather than a development one. Of course, in different environments we have to implement these capabilities differently, and in some it may not be possible. For example, in SQL-based environments, it is difficult to separate CS and DAS tiers, let alone have similarity between remote and local interfaces. On the other hand, an environment such as DCE allows interfaces to be implemented (albeit at some cost when compared with a local procedure call) as RPCs. Once implemented as RPCs, two functions may well reside at the same physical location, however the location information is obtained at runtime via the distributed directory. Recently, one of the authors designed a system with flexible deployment capability in a Progress environment. In Progress, the middleware capability is provided by the "AppServer", a synchronous and conversational connection. The system was constructed with UI, CS and DAS tiers. At runtime, the startup code associated with a client was able to detect if an AppServer was available; if so the CS tier was instantiated via the AppServer, otherwise (only for a two-tier fat client configuration) locally. Similarly, the CS tier was able to detect if an AppServer was required for the DAS. This feature, plus strict procedure call based interfaces between client, CS and DAS components, made flexible deployment possible for this system.

Versioning

It is very important to manage the enhancement of software by strict versioning, so that under "normal" business conditions, change requests over some set period are all rolled into a new version, with new versions rolled out at predetermined intervals. A related issue is for each jurisdiction responsible for administering software, as far as possible, to manage a single version at any given time, with all users in the jurisdiction cutting over to the new version in the shortest possible period of time. Response to a major change of business requirements will perhaps be handled as a new release, with accompanying training and possible parallel operations.

Widget Master Revisited

The sources of Widget Master's woes can be traced to issues of deployment and response to change. In response to their troubles, they should:

- never deploy client software to PCs – always deploy to a drive at a server, accessible by the PC as a remote drive;
- deploy to a central location, from then (using a push or pull mechanism) to the final destinations;

- fix the software so that flexible deployment is possible – deployment information not to be hard-coded into the software;
- minimize their exposure to maintaining multiple executable versions of software: e.g. negotiate with the users to have the bill-to address on all clients, so that a single version of client and server software is maintained. If this is not possible, maintain the bill-to address service on all customer servers, even though some clients may not use this service (this requires spawning two versions of the old client, but maintains the single server copy).

Response to Change Requirements

As with centralized applications, managing change is the bugbear of client/server systems. With distributed systems though, the issues are different, and with good application design and infrastructure tools, it is possible to perform efficiently in this area.

Unlike centralized applications, deployment is a major task in the change management of distributed applications. As we have seen, the way to manage the physical aspects of deployment is to adhere to the flexible deployment principles we have discussed – designing the software to be capable of flexible deployment, employing appropriate systems management tools, deploying to central sites and never deploying application code to client PCs.

Let us now look at the types of possible changes to which client/server applications are subject, and the capability of applications to weather these change requirements.

These changes are summarized in Figure 3.8. We observe that as we go from left to right, the complexity and the effort increases; also that the bottom half involves more effort than its top half equivalent.

Because of the modular nature of the software, some changes – changes that are confined to a module – are relatively easy to apply. If the design and the deployment environment is as we have suggested, then this type of change can be readily responded to. However, there are two sources of complexity:

- When changes ripple through – these are essentially changes to the service interfaces. Changes that ripple through involves identifying, changing, and re-deploying all affected components. A "where-used" cross referencing capability will make identification of affected components easier, and good design should eliminate all but data-only interfaces, making for easier maintenance.
- When changes require what was the single component in the development environment, now to be maintained as two versions or components. If this tendency is not managed carefully, it can be a major source of component proliferation. Good initial design of server components and negotiation with all stakeholders will go some way to control the emergence of multiple executable versions. If all else fails, we can use method overloading or an equivalent capability to achieve this aim. Method overloading enables the same service to be called via different calls using different argument lists. Therefore, rather than two versions of the same service (with a difference of one or two arguments) we can specify two calls that refer to the same (overloaded) service.

	Change confined to a client only	Change confined to internals of CS component	Change confined to internals of DAS component	Change affects CS or DAS service interface
Change applicable to all affected components	Modify client, re-deploy modified client, replacing all deployed instances of the old version.	Modify CS service, re-deploy modified CS service, replacing all deployed instances of the old version. Since change confined to within CS service, no other changes necessary.	Modify DAS server, re-deploy modified DAS server, replacing all deployed instances of the old version. Since change confined to within DAS server, no other changes necessary.	Modify server component. Modify all clients using the affected service(s). Re-deploy all modified components, replacing all deployed instances of the old versions.
Change applicable to some affected components only	Negotiate with stakeholders to see if change can be incorporated in all client instances – if so, as above. Else install new version (or new client depending on type of change) for affected users. Others to continue with old version. Maintain new and old in conjunction in development environment.	Attempt to accommodate new requirement with conditional statements etc within the single development copy. Else deploy as a new version to required sites. Maintain new and old in conjunction in development environment.	Attempt to accommodate new requirement with conditional statements etc within the single development copy. Else deploy as a new version to required sites. Maintain new and old in conjunction in development environment.	Use method overloading or equivalent capability to accommodate the changes within the same development copy of the service. Modify all clients using the new call to the service. This spawns new version for each affected client. Re-deploy all modified components, replacing all deployed instances of the old versions.

Figure 3.8: Dealing with change requirements

Deployment Configurations

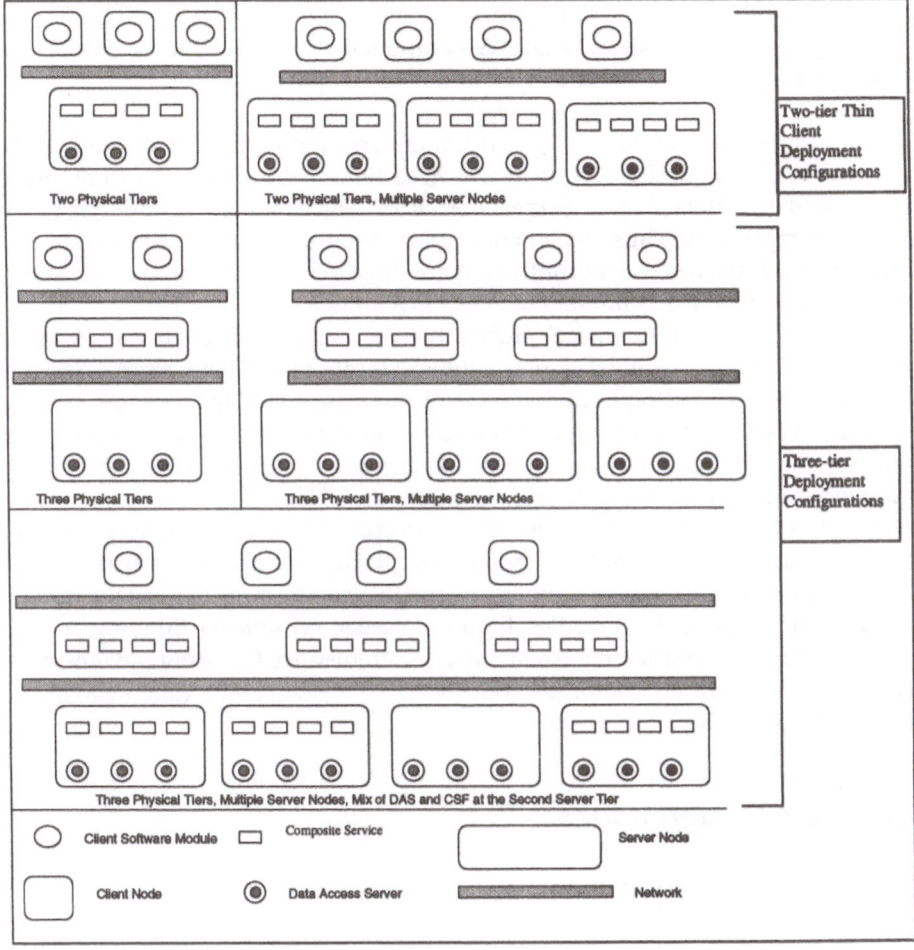

Figure 3.9: Deployment alternatives

With appropriate infrastructure capabilities, we can physically incarnate applications compliant with this architecture in several ways. Figure 3.9 depicts different types of physical manifestations. In increasing complexity, these are:

- The trivial physical arrangement (not depicted in the diagram) is the single platform case, where all three tiers are housed in a single, single user machine.
- The simplest distributed physical architecture is a two physical tier architecture, where the two server tiers are implemented in a single server machine (we do not implement the CS tier at a client machine since it contains components shared by several clients). This is the two-tier thin client deployment mode increasingly mentioned in the context of Web-based clients. Next in complexity is the architecture where there are many such server nodes.

- A single "middle" physical node – CSs housed in their own separate physical machine.
- Many instances of this "middle" physical node.
- Finally, nodes exclusively with CS components, others with CS and DAS components, still others exclusively with DAS components.

We can now resolve some of the confusion surrounding the "three-tier" label: applications can be designed to contain three tiers – the client, the Composite Service, and the Data Access Server – each of which houses specific types of software components. Thus, for an application, the three tiers are determined at development. Infrastructure permitting, these three tiers can be deployed at two or three physical tiers, at any number of actual machines.

In general, for a given logical architecture, as we step through the physical alternatives from the simple to the complex, locations of Data Access Servers containing partitioned/replicated data will increase. The number of remote interfaces, WAN traffic, distributed transactional dependencies, are all likely to increase, and the required distributed infrastructure is likely to require richer capability. In common with formulating the logical architecture, when determining the most suitable physical architecture, we need to be very wary of this propensity of the system to balloon in complexity. We need to ensure that the system is implemented with the minimum possible components to fulfil the design criteria. In addition to the remedies discussed earlier, sensible partitioning of data (to minimize WAN traffic), choice of suitable middleware (for example message-oriented middleware for communication that can tolerate some time delay), can all help to achieve this aim.

3.4 More Design Issues

DAS and Business Objects

There is a great deal of interest, especially in the object-oriented schools of thought, in the notion of business objects. A business object is a representation of some active component in the business domain, for example "Invoice" "Customer", "Product". A business object encapsulates the data, the processing on that data, and the rules to preserve its integrity. See, for example, Orfali et al. (1996) for a discussion on business objects.

Let us now turn to the Data Access Server construct, the encapsulation of data and process that we defined in this chapter. We encapsulate data that is related in a business sense and the functions responsible for maintaining this data as a single DAS; any rules needed for maintaining the integrity of the encapsulated data are also contained within the DAS. Take the customer DAS of Figure 3.3. This DAS contains data pertaining to the customer. It also contains all the components that carry out the access and storage operations on the data. In addition, our principles of partitioning place rules such as: "a bill-to address is mandatory for a customer"; "the customer code contains a two digit prefix signifying the main type of business they conduct with us plus a six digit numeric code"; "if a wholesale customer, the discount types that apply are…, if retail the discount types are…" in the customer DAS.

Therefore, a DAS is functionally equivalent to a business object. However, the way we have defined the DAS makes possible its implementation either with object-oriented technology or without object-oriented technology. True, with the latter approach we will lose some of the richness of object capabilities such as inheritance, but there is nothing to prevent us from implementing a customer DAS in the manner specified with, say, COBOL and an IMS database.

Business Rules and the Three Tiers

Another common term used in discussions about client/server computing is "business rules". People often talk about a "business rules tier" or a "business application tier". What are these business rules, and where do they fit in the architecture that we have described?

A business rule expresses some truth about the business – business structure, operation, or relationships. Malik (1996) puts forward the following typology of business rules:

- A definition: introduces a business concept.
- A fact: relates business concepts, for example relates two or more facts in a meaningful way.
- A constraint: specifies a mandatory condition that must be imposed on some item(s) of data.
- A derivation: describes how one fact can be inferred from or derived from another.
- An action: describes some activity that must be carried out under some conditions.

Let us take some examples, and try to relate them to the business rules classification, as well as the component type classification introduced in this chapter.

Statements such as "a business rules tier" or "a business application plus a data tier" are misleading. Figure 3.10 indicates that "business rules" can map into three of our component types:

- maintaining relationships among data items;
- calculate/operate on corporate data;
- configuration and security information.

It follows that business rules are never housed at the UI tier, but implemented at appropriate server tiers. A business rule can be located in the CS tier or at the DAS tier, depending on the type of component into which it maps: if the rule is about the integrity of a single DAS, then it should be housed within that DAS; otherwise it is typically a CS component.

Used in this manner, a business rules perspective becomes a useful complement to the component typology we propose in this chapter, providing additional richness in a partitioning analysis.

Example	Business rule type	Where used	Component type and tier
"A general ledger account is defined as follows: the first two digits define the entity, the second four digits define the type, the last four digits determine the account number".	A definition.	Used in the creation of a new account and in the validation of input.	Calculate/operate on corporate data. DAS (since it is about a single DAS).
"a payment is related to an invoice as follows: a single payment can pay one or more invoices".	A fact.	Used in maintaining a relationship between the payment and invoice DASs.	Maintaining relationships among data items. CS.
"only the credit control manager can alter a customer's credit limit" (or "before allowing alterations to a customer's credit limit, check that the user is the credit control manager").	A fact (an action).	Used in allowing access to parts of customer maintenance – either allowing access to the credit limit tab, or update access to the relevant fields on that tab.	Providing configuration and security information. CS.
"An entry in the customer master file should either be a customer or a prospect".	A definition.	In validating customer/prospect data entry or maintenance.	Calculate/operate on corporate data. DAS (since it is about a single DAS).
"Before deleting a customer, check that there are no outstanding orders.	An action.	Used in maintaining a relationship between customer and order; specifically as part of validation of deletion of customer.	Maintaining relationships among data items. CS.
"The reorder quantity is calculated from the demand, the reorder frequency, and the reorder level, as follows…"	A derivation.	Used in the processing associated with generating the reorder quantity.	Calculate/operate on corporate data. CS.

Figure 3.10: Business rules and component types

Application Development Revisited

We now illustrate some common design issues in three-tier systems. We use two familiar tasks in business systems, order entry and payment entry.

Order Entry

Imagine an order entry process that interacts with the customer: the order entry clerk takes the order from a customer; goes through each order line, and then upon acceptance by the customer (of each item and the total) completes the order. The stock has to be allocated immediately to the order, since the customer's next step in the process is to walk over to the delivery counter and take the ordered goods; picking the order has to follow immediately after order entry.

Figure 3.11 illustrates the first design approach. With this approach, the CS component "Create and Commit Order Line" manages a commit of each order line as it is entered. The "Complete Order" service at the DAS totals the order; and the "Accept Order" Composite Service manages an acceptance request to the Order and Inventory DASs. There are two issues with this design: first, a customer changing his mind (a) about an order item once committed or (b) the order once completed, necessitates roll-back of committed records in the order and inventory databases. The second issue is that it is difficult to implement this design without state-aware (conversational) links between the tiers. For the Order DAS, committing each order line is not a complete action: it is part of creating an order on behalf of customer Higginbottom. If the link were stateless, then with each new order line request, the order DAS needs to receive sufficient information for it to re-create the context of the current order.

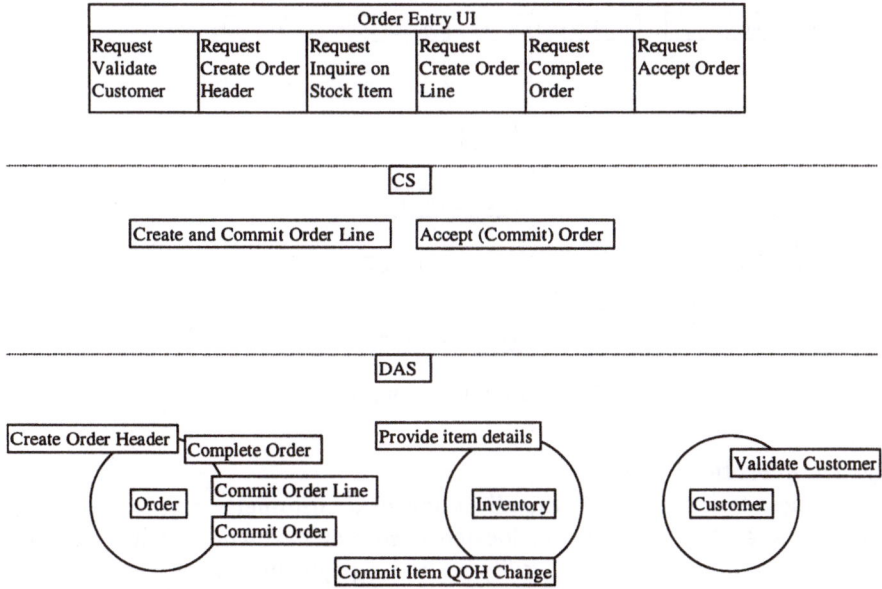

Figure 3.11: Design approach 1

In the second approach (Figure 3.12) we build the details of the uncommitted order in client memory as we take down each order line. The order header and each order line is now *validated* rather than committed (with a request to the relevant CS component) on leave of that field (or group of fields) in the UI. After the last line, an order pricing request is sent to the order DAS with the unit prices and quantities (the entire order information need not traverse the network at this time). Alternatively, if pricing requires customer and product based discounts, then the pricing component can be located at the CS tier. If the customer now rejects the order, then it is discarded from UI memory, without having to undo any committed actions anywhere else in the system; if the customer requests a change to an order line, this too can be accommodated easily. On acceptance by the customer, the entire order is sent down to the CS commit function, which manages the commit across the relevant DASs. This type of design is easier to implement without state-aware links than the former.

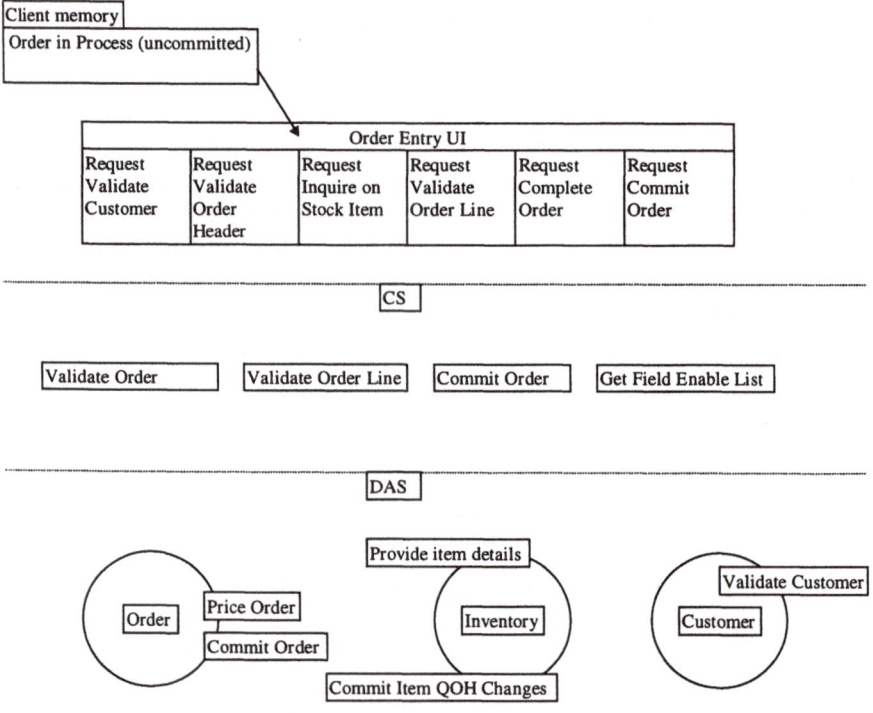

Figure 3.12: Design approach 2

Payment Allocation

The business task scenario is the allocation of a customer's payment to one or more invoices. We select an unallocated customer payment that we previously entered. Therefore, we have a facility to find a payment – given some selection criteria – display a list of payments, select one from the list (for simplicity assume that payments are entered elsewhere). We then get a list of open invoices (again given some selection criteria display a list of open invoices). We then select the invoices to which we want the payment to apply. We view the results, if we are not satisfied we change the allocation; finally we commit the results (see Figure 3.13).

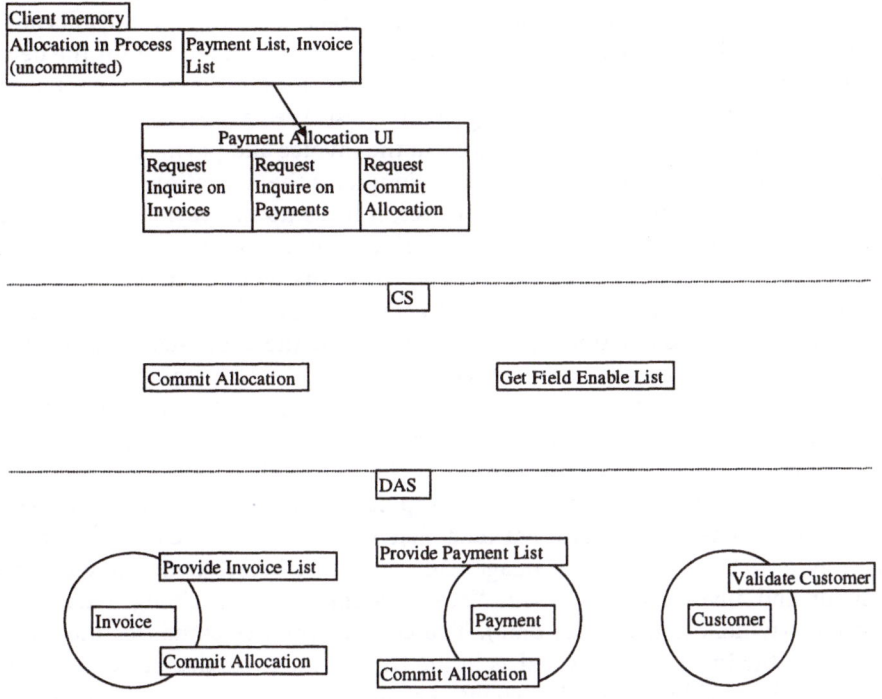

Figure 3.13: Payment allocation

Here too, we maintain the work in process data in client memory. Once the entire allocation is finished, we pass the allocation data to the commit component in the CS tier, which manages the commit across the Invoice DAS and the Payment DAS. In common with the earlier example, this approach affords a way of providing flexibility at the user interface that is a good deal more simple than with committing each step of the allocation process.

We also have to perform traversal of data across the network efficiently. The lists we provide for browsing need only contain important details of payment and invoice, enough detail for the user to make an informed choice. We can then request and bring across the network the detail of the selected payment and the selected invoices. In this way, we conserve network resources, as well as provide the user the necessary detail for the allocation process. We also need to manage the loading of data into the browse lists. One way (as we have suggested) is to have a filter/selection capability that lets the user determine a subset of all invoices, payments etc. Another useful capability is to have a way of managing "behind the scenes", the number of list items that traverse the network at a time: for example, we bring some predetermined number of list items, which append to the existing list in client memory. An event that occurs when the user scrolls to (or near) the end of the browser/listbox will send a request to bring the next batch of list items. This type of operation can be managed very easily with a conversational connection between tiers; if a stateless connection exists, we need to send the selection criteria plus "last key" type information with each new request, so that the server can reassemble the total list and position the beginning of the next batch.

An important issue in applications like this is record locking. In the allocation example, when the user selects a payment item from the list a request for the detail information is sent to the payment DAS. We can lock the records containing payment data at the time of providing this request. We can also follow a similar approach to locking the selected invoices. In the invoice and payment DASs, these records will remain locked until the user completes the allocation. This strategy may be suitable in some situations. However, it locks up the payment record and one or more invoices at the beginning of each allocation exercise until its end, an outcome that may not always be attractive. Also, this type of strategy sits better with a state-aware link between tiers than with stateless links. A better alternative is not to lock records at this time; the DASs send the requested data without locking the data, if an allocation proceeds to an end and a commit request is issued, then we ascertain if the relevant data has been changed in the meantime. In this way, the scope of the record lock narrows to be within the commit process. A common way of establishing if a record has changed is via a date and time stamp for the record. Another, slightly more sophisticated way is by maintaining a before-image. That is, the original data that was sent to the UI is maintained (possibly in the UI) as a before image. On saving, the before image (the original payment and invoice data) is sent "down" along with the changed data (the allocated payment and invoice data). The commit process compares the before image with the image that now exists in the DAS. If those particular items of data have been changed by some other client, the commit process can ascertain exactly what changes have taken place. If the changes that have taken place do not change the integrity of the allocation exercise, the allocation results can still be committed. For example, the date of the check was mis-keyed and was altered by the payment entry clerk, while the payment allocation was in process. A record-level date and time stamp mechanism would disallow the commit; but the before/after image comparison leaves the decision to the commit process – in this case, the commit could go ahead. The astute reader will notice that this before image comparison scheme is the equivalent of field-level time stamping.

In summary, with this approach we:

- Create changes in client memory, in effect creating in client memory the transaction to be committed, rather than engaging the DASs in partial commits of work in process. We thereby clearly define the scope of the "logical unit of work", and assemble its elements in client memory.
- Restrict the scope of an exclusive lock on data to the commit logic, deferring seizing of database resources as late as possible, to commit time.

This scheme has the following advantages:

- It enables the provision of a non-procedural way for the user to attend to the task. Within the scope of the transaction, the user can navigate through the activities of the task in a non-procedural manner. Of course, we should have on-leave-of-field validations, but these should give an indication of the error against the field but not stop the user from doing other things within the scope of the transaction (obviously, errors should prevent the user from saving [committing] the work).

- It is network efficient since it minimizes network traffic between the tiers: with this arrangement, we would have the initial load of the data, the individual on-leave-of-field validation requests, and the final data to be committed as the substantive network traffic. An approach involving partial commits will add to this volume of traffic in two ways: each partial commit and each undo will generate additional traffic.

- It insulates the DAS from actions of the UI, until the final commit of the changed data. This is very useful for recovery, because the entire transaction (the order, or the payment allocation) is either fully un-committed or fully committed – there is no intermediate or partially committed state (apart from within the commit logic). This is very useful in heterogeneous environments, where there may not be strong recovery facilities of global scope.

One thing we need to ensure is to keep the size of the transaction to a manageable level. For example, imagine that you are entering orders that are batched. There are three levels of data here: that of the batch, that of the order, and that of the order line. A transaction whose scope encompasses all three levels will typically be too much: if you are committing batches, and on average if a batch has 25 orders and an order has 10 lines, then potentially you will be creating a transaction of 25 orders containing a total of 250 order lines. We therefore need to partition the task to create transactions of manageable scope. A maximum of two levels is a useful rule of thumb: in this case creation and maintenance of batches (batch headers) is one task, creation and maintenance of orders (with their order lines) is another.

Separation of Presentation/Delivery from Business Rules and Data

In the last two years or so, the Web browser has made a significant impact as, among other things, a vehicle of delivery and presentation for certain business applications. There is a good deal of discussion about web-enabling business applications, that is extending functions to users via the Internet or an Intranet.

An application that is compliant with the architecture we have proposed is well-placed to satisfy this requirement with the minimum of change. The proposed architecture separates all business-related processing plus database access from the user interface; the user interface is concerned only with the presentation of data (also task navigation – which is minimal in a non-procedural design). Furthermore, the approach we discussed above, of creating in client memory the transaction we want to commit (rather than making a series of partial commits) sits well with the style suitable to HTML/CGI type applications. It is possible to maintain the same CS and DASs, but to have two UIs, one a "conventional" GUI, and the other for delivery via an Intranet or the Internet (see Figure 3.14). Among other benefits, this approach minimizes component proliferation, since we now have the same server components servicing two types of client, rather than two separate applications.

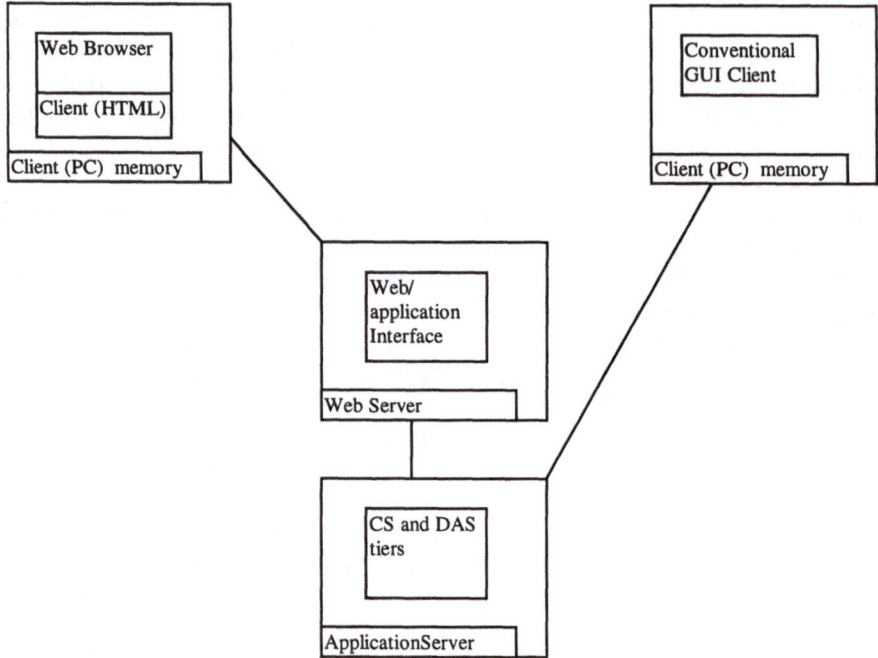

Figure 3.14: Web browser and conventional clients with two-tier thin client deployment

Building with Components

Component frameworks are another oft-discussed capability. There is a good deal of interest in component frameworks in the object-oriented literature. An object framework is a set of objects that collaborate to carry out certain duties. An application-level framework provides a superstructure for the application designer and builder. The application development process, rather than starting from scratch, now starts from this prefabricated superstructure – putting flesh on it by modifying it, enhancing it and extending it as appropriate to the situation. (For a useful introduction to object frameworks, refer to Orfali *et al.*, 1996.)

However, while the framework concept grew out of the object-oriented camp, it is not essential that frameworks be object-oriented. We can deliver similar functionality in environments that are not object-oriented. The fundamental requirement is to incarnate an architecture as code components that provide default behaviours and serves as a template/superstructure for compliant applications (Figure 3.15).

Recently, one of the authors was associated with a project where just this objective was accomplished. We had to re-engineer a large, stable application from a centralized character-based form to a GUI client/server form.

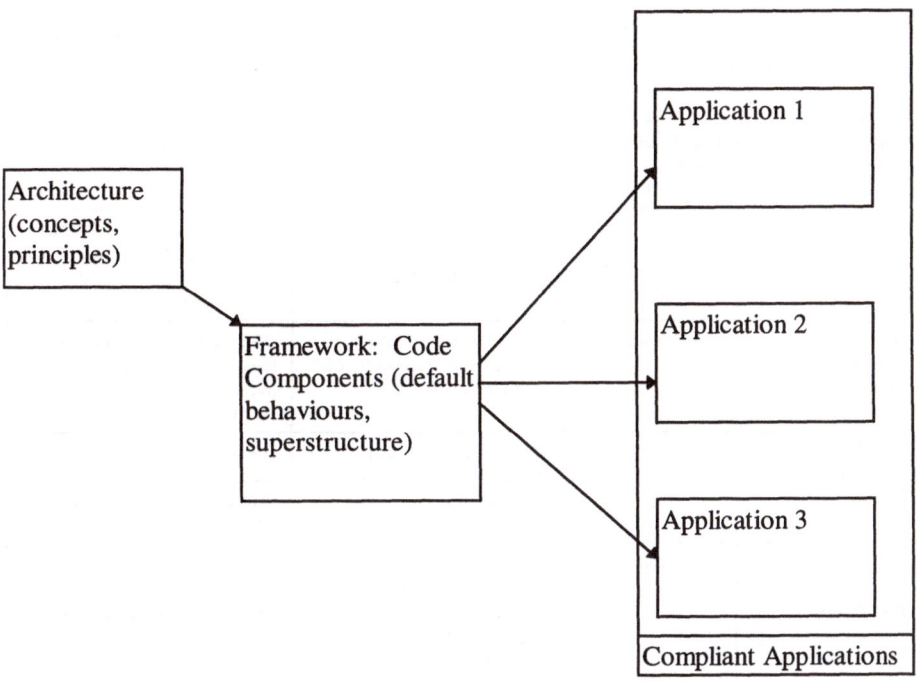

Figure 3.15: Architecture, framework and compliant applications

The three-tier architecture, as proposed in this chapter, was tailored to suit the development environment. The development environment consisted of a 4GL that was suited for both client and server code. The 4GL provided a proprietary connection between client and server (over a TCP/IP communications protocol), which was a conversational or state-aware link.

We next built the superstructure, which consisted of the components displayed in Figure 3.16. We identified six distinct application-level component types that were required. For each of these components, we built a superstructure of UI, CS and DAS components. Typically, a task-based client fell into one of the six application-level components. For example, the task "General Ledger Journal Entry" fell into the transaction maintenance category, as did the task "Enter Invoices". Because of the conversational nature of the middleware connection, it was convenient to create a CS and a DAS session on behalf of each instantiated client. The common CS and DAS business components (for example, Customer, Vendor, Invoice, Order etc. DAS components) were in libraries shared across these sessions.

An explicit framework-building phase can be incorporated into the project. A useful way of creating a framework is to build it in conjunction with constructing the first compliant application. In this way, the framework can be built by abstracting from the real application components – by abstracting from the application the reusable superstructure components. We took this approach in the project. From the second application onwards, we used the framework as the starting point. In addition, as the common DASs (for example, Customer, Vendor,

Invoice, Order etc.) were fleshed out, new applications reused more and more of these components, and required less and less of new DAS level code.

Application-level component	Examples of UI superstructure components	Examples of CS superstructure capabilities	Examples of DAS superstructure capabilities
Transaction maintenance	UI templates	CS instantiation and destroy logic; generic load and commit logic	DAS destroy logic, generic load and commit logic including before-image comparison
Simple maintenance (type 1)	UI templates	CS instantiation and destroy logic; generic load and commit logic	DAS destroy logic, generic load and commit logic including before-image comparison
Simple maintenance (type 2)	UI templates	CS instantiation and destroy logic; generic load and commit logic	DAS destroy logic, generic load and commit logic including before-image comparison
Reports and background processing	UI templates	CS instantiation and destroy logic; generic mechanism for passing selection and scheduling criteria; managing report execution	DAS destroy logic, generic mechanism for saving selection and scheduling criteria
Simple inquiry	UI templates	CS instantiation and destroy logic; generic mechanism for passing selection criteria to inquiry; managing inquiry execution	DAS destroy logic
Drill-down inquiry	UI templates	CS instantiation and destroy logic; generic mechanism for passing selection criteria to inquiry; managing inquiry execution	DAS destroy logic

Figure 3.16: Superstructure for application-level component types

The Architecture and the Business Model

Partitioning software on the basis of tasks enables software to shadow the distribution of work in the business very closely. However, this does *not* imply that the application is restricted to fitting in with an existing business model. On the contrary, this architecture provides a powerful means of supporting the transformation or enhancement of work organization – for example through business process re-engineering, and also of responding rapidly to subsequent organizational changes.

This partitioning places the onus upon the enterprise to distribute work in a rational and effective manner. Task-based client software will mirror the work organization in the enterprise, linking the effective organization of the information system to the effective organization of business processes. If that work organization is flawed, *and if there is no mandate to improve the work organization*, then the software that is developed will reflect those flaws. However, where there is the organizational will to improve or enhance the business processes, then this architectural style has the potential to provide a software solution to mirror the improved business processes and the new distribution of tasks therein. The new task specifications of the transformed or enhanced businesses process is the starting point for the new client software and the new application(s). Indeed, the same model used to represent the business in terms of processes and tasks for a process re-engineering exercise can be taken further as the blueprint for the systems design.

3.5 Conclusion

A distinctive feature of the proposed architecture is the central role of the task: the application is a set of cooperating software components that support human beings in their work, work related to performing some organizational or business activity. That is, the typical business or commercial information system. This structure is not suitable for other types of systems – such as command and control systems, process automation systems, system software such as communication or operating system software – where there is no notion of one or more humans engaged in purposeful activity that the system is designed to support.

Strictly speaking, the way we partition software here renders meaningless the traditional notion of an "application": each client and server software module can be a unit of administration/maintenance. Nevertheless, we can still call the group of software components that supports some business objective "the application", to retain a sense of continuity and for administrative convenience. Such a grouping will generally consist of a whole number of task-based client software modules, some number of Composite Services and Data Access Servers. The non-client components of the system will, in general, be shared among several such "applications". Product capabilities permitting, we can provide access to users to the system at the level of the tasks they perform: For example, we can display a set of icons at the user's computer interface for the tasks he or she performs: the order entry clerk's PC may display an icon for the order entry task and an icon for the company's internal mail. This contrasts with accessing the *applications* used, and dispenses with the need to routinely see and navigate through functions the user never employs.

In this chapter, an attempt was made to provide a reasonably complete description of a three-tier architectural style for client/server applications. Principles for scoping, organizing, and partitioning application components have been elucidated, and the nature of the three tiers has been established. Physical deployment has been discussed, as have been several requirements, implications, and possibilities of the architecture. In essence, the architecture contains principles of application component partitioning, principles of deferred deployment, and guidelines for design. Befitting an architectural *style*, the principles are general ones, providing a "template" for designing individual applications compliant with this style. It is open for individual systems designs to comply with this architecture by employing the principles proposed here in the design activities of a systems life cycle. We have shown one useful approach to developing compliant applications in the discussion on component frameworks.

The various threads of argument presented in this chapter point to the following main areas of potential benefit from the architecture we discuss.

- The proposed architecture attempts to realize the potential of client/server technology to distribute the user interface and supporting logic across the enterprise. The partitioning of client software on the basis of tasks, units of work that individuals (in organizational roles) carry out, supplies the underpinning to shape the application closely to the distribution of work in the enterprise.
- One of the main concerns with client/server computing is the potential for components to proliferate, and for deployment, maintenance and operational costs to grow. We have discussed ways in which an application can be designed to counter this tendency, by maximizing reuse, designing for flexible deployment, and for accommodating different information presentation/ delivery mechanisms.
- There is a tendency, especially in the industry, to associate "client/server" with a particular technology or product. We have demonstrated in this chapter that "client/server" is primarily about the way the application is organized, and that this organization can be supported not by one particular technology, but (with various degrees of compliance) by a number of different technologies.

The three-tier architecture is suitable for a single "application", or a closely related group of applications. We reason later in this book that it may not scale up very well to the level of the enterprise, where a higher architectural stratum (comprising of relatively autonomous groups of applications, perhaps with different intra and inter group organizing principles) is needed. Also, the architecture is not cast in stone. Evidence shows that distributed computing is an area where capabilities change rapidly. New capabilities may emerge that may well have an impact upon this architectural style or result in the emergence of other, complementary, architectural styles.

4. *The Three-Tier Architecture:*
An Object-Oriented Perspective

Paul Taylor

4.1 Background

In this chapter, we take an object-oriented perspective of the three-tier architecture described in the previous chapter. The partitioning of the application discussed in section 3.1 is based on a behavioural decomposition, where typical system behaviours are classified into general groups. The assignment of these behavioural categories to various physical architectures is outlined in Figure 3.4. The following discussion identifies if, and how, an object-oriented decomposition might differ, and the implications for the proposed three-tier client/server architecture of using an object-oriented architectural view.

Object-oriented technology provides analysis, modelling and descriptive techniques which overlap to various degrees with the proposed architecture and its development process; these are introduced and explained.

Basis of the Object Paradigm

The object paradigm distinguishes itself on the basis of its treatment of function and data. In a traditional functional view, functions transform data values by operating on them – an application's requirements are met by designing functions which provide the appropriate data transformation, and functions are designed for complex applications by successively decomposing abstract functions to more specific, implementable functions. Functional decomposition has been criticized because the decomposition is based on a perception of system requirements at analysis time, and this decomposition does not yield to change and evolution during a system's operational lifetime. This inflexibility impacts software system evolution in the face of changing requirements, both technological (such as operating system and platform changes) and application related (such as business domain or requirements changes).

On the other hand, the object paradigm views functions, and the data upon which they operate, as inseparable cohesive abstractions. An object is an instance of a class of like abstractions; objects encapsulate their state (or data attributes) and provide access to their functionality via a public interface. Functions available at an object's interface typically manipulate the object's data attributes – this effect is called "behaviour". Individual objects provide behaviour specific to their abstraction, while clusters of objects are usually designed to collaborate to provide system level behaviours, which directly meet end user requirements.

Classes and Objects

A "class" is a set of indistinguishable objects, and is somewhat synonymous with "type". Object-oriented programming languages support the definition of classes with names, attributes and methods (or functions, the callable code fragments), from which the program instantiates objects at runtime. Object-oriented programs or software components in typical business domains typically consist of hundreds of classes, with hundreds or thousands of interacting objects in an executing program. Since the design of classes is entirely at the discretion of the modeller and the programmer, classes may represent very small and numerous elements of the problem domain (such as a complex number, or a date), very large elements (such as a warehouse or nuclear reactor), or something in between (a bank account, with twenty to thirty attributes such as names, identifications, dates, amounts and interest rates). As is the case with all conceptual modelling, only those elements of the problem domain which are relevant to current and foreseeable systems are included in the classes' definition.

Not all objects in an object-oriented program are directly recognizable elements of the business domain, such as customers, accounts or orders. During design, the implementation concerns of the system or component impact the actual classes which get programmed, resulting in the specification of additional design and implementation classes. A commonly recognized rule of thumb is that for each business object in the analysis model, two additional classes will be defined to provide the program's infrastructure and scaffolding during detailed design and implementation. For example, an order object may require a related object to load it in from, and out to a database or file, and another family of objects to print it out in various forms (in plain ASCII characters for a report, or in HTML for a browser).

Encapsulation

A class typically hides its internal attributes (and some of its methods) from other objects, and provides a set of "public" methods to access its behaviours. The practice of hiding internal state and behaviour is called "encapsulation", and the set of public methods define the classes' "public interface". A well-designed class presents a simple and logically consistent business abstraction through its public interface, while encapsulating the internal state and processing required to implement its public services. Users of an object should be able to request its services without having to know how they are provided – this decouples collaborating objects in a system, supporting easier change and evolution.

Many relationships between objects have attributes and behaviour of their own, so it is common for one to many and many to many relationships to be implemented as objects (which hold collections of object references, and have insertion and removal methods to constrain the relationship's integrity).

Inheritance and Polymorphism

Object-oriented programming languages are well known for their support for inheritance, which declares a parent/child relationship between two classes. The child (or sub-class) inherits all of the parent's (or super-classes') attributes and methods, and can add its own attributes and methods, or overload inherited ones to change their implementation, without changing their meaning. Inheritance is clearly a powerful mechanism for representing classification and type/sub-type relationships in the implementation. For example, the sub-classes ChequeAccount and SavingsAccount are unambiguously related to their parent class Account. Additionally, the programming language semantics of inheritance allow attributes and methods common to all sub-classes to be defined once in the super-class, thereby facilitating a form of design and code reuse.

Inheritance is practically used to allow detailed implementations of particular methods to change without varying the calling code in other classes. The runtime substitution of a sub-class object for its super-class is a fundamental property of object-orientation, and its most powerful facilitator of code stability and reuse. For example, all account objects have a balance, and a method for calculating an amount of interest based on current rate, balance and other business rules. But the actual percentage rates and business rules for calculating interest are different for cheque accounts and savings accounts. If these account objects are sub-classes of the Account class, they can each provide their own implementation of the method to get the account balance. The other classes in the system which use accounts need only know about the generic account object (as defined by the Account class), even though their actual account object instance in the executing program may be a ChequeAccount object or a SavingsAccount object.

The routing of method invocation to the actual object's overloaded method at runtime is called "dynamic binding", and facilitates "polymorphism". Polymorphism is used by object-oriented designers as a way of isolating client code from areas elsewhere in the system that are prone to change; in fact, the solutions of many of the popular "design patterns" (Gamma, 1994) rely heavily on polymorphism for their operation.

4.2 Models

Object modelling, the activity which delivers requirements and analysis models consisting of scenarios, classes and their relationships, unifies the formerly separate views during the development of a logical architecture, and subsequent detailed design and implementation. An object-oriented view has the potential to impact our view of client/server architecture in a number of ways.

Client/Server Roles

Two common views of client/server behaviour (introduced in Chapter 2) are the interaction-based view, where the client and server labels are associated with the peer entities for the lifetime of a particular interaction, and the role-based view, which attaches client and server labels to the entities based on their long term or predominant behaviour. An object-oriented view introduces these exact same interactions down to individual objects at the lowest level of software construction, allowing both these interpretations of client/server behaviour at a new level of abstraction. It is therefore necessary to distinguish these interactions from those which mark the architecture as client/server.

An executable program or process consists of a group of objects which interact in order to collectively provide a required system behaviour. In object-oriented terminology, these interactions are called "collaborations" (Wirfs-Brock *et al.*, 1990). Collaborations are necessitated by encapsulation – objects need to interact in order to access data and associated behaviour. The patterns of collaboration depend on the behaviour provided by individual objects, and the task which the collaboration must perform. Tasks are associated with the Organizational Model, and are discussed below.

The abstract mechanism which supports object interactions is called "message passing". An object which collaborates with another sends a message to its collaborator, which provides the requested service and returns a second message indicating completion and optionally containing returned data. In all of the popular object-oriented programming languages (including C++, Smalltalk and Java), message passing is implemented as a synchronous (blocking) procedure call. If objects need to implement an asynchronous exchange, the caller must either poll the called object, or use threads (explicitly supported by some object-oriented programming languages – Java being the obvious example) to support true asynchrony.

It is generally not useful to associate client and server roles with individual objects, but rather with groups of cohesive, collaborating objects, which constitute services within the client/server architecture. Services and their boundaries are described with object interaction models.

Modelling Object Interactions

Most object-oriented methodologies provide three categories of models: the class model, which shows classes and their static relationships (the object-oriented equivalent of an entity-relationship model); the dynamic model, which describes a particular sequence of interactions between collaborating objects, and state models, which model the allowable states and attribute value transitions of specific objects (Rumbaugh *et al.*, 1991; Booch, 1994; Jacobson *et al.*, 1992). Figure 4.1 illustrates the elements of a typical dynamic model.

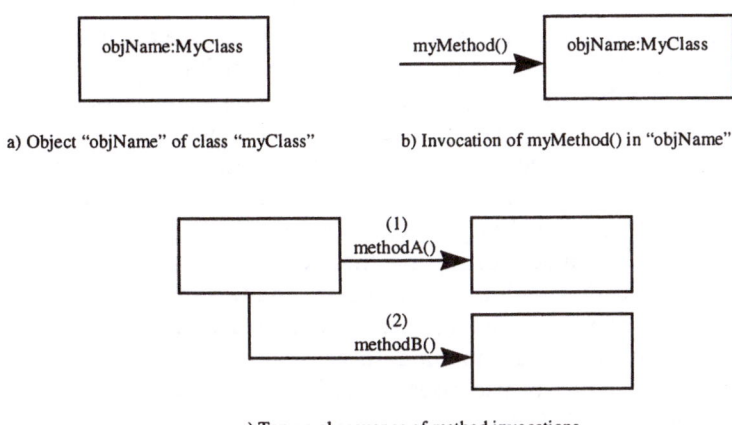

a) Object "objName" of class "myClass"   b) Invocation of myMethod() in "objName"

c) Temporal sequence of method invocations

Figure 4.1: Elements of an object interaction model for a scenario

In a simple exchange, an object may call an accessor method on another object to retrieve a value, or a modifier method to set a value or change the called object's state. The called object may at times need to request information from another object in order to service its call; this object may be a third collaborator, or the original caller. In message passing implemented by synchronous procedure calls, a called object must return control to its caller. Apart from this obvious rule, the interactions between collaborating objects follow no formalisms. An object may participate in simple exchanges, chain calls, call back its caller, or call one of its caller's callers. In object-oriented design, creating long sequences of calls from an initiating or central object in order to accomplish a particular system requirement is discouraged, as it can represent a centralization of control. The general principle of "responsibility-driven design" (Wirfs-Brock *et al.*, 1990) encourages a system's behaviours to be evenly spread around the business abstractions in an object-oriented architecture. Metrics have been designed to measure the degree of distribution of a system's collaborations around key objects, so as to encourage properly distributed responsibilities (Fenton, 1991).

There is little use in labelling the calling and called objects "client" and "server" objects, due to the typically very short span of interactions between pairs of collaborators, and the fact that in a well-designed object-oriented architecture, hundreds or even thousands of objects of perhaps hundreds of classes often collaborate in complex interaction patterns to perform a business function or a particular system requirement.

4.3   Organizational Model

In "An Organizational Model" in section 2.5 the organization was presented as a collection of units (divisions, sections, departments) containing employees in various roles, who are assigned to tasks. The term "task" was defined as "an element of work consisting of a set of activities, producing a deliverable that contributes to a business process, and performed by an individual in a single organizational role". This view is closely aligned with the principal business process modelling technique from the domain of object-oriented methods – Ivar Jacobson's use case modelling (Jacobson *et al.*, 1992). Use case modelling was introduced as a component of Jacobson's Object-Oriented Software Engineering methodology, a first generation object-oriented methodology based on the definition and application of use cases to drive the entire software development process. Use cases were widely accepted during the first few years after publication as an appropriate way of capturing business processes and tasks for information system development. Jacobson followed up his launch of use cases as the core of a software system development method three years later with a second book describing the application of use cases to modelling and re-engineering business processes (Jacobson *et al.*, 1994).

Use cases are particularly useful for modelling the task and process behaviour of an enterprise. As will become clear from the following description, a use case model of processes and tasks corresponds directly with the organizational model of processes, tasks and activities introduced in the previous chapter.

Overview of Use Cases

Use cases relate specific activities within a "system" to "actors". A use case is a business scenario, task, or event and action sequence which is initiated by an actor, and returns an outcome to an actor. Use cases emphasize the modelling of system behaviours from a user's or client's perspective, by associating every system behaviour with a business task which is anchored on one or more actors. Use cases are event driven, where the events are initiated by user actions. This event driven characteristic maps naturally to an object-oriented design based on message passing and collaborating objects. Figure 4.2 illustrates the basic elements of a simple use case model.

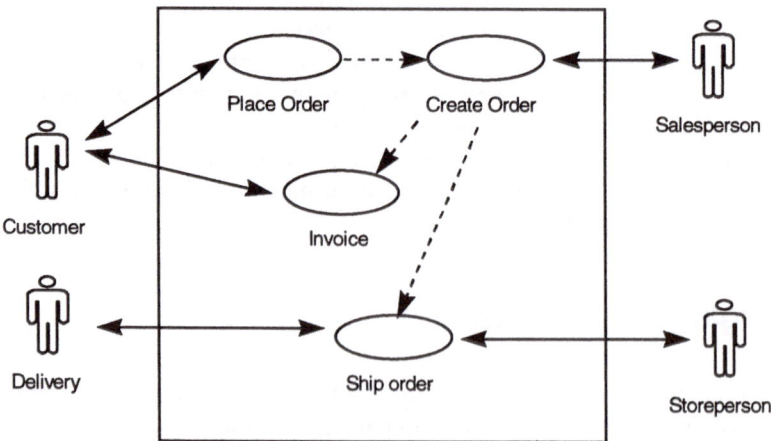

Figure 4.2: Simple use case model

This model depicts four use cases which represent the sales processes of a wholesale business. Four actors, depicted by "person" symbols, represent the customer, salesperson, store-person and delivery roles. The same individual may play two or more roles; for example, the salesperson may also pack or deliver orders. These actors exist outside the system boundary, demarcated by the solid box, defining the scope of the model. Use cases, shown as named oval symbols, exist within the system boundary in this model, although in other models the processes being modelled may require use cases to be drawn outside the system boundary. Use cases shown within the system typically translate into requirements for a software system. Solid, double-ended arrows associate actors with use cases, and may represent a one way or two way flow of control and/or information. Broken, single ended arrows link use cases together, indicating a dependency or sequencing relationship.

Use cases, like classes in an object-oriented program, are said to be instantiated when an actor raises the appropriate commencement event. In this model, the Place Order use case instantiates when a Customer actor presents with a list of required items (note that data attributes such as product names or descriptions are not explicitly shown on this model). The Salesperson actor takes the order and initiates the Create Order use case, which is a named sequence of steps required to generate an order (see Figure 4.3 for an example of how a use case body is expressed), from which the Invoice and Ship Order use cases are invoked, so that the Customer is billed and the order is packed, and finally delivered. Use cases are expressed as a simple sequence of free text descriptions. Use case boundaries are somewhat arbitrary, and need to be drawn after extensive scenario playing with the developing requirements model. Once developed, the inherent simplicity of a use case model makes it particularly open to review by its actors – the end users and business process owners. Use case models are typically created and then reviewed in workshop situations with extensive participation from stakeholders.

Place Order:

- present at point of sale during business hours
- queue for service
- for each required purchase, check description and availability and price
- review total price
- commit purchase

Figure 4.3: Use case body

Tasks can be classified into "strongly structured" tasks which have a distinct sequence of well defined steps, and "weakly structured" tasks which have a comparably weak definition and allow the performer a wider range of freedom to interpret and select steps and sequences. As with any task or process model, strongly structured tasks are ideal material for use case modelling.

Of the contributions made by Jacobson's methodology, use cases have proven to be the most enduring, and have been incorporated into a number of public domain object-oriented methodologies, most notably the Unified Modeling Language (UML, 1997).

4.4 Logical Architecture

Organizing Principles

An object-oriented view of client/server architecture introduces two organizing principles relevant to software architecture – seamless models and components. Object models and implementations provide a degree of seamlessness which is unavailable in other models. In functional decomposition, interfaces, services and layer boundaries need to be defined earlier than in object-oriented decomposition, and once set, are significantly harder to move as a result of inappropriate positioning of services, unanticipated design or implementation complexity, or system evolution. As well, a "seam" is usually created when the function and data models are implemented in database schema and functional programming languages. In object models, all application requirements expressed as use cases are further refined to produce object collaboration models. A number of benefits result from the fact that the basic structure of both the logical and physical designs involve client/server style interactions (between objects and object clusters).

First, decisions about system interfaces and system partitioning can be deferred, until all collaboration models have been designed from the set of essential use cases have been completed. Deferring decisions about implementation is a recurring theme in the object literature. The paradigm supports deferring implementation through encapsulation of implementation mechanisms, at the cost of defining public interfaces to classes and clusters early. The obvious assumption here, that interfaces to abstract state and behaviour change infrequently whereas implementations change more frequently, parallels that of functional composition discussed earlier. In fact, some authors recommend measuring the stability of class interfaces – but definitely *not* their implementa-tions – as a useful metric of system completion during periods of highly iterative development (Meyer, 1988). Making logical and physical partitioning decisions later, rather than sooner, means that decisions can be informed by a better understanding of overall system behaviour, and a more detailed knowledge of implementation constraints. It also means that the most critical system partitioning and structuring decisions are made independent of implementation concerns, which de-couples implementation from logical architecture.

Secondly, object-oriented models provide more options for partitioning and decomposition. In simple terms, an object-oriented software architecture distributes almost anywhere, in that a tier partition can be drawn at any point in the continuum of client, business, or persistence objects and their interactions, subject to the appropriate preservation of regions of cohesion.

Finally, object-oriented models and architectures are more flexible and maintainable, since changes to the positioning of a client/server partition within the architecture have minimal impact because the partition already existed as a part of the internal structure of the tier. Changes to an interface's protocol impact only those objects which implement the interface, and do not propagate to their collaborators, or further around the architecture.

Reuse and Components

Attempts to achieve enterprise-wide and economic software reuse over the past 20 years have met with only limited success. It was widely thought that the initial success with reuse of individual classes achieved with object-oriented programming languages (particularly Smalltalk) would scale up as these languages were adopted by industry. However, the last six to eight years have produced little evidence of class reuse on any significant scale, other than classes from lower layer infrastructure libraries, such as the ubiquitous GUI user interface classes, and simple abstract data types such as collections, strings, dates, etc.

An alternate approach to object-oriented software reuse involves the generalization of "vertical" slices through representative application or system architectures called "frameworks" (Johnson and Foote, 1988). To turn a framework into an application, the user must understand large areas of the skeleton architecture, then derive sub-classes from existing framework classes to provide customized behaviour. Clearly, if a suitable framework can be found from the application domain which implements a significant amount of the required application, impressive amounts of software reuse can occur (typically 50–70 per cent), along with correspondingly impressive development times. But these gains must be balanced against the time required to locate, evaluate and use the framework, and the dependency upon the framework source and its suppliers.

While some standardization and industry acceptance of low level components and frameworks has been achieved, we are still a long way from application development from reusable components, the ultimate goal. More recently, as a result of the current focus on business processes re-engineering, the importance of business application flexibility and extensibility have risen over the more economic drivers of software reuse. Flexible business processes need flexible and responsive system support, particularly from information technology. A new type of "component" is currently being pursued as a solution to large scale software reuse, and enterprise-wide application flexibility.

Enterprise software components are software "blocks" or sub-systems which encapsulate significant chunks of application level functionality. Enterprise components provide their functionality via an object-oriented public interface, which makes them available to enterprise application designers for black-box reuse. Some typical components might be an encapsulated set of data files or database, a computational engine for computing retirement benefits, an encapsulated interface to external devices or systems, a directory or name look-up service, or a mapping service to convert file or data formats, currencies or resource locators.

The interest in enterprise components has been facilitated by the standardization and commercial maturing of object request brokers and products (the Common Object Request Broker Architecture [CORBA] and its Interface

Definition Language [IDL] standard and their family of products, and Microsoft's Component Object Model [COM]). These distributed system interfaces are clearly nothing new – it is the integration of CORBA support into many of the popular object-oriented and object-based integrated development environments which has fuelled the movement. It now costs no extra money, and little additional design or development effort, to distribute an object-oriented application using CORBA at several key places. Additionally, the adoption of CORBA interfaces by both client development languages (such as Java, VisualBasic, Smalltalk and PowerBuilder) and the traditional back end and server platform languages (C, C++) brings true multi-tier and platform independence into scope for common business application development teams.

In-built ORB toolkits break the traditional two-tier architecture, which has dominated business application designer's client/server thinking over the past five years. In the classic client/server architecture, the client managed a combination of graphical user interface and business logic, while the server provided database access (usually via SQL). Back end business processing was often tied to the database via stored procedures or triggers. Support for platform-independent object interactions now opens up the designer's options for placing application functionality on any tier, resulting in new interest in separate business object tiers. By following some design considerations, these business object tiers are yielding shared and reusable enterprise components.

Services, Components and Objects

Recently, the term "enterprise component" or "software component" has become popular. Components are more than graphical user interface widgets or the source code to implement a single class. Enterprise "components" provide the mechanism for implementing enterprise wide services, the building blocks of client/server architectures. Like classes in an object-oriented programming language, services are available from the component's interface. Since many client/server architectures are implemented using object-oriented programming languages and environments, both the service interfaces and their components are implemented using objects. Objects themselves are usually too fine grained to provide enterprise level software components, but are an ideal fabric from which enterprise components are built. Since components only need to implement an (IDL or COM) interface, it is possible that components may be built in non object-oriented programming languages, although this would likely be the exception.

A typical component implements a free standing, self contained business function required by one or more business applications. In terms of the three-tier logical software architecture described in the previous chapter, components implement servers. For example, the Order server (which provides the "Create Order Header", "Complete Order", "Commit Order Line" and "Commit Order" services in the Data Access Servers tier) may be implemented by an Order handling component which manages creation, retrieval, deletion and updating of orders. More generic components will typically include schedulers, sorters, dispatchers, query or search engines, all with customized or configured knowledge of specific business objects, such as orders, invoices, customers, items and products. Components can be thought of as large grained objects – they have identity, internal state, a knowledge of the application or business context, a public interface, and relationships with other components, but no ability to be externally sub-classed for customization.

In an enterprise component based client/server architecture, services fall into several classifications. The popular service classification model is presented graphically in Figure 4.4.

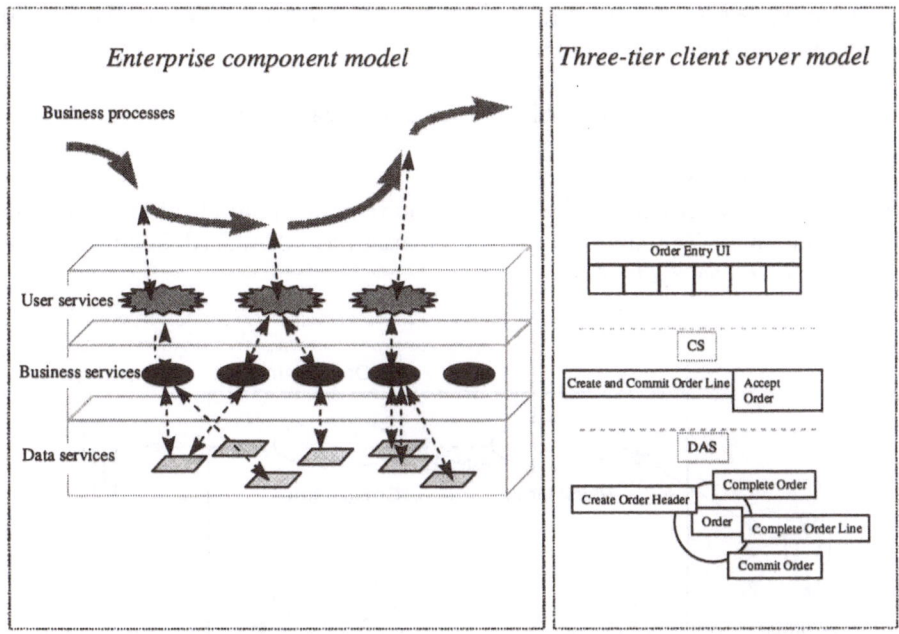

Figure 4.4: Service categories and their support of business processes

Some services exist to directly support business processes, and are defined from the use case requirements model. These have been called "user services". Services may have other, less green-fields, origins. Services may be defined by coalescing similar elements of functions from multiple use cases. In these cases, the service may have no direct association with an actor. These services typically encapsulate business rules or logic, and have been called "business services". Other services may be defined to provide a business oriented view of external devices, systems or databases ("data services").

These service categories have a straightforward mapping to the categories of the three-tier architecture described in the previous chapter. "User services" in Figure 4.4 directly support a task, so they must have user interface, and whatever task navigation is required – they are Client services in our three-tier logical model. "Business services" in Figure 4.4, identified as being service elements common to two use cases, with more general business behaviour incorporating business rules and logic, are Composite Services in the three-tier model. "Data Services" in Figure 4.4 encapsulate basic database, file and interface access to provide a business oriented view – these are Data Access Services in the three-tier model.

Designing with Components

The process of designing with components follows the service model of client/server architecture closely. The steps are as follows:

1. Model the use cases.
2. Define and scope the architectural dependencies by defining packages.
3. Model the object (and therefore package) collaborations.
4. Model the classes involved in the collaboration, refining existing classes with new responsibilities as required.

These steps are outlined with the help of a worked example.

Model the Use Cases
The use case model defines the system requirements, and all other models are dependent on it. The simple order entry example introduced in the previous chapter is used (see Figure 4.5).

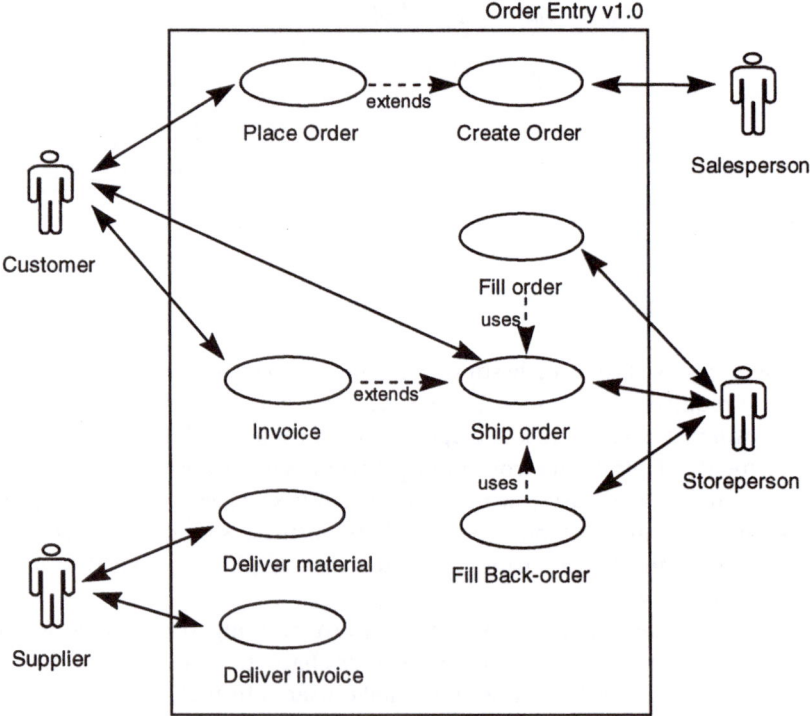

Figure 4.5: Use case model for "Order Entry v1.0"

The set of use cases constitute a specification of a named system, which is bounded by the solid box labelled "Order Entry v1.0". Each use case represents a named region of system behaviour, initiated by an actor, and returning control to the same, or another actor. The use case Place Order (Figure 4.3) describes the system's behaviour in accepting order items from a customer, which chains to use case Create Order, which describes the creation of an order for immediate, partial or complete filling. The actors Salesperson and Storeperson interact (remembering that actors are roles, not necessarily different individuals) to fill and ship the order (use cases Fill Order and Ship Order), which may result in the creation of back orders for out of stock items. Shipping or dispatch of partially or fully completed orders result in execution of the Invoice use case, which names the system's behaviour and business rules regarding invoicing.

Newcomers to use case requirements modelling often query the soft boundary demarcation of a specific use case – for example, why not model order placing and creation as one use case? Jacobson's definition of use cases as the set of behaviours which facilitate an end-to-end interaction with an actor provides one guideline. Another possibility is to reference one use case from several others in the model, either now or in the future.

It is important to note that the use case model does *not* dictate the logical architecture of the system. Rather, it provides an overlay over the traditional English language requirements specification which reduces ambiguity and provides a useful structure. The use case model serves logical architecture development by providing named scenarios to exercise the candidate architecture which follows.

Define Packages

We now turn to the creation of the software architecture. Packages were introduced earlier as a high level class modeling element, which provide a first level of decomposition in a class model, and group cohesive clusters of tightly related classes. Packages provide a manageable abstraction for developing the software architecture – when modelling client/server architectures based on services, packages provide an appropriate level to group service classes (user, business and data services) into servers. Figure 4.6 shows a candidate package diagram for the model.

Candidate packages are selected by considering key abstractions which appear in both the business domain, and the textual bodies of use cases in the requirements model. Other factors which influence the selection packages in this first architectural model include:

- the integration of existing systems or software components;
- the likelihood that a package will be multiply used (i.e. reused) in the architecture; and
- the opportunity for current or future distribution which a package boundary presents.

The candidate package model in Figure 4.6 has been supplemented with a likely assignment of packages to architectural tiers – the POINT_OF_SALE and DELIVERY packages contain user interface and task logic which must sit in the client tier, the ORDER package contains elements for creating, deleting and updating orders, along with significant business rules for order handling. This package will be used by both client tier packages (interactive requests on orders from the system's user interface), and single, periodic off-line clients (such as those which handle stock delivery, inventory updates and back order processing), and in turn relies of Data Access Servers for storing and retrieving orders – it most likely belongs on the Composite Services tier. The PRODUCT_INFORMATION and INVENTORY packages contain Data Access Services.

The package model now provides a scaffolding for assigning more specific and detailed behaviours. We identify these in the next level of object modelling.

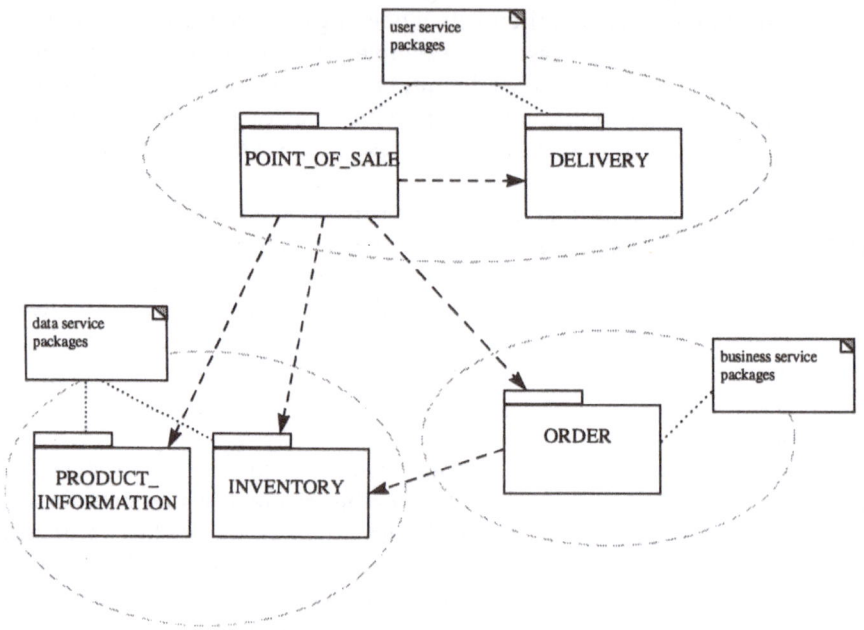

Figure 4.6: Package model for "Order Entry" services

Model the Package and Object Collaborations
Given the package model, the assignment of packages to architectural tiers, and the use case model, the detailed work of object modelling can begin. The entire use case model is now manually walked through and mapped to the package model, use case by use case, step by step. Candidate objects (classes in the static sense) are identified from the text of each case, and assigned to a package. As objects are built up inside packages, their interactions are drawn in, illustrating the necessary collaborations between objects to support a use case step. Figure 4.7 illustrates the result for the Place Order use case.

This process usually results in a high degree of reiteration. As new responsibilities are identified, they may readily find a "home" in an existing object, split an existing object into two, or they may require the creation of new, unrelated objects in the model (ORDER::ORDER_QUEUE is an example). As modelling proceeds, the association between an object and its package may weaken, necessitating its movement to another package. Some packages may end up with few or no objects. Similarly, the assignment of objects to packages may invalidate the current assignment of package to tier – this is perfectly legitimate, since the packages were initially created as "platforms" in the model's scaffolding. The aim of this modelling step is to produce an understandable and feasible package and class model which demonstrably supports the requirements model. Once this has been done, the candidate classes can be more fully specified, even to the point of coding class headers for a more formal review.

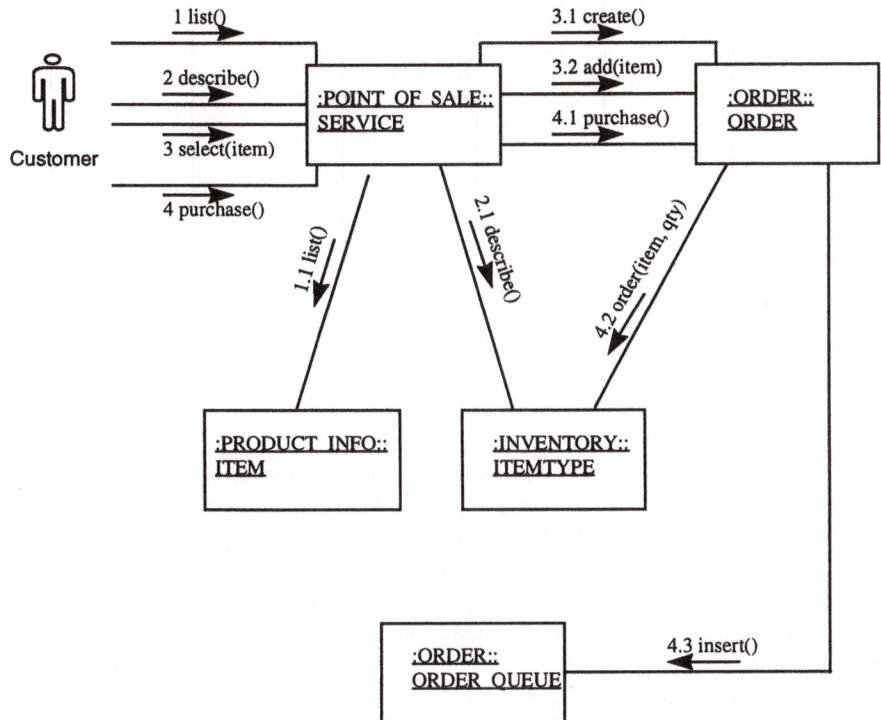

Figure 4.7: Object collaboration model for "Place Order" use case

Define Services
The final step in developing the class model involves reviewing the package interfaces. During the object modelling activity, many object interactions will have been identified and drawn in which span package boundaries. These interactions must be rationalized into a well defined and logically consistent interface for each package, thereby defining the services available from each package (Figure 4.8).

Service interfaces must uphold the principles of good interface design. The interface must be as simple as possible, must strongly support the function of the package, but must not reveal the package's internal workings or implementation. If it is likely that the package will be reused now or in the future, suitable configuration options must be planned. As with all design for reuse on any level of abstraction, the best time to get package interfaces right is at design time, before implementation and package client software dependencies are in place.

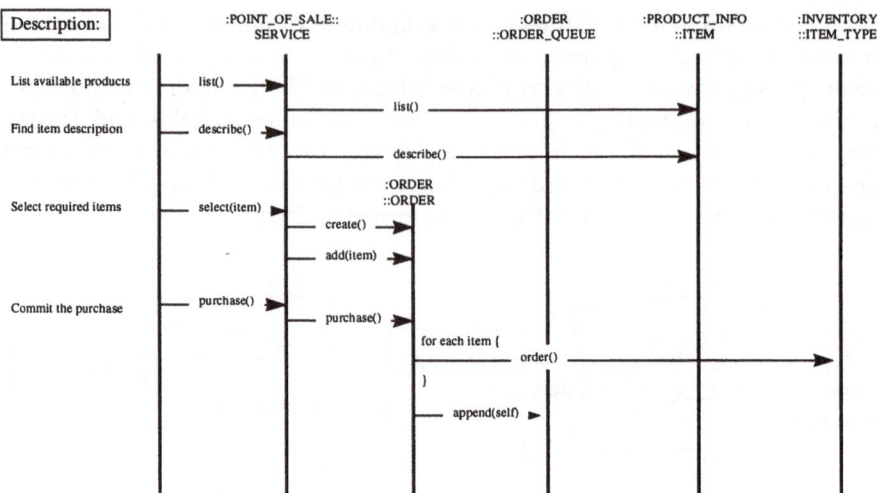

Figure 4.8: Service boundaries from object interactions

4.5 Summary

Both object-oriented software technologies and the established object-oriented analysis and design techniques support the logical design and implementation of three-tier client/server architectures strongly. Use case requirements modelling aligns closely with the task-based organizational model presented in the previous chapter. Object modelling with packages, classes and objects provides a natural way of translating a complex set of business requirements into a logical software architecture. Using this approach, decisions about allocation of modules to tiers (client, composite and data access) can be made from early on in the modelling process, through to relatively late, as the fine detail of object abstractions are being discovered. A by-product of object modelling is the opportunity to treat each package as a potential software component for reuse in the current or future architecture.

Part 3

Coupling and Dependency

5. Coupling in Distributed Systems

5.1 Introduction

The concept of *coupling* was introduced by Yourdon and Constantine in their book, *Structured Design: Fundamentals of a Discipline of Computer Program and Systems Design*, in 1979. Over the years coupling, and the related notion of cohesion, have become established tenets of software engineering (see, for example, Pressman, 1994). As we shall see, coupling is the strength of interconnection between two software modules: the higher the strength of interconnection, the higher the coupling. For software to be easier to understand, correct and maintain, a system should be partitioned so that the coupling between modules is as loose as possible.

In introducing coupling, Yourdon and Constantine state:

"How much of one module must be known in order to understand another module? The more that we must know of module B in order to understand module A, the more closely connected A is to B... The measure that we are seeking is known as *coupling*; it is a measure of the *strength* of the interconnection. Highly coupled modules are joined by strong interconnections; loosely coupled ones by weak interconnections. We aim for loosely coupled systems, that is systems in which we can study (debug or maintain) one module without having to know very much about any other module in the system."

Recognizing that it is difficult to quantify the concept of knowledge directly, they reason that to arrive at an operational method of establishing the degree of interconnection, "Coupling...may be operationalized as the probability that in coding, debugging or modifying one module, the programmer will have to take into account something in another module. If two modules are highly coupled, then there is a high probability that a programmer trying to modify one of them will have to make a change in another". They put forward the following factors that influence coupling:

- Type of information flow along the connection: data and control can flow across the interface, and control information induces stronger coupling than data.
- Complexity of the interface: the greater the number of different items being passed the stronger the coupling.
- Binding time of the connection: the earlier the binding the stronger the coupling.
- Type of connection between modules: minimally connected modules (containing a single, fully parameterized interface) exhibit the least coupling. Normal connections and pathological connections possess progressively stronger coupling.

When Yourdon and Constantine put forward the concepts of coupling and cohesion, distributed systems as we know them today did not exist. In a non-distributed system, we are essentially addressing the problem of modularizing a single large program. In today's distributed systems, we are confronted with a problem domain that is more complex, encompassing application components that are distributed over heterogeneous environments – possibly written in different languages and housed at different network nodes on different machines – that nevertheless need to communicate dynamically to achieve some purpose. A distributed environment is also characterized by the communication infra-structure, middleware, which provides services to the application enabling the distributed application components to interact with each other.

A distributed environment has its own characteristic development and maintenance issues. For example,

- Once designed, subsequent changes for shared software components in a distributed application – especially changes involving the external interfaces of distributed application components – become especially difficult, since a service may be used by any number of other components in disparate locations. Therefore, designing these interfaces to minimize a module's exposure to remote components (maximizing the autonomy and local control) is of critical importance.
- Development and upkeep of the software in a distributed system often requires the agreement of geographically distributed groups and constituencies, requiring consensus over the design of the external interfaces. Therefore, each mistake in the design of the inter-module interactions becomes doubly significant, since it attracts not only a hefty redevelopment penalty (possibly including effects of technology change and performance), but also because the penalty may be compounded by the need for re-negotiation between groups with different interests.
- An executing module of a distributed application calling upon remote modules and resources can raise robustness implications – for example, the performance penalty that a poorly performing server can cause to a blocked calling module or the consequences of the unavailability of a remote resource to a calling module's ability to continue processing. These implications can be compounded – where these remote resources are beyond the jurisdiction of the

owners/users of the calling module, neither the calling module nor its owner may be able to do much about rectifying the problem.

These and similar issues mean that the choice of appropriate types and levels of interaction between cooperating remote software modules becomes critical to the success or otherwise of the distributed application. Since executing modules, with the assistance of middleware infrastructures, communicate over a network mimicking local interaction, one can reasonably expect to extend the notion of coupling to a distributed environment. If we can – so that types and levels of remote interaction can be expressed in terms of coupling – then coupling and its consequences assume a critical importance in designing "good" distributed applications.

In this chapter, we aim to extend the notion of coupling into the distributed application environment, to provide a practical framework for the application architect or designer to assist making effective design choices.

5.2 Operationalizing Coupling in Distributed Systems

We begin by discussing the four factors influencing coupling itemized in the previous section, in the context of distributed applications.

Types of Information Flow along the Connection

The more we must know about the "outside world" in order to understand how any one module works, the greater the coupling in the system. In general, there are three types of information that flow within a distributed application system. For any one module, these three types of information flow contribute to its interaction with the "outside world".

1. Data.
2. Control information: information originating in one application module that is used to influence the flow of control in another application module.
3. Administrative information: information not directly part of application execution logic, nevertheless needed for the distributed application system to operate successfully. Types of administrative information are:

    - Naming: the names by which application components are identified need to be known, where there is a variation, local variants need to be correctly resolved;
    - Location: the association between the application module and the network node at which it resides (the network address, protocols etc);
    - Usage: the users authorized to access an application module;
    - Time: the time associated with a location. We cannot assume that all locations of a distributed environment operate within the same time zone or keep time in the same way;

- Formats: the low-level data formats (such as ASCII and EBCDC, Little Endian and Big Endian) associated with a location (specifically with the hardware and system software platform). We cannot assume homogeneity in a distributed computing environment; different platforms have different representations for data.

Data and Control Information
The roles of data and control in inducing coupling were introduced by Yourdon and Constantine and are now well established. It is commonly accepted now that coupling is minimized when only data is communicated between two interacting modules; other things being equal control induces a greater degree of dependency between modules – and hence coupling – than does data. In the interaction between two physically distributed application modules, the coupling issues that are raised by the passage of control and data are essentially similar to those in a non-distributed situation.

There is a difference however. Yourdon and Constantine were focusing upon preferred ways of modularizing a single large program, where among other things the designer/programmer has a good deal of freedom in how the program was partitioned. In a distributed setting however, we would use some type of middleware – SQL, RPC, ORB, MOM, DTP etc. – to effect communications between distributed application components. A middleware product typically offers one or more programming interface types. For example, an RPC-based middleware product may offer a synchronous or asynchronous RPC. An SQL product may offer embedded SQL, dynamic SQL, or SQL stored procedures. In designing the communication between distributed application components, the designer is limited to the interface types provided by the middleware product(s) of choice. Hence the form of the interfaces between the distributed application components is strongly conditioned by the middleware product or technology with which we work.

Therefore we can argue that in a distributed environment:

- Coupling is minimized when only data passes through the interface between interacting application components. Other things being equal, control information induces a greater degree of coupling between distributed application modules than data.
- Interface types that (a) require the passage of control or (b) enable control information to be easily woven into the logic governing the behaviour of the two modules are capable of inducing a greater level of coupling than those interfaces whose model of behaviour presumes only a flow of data.

Administrative Information
The third type, administrative information, not part of Yourdon and Constantine's original coupling framework, comes into its own in distributed systems. This class of information is very much part of a module's interaction with the "outside world" *since that module needs to rely upon naming, location, and usage information in order to make a connection with any other module.* In addition to this, time and formatting information can be relevant in some circumstances.

Take an RPC-like interaction. The calling module makes what appears to be a local call. The infrastructure, using its knowledge of the location of the service provider module, the protocols and routing information, and possibly the authorized users for that module, takes the arguments of the call, marshalls them, routes them to the destination, and routes the response back to the origin. Figure 5.1 models the role of administrative information in effecting an interaction between two remote application components.

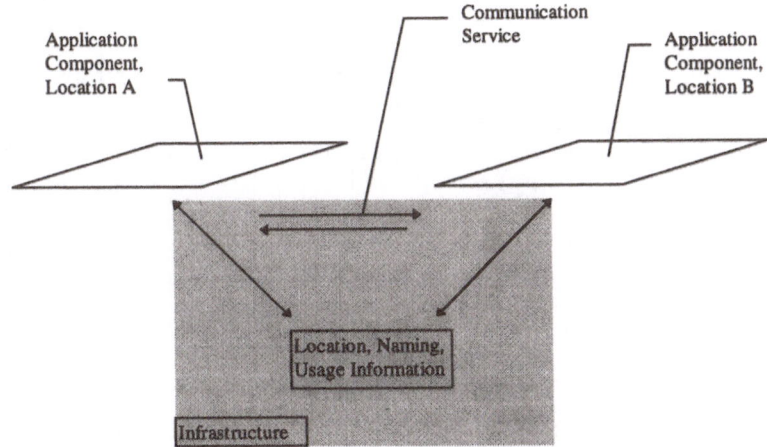

Figure 5.1: Remote Procedure Call: interplay between application components and administrative information and services

What are the consequences for maintenance? Consider a set of PC-based clients that communicate with a SQL DBMS via stored procedure calls. As a result of a data reorganization, some of the stored procedure calls are moved to another DBMS, at a different network node. Apart from the work necessary to develop/ install the new stored procedures at the new database, this change effort could include the following additional duties: (a) change to client code, since the new configuration requires the client software to distinguish between the two databases when referring to the respective stored procedures; (b) changes to the information in configuration files in the infrastructure software at each client – to provide the new DBMS address; (c) at the second DBMS, creating references to the new stored procedures (if not automatically created), and registering access rules (who can use what) for the new stored procedures. In contrast, in a DCE environment, when the providers of some RPCs are moved from location A to location B, it only requires the affected servers to register their new location/host information at initialization with the name service system. Another illustration is contained in Figure 5.2. The top diagram shows an include process, where location information is embedded in the source code. This carries relatively little coupling penalty, since normally inclusion is a development environment (compile time) activity; a wrong reference (or a change) can be relatively easily accommodated. The remote connection (bottom) has more severe coupling implications – the connection is only made at runtime, and any source code reference changes need to be effected in the development environment.

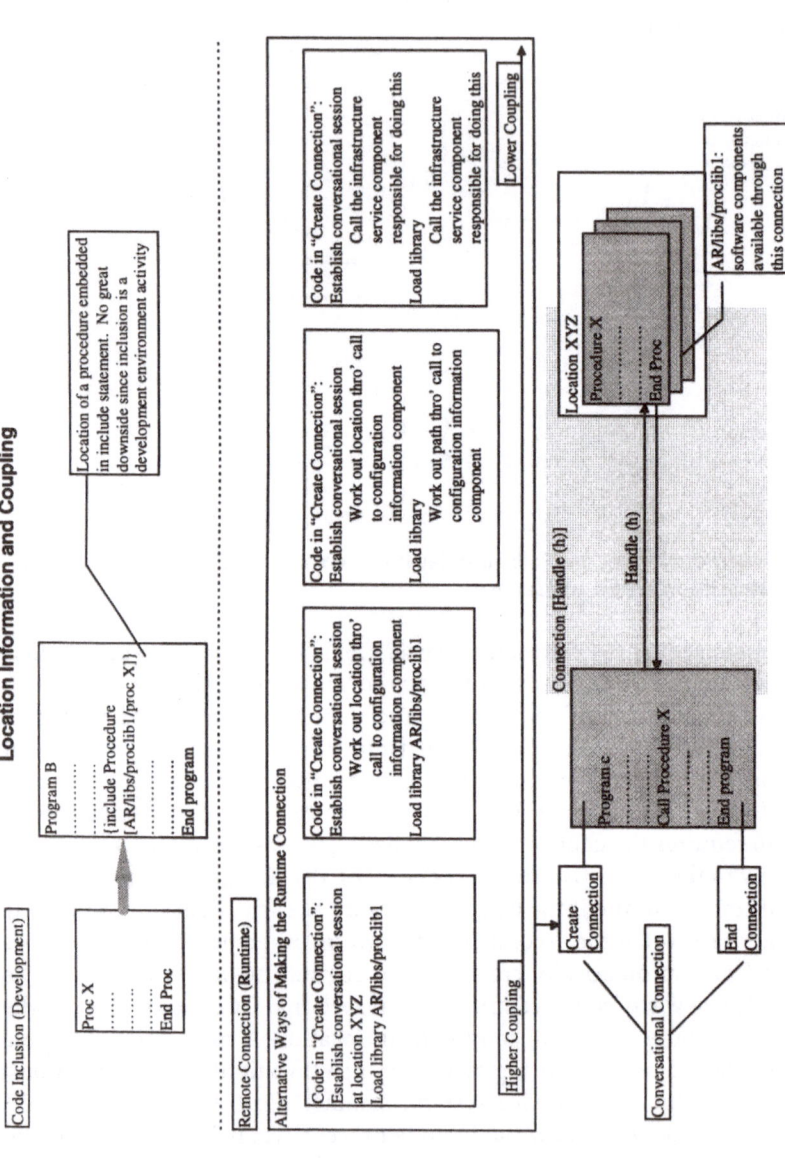

Figure 5.2: Location information and coupling. Top: code inclusion – little coupling penalty; Bottom: different ways of making a conversational connection with different coupling implications

These examples show that the resolution of naming, location and usage information is not a trivial matter in a distributed system. Administrative information – this knowledge about naming, physical location and usage attributes of an application component – can be housed at application level or at infrastructure level, the mix of locations depends on the distributed computing product used. We can make two conclusions. Typically, a modification to administrative information embedded at application level requires a development time change, whereas a modification to information located at infrastructure level need not require any changes to the application. Where this information is housed at the infrastructure level, it is usually available to the application as a service, and the information is usually configurable. Furthermore, extrapolating from the previous example, the same set of administrative information items housed say at three locations – the application, a client-based .INI file, and the database – requires a great deal more effort to maintain than the same information housed at a single location. Accordingly, the greater the fragmentation of administrative information required for application component A to communicate with remote application component B, the greater the effort required to effect changes to that information. Therefore, other things being equal:

- administrative information housed at application level induces closer coupling than at infrastructure level;
- fragmented administrative information induces closer (higher) coupling than that housed at a single location.

Interface Complexity

Yourdon and Constantine's relationship between interface complexity and coupling – other things being equal, the number of different items (not the volume of data) passing through the interface is an indicator of the strength of coupling – can be directly applied to a distributed setting. Therefore,

- The higher the number of different items of (a) data, (b) control, and (c) administration information involved in application component A communicating with a remote application component B, the higher the strength of coupling.
- As a corollary, interface coupling increases with the number of interfaces in the system.

Binding

In information technology, we use the term binding in several contexts. An example is in referring to the resolution of variables to values. Another is in describing the behaviour of RPC and allied communication to refer to the association of a client with a specific server or service provider. We can regard binding pertaining to a distributed environment as the resolution of aspects of contact between modules, such as mapping a name to a runtime instance of an application component located at a specific network node, or matching the parameter list of a called module. Binding is therefore the act of associating some aspect of one software module with another remote module. In terms of coupling, the concern is *when* binding takes place. We identify three types of binding.

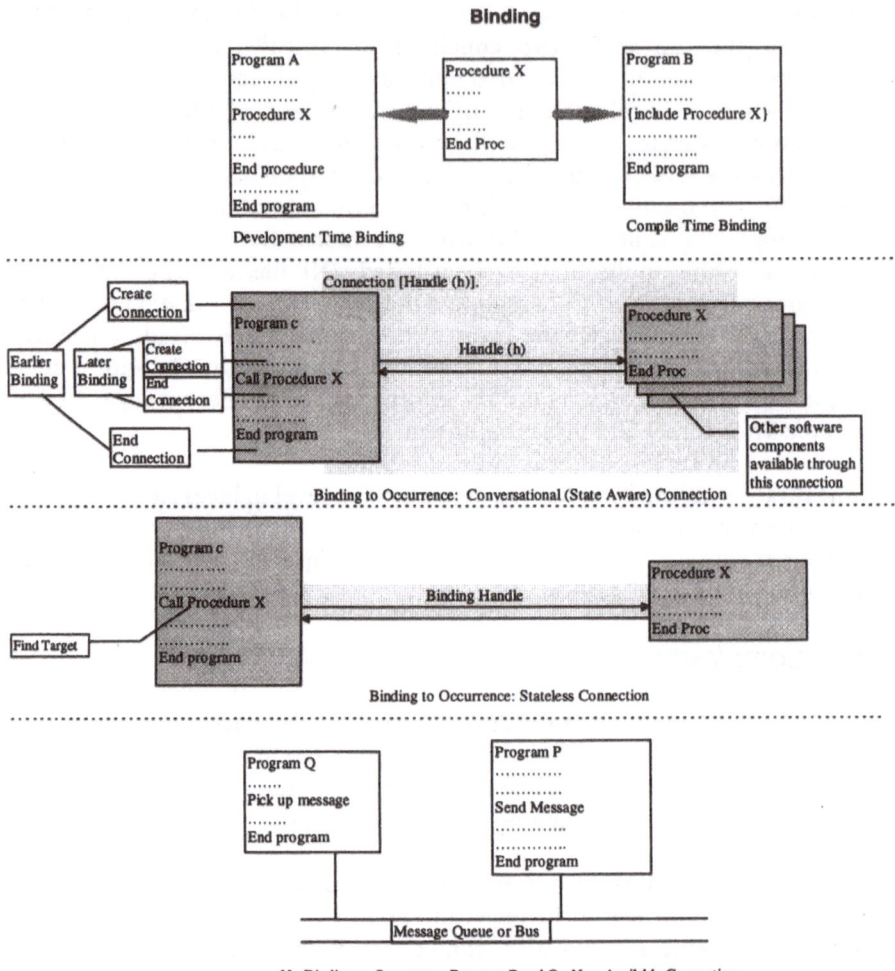

Binding

Development Time Binding

Compile Time Binding

Binding to Occurrence: Conversational (State Aware) Connection

Binding to Occurrence: Stateless Connection

No Binding to Occurrence Between P and Q: Non-Available Connection

Figure 5.3: Binding effects with different types of middleware

Binding to a Form/Structure

We can illustrate the binding of one module to some form associated with another software module as follows. At development time the client RPC needs to match exactly the specification of the call interface – the identifier, the number and order of the arguments – binding the client to the form of the provider, even though this procedure may not yet exist in code. Also, with CORBA's static invocation, the precision that is enabled by method overloading has its cost in the demand for an exact specification in the calling module. In contrast, with dynamic invocation, CORBA allows the client to build and execute a request dynamically at runtime:

the client can obtain the method description, create the argument list, and then create and invoke the request – binding it to the form of the method late, only at runtime. With a MOM-based message, the recipient modules need to know the message format, binding it early since a change to this format will require changes to the recipients. However, with a MOM-based self-describing message there is no form/structure binding between sender and recipient(s) at all.

Therefore, the later the binding to a form or structure, the lower the probability that a module A needs to take account of form/structure changes in another remote module B with which A communicates, and hence the looser the coupling between the two.

Binding to an Implementation

Binding of a module to an implementation of another module is about language dependency.

A distributed environment is not required to be homogeneous: it is a distinct advantage if application components on different machine environments on different geographic locations could also be developed in different languages, enabling the language of choice at a site to be used in developing and maintaining their part of the application. This is only possible where a module is bound late to the implementation of another module.

With embedded SQL, the embedded portions must be precompiled, thus binding them at that time to a vendor specific dialect of SQL at the server. A stored procedure call, even though there is no actual precompilation, nevertheless is likely to exhibit some early binding to the implementation dialect through the manifestation of dialect specific features in the call. For example, a client software module using Transact SQL stored procedure calls to communicate with a Sybase server binds the client early to Transact SQL – in general not supporting a functionally equivalent set of stored procedures on an Oracle database, coded in PL/SQL. If this type of change occurs, the client too will need modification. Arguably, in a DCE style RPC this aspect of binding does not occur at all, since the abstract IDL specification of the interface insulates the client from language specifics of the server. This means that a change can occur to the implementation language of one or more server functions, without any change to any of the calling modules.

Therefore, where a module is bound late or not at all to the implementation of a remote module insulates one from language changes to the other, inducing looser coupling between the two than otherwise.

Binding to an Occurrence

The third form of binding occurs where a module is bound to an occurrence of another module at a physical location. For example when an RPC is invoked by the client, the call is resolved to a particular server at a particular network address by the directory/name service late, at runtime. With some SQL implementations certain facets of the occurrence, for example a stored procedure qualification with a database name, may be exposed at application level, causing some early binding. In other distributed environments, the connection call to a remote server may require the latter's physical location details. Where occurrence details are bound early, there is less flexibility to change them. In general the appearance of location information, such as physical names network addresses and protocols, at application level signals early binding to the occurrence of the remote module. A change to any of these attributes then requires a modification at development time. Alternatively, where these attributes are separate from the application, housed either in a runtime accessible directory, a .INI file, etc. makes this information available at runtime, signalling late binding. In this scenario, a change to occurrence information is able to be associated with application components as a matter of runtime configuration, not requiring application changes.

It is interesting that we reached a similar conclusion in the analysis of administrative information. These two criteria are really two perspectives on the same phenomenon: early binding to an occurrence happens where administrative information is housed at application level.

Binding – Summary
Therefore, the earlier the binding to (a) a form, (b) an implementation, or (c) an occurrence occurs, the stronger the coupling between the application components.

Types of Connection between Modules

By examining ways of minimizing the number and variety of interfaces per module – using as the main criteria (a) the number of entry/exit points to a module, (b) the parameterization of information items passing across the interface, and (c) conditioned transfer of control – Yourdon and Constantine classified connections into minimal, normal and pathological types, with progressively higher coupling. This approach is appropriate when analyzing ways in which we modularize a single large program. A distributed setting, however, presents a somewhat different problem. As we indicated earlier, the form of the interface to a remote component is strongly conditioned by the middleware product or technology with which you work. For example, a designer working with CORBA and a CORBA compliant development/runtime environment is confronted with either a static or a dynamic object request broker (ORB) connection type. Another designer, working in an SQL-based environment encounters embedded SQL, an SQL call level interface, or stored procedures as the means of remote communication. Another, working with an RPC-based product, may be provided with the choice of synchronous or asynchronous RPCs. Accordingly in designing the communication between distributed application components, the designer is limited to the interface types provided by the middleware product(s) of choice. Moreover (with the possible exception of the SQL command, which contain static references to data), most interface types conform to the minimal and normal connection criteria specified by Yourdon and Constantine. Hence we need a different set of criteria to differentiate between modes of remote communication on the basis of coupling.

Classification of Communication Types
First though, what are the different types of communication between remote application components that are available in a distributed setting? Thus far, we

have used middleware product/technology types (e.g. RPC, ORB, MOM etc.) as an informal way of distinguishing between types of remote interface. It is now appropriate to develop a more formal classification.

What follows is a typology of properties that shape the interaction between two remote application modules. As we will see, a particular type of interface offered by a middleware product (e.g. DCE RPC) will exhibit some combination of these properties. Of course, only some of these combinations are valid.

- Available versus Non-Available

  In Available communication a remote application component needs to be available for communication to take place. For example, for a client module to execute an RPC, an SQL stored procedure, an object request, the server module providing the service needs to be available.

  In Non-Available communication, a remote application component need not be available for communication to take place. For instance, with a Message-Oriented Middleware product using a queue or a publish/subscribe mechanism, the sending application module is not dependent on the availability of a recipient module(s) in order to put a message in a queue or to publish a message.

- Conversational versus Non-Conversational

  In the Conversational class, a "connection" between requester and provider modules need to be established, for communication to take place: typically a handle, session, or conversation identifier is established that ties the calling instance to the provider instance (e.g. Coulouris et al., 1994). Once this identifier is created, the two modules can carry out a conversation that may consist of one or more request/reply interactions; data may be transferred, and state may be shared between calling and providing modules. Typically, the connection will persist until (usually the module that established the connection) explicitly closes it down. Accordingly, this type of communication is also termed Persistent. This type of communication is sometimes termed State Aware because it is conducive to sharing state. Products such as CICS or Progress provide the capability for conversational communication.

  In Non-Conversational communication, a "connection" between the calling and called modules does not exist. That is, typically, there is no session or conversation identifier that needs to be established for communication between two remote application components to take place. Usually, based on the request identifier, the infrastructure handles the marshalling of arguments and transportation of the request. The server services the complete request providing the complete result; then, discarding all information about that request, waits for the next request which may be from the same or a different client. Hence, this type of communication is also said to be Stateless. It has sometimes been termed Connectionless Request/Reply or CLRR (Hesselgrave, 1990). RPC or ORB-based communication is a good example of this category.

- Synchronous versus Asynchronous

  In Synchronous communication, once it makes a request the calling module is blocked for the duration of the call. That is, until it receives the reply that the recipient module sends back after servicing the request.

In Asynchronous communication, the calling module can carry out other work after the request is sent. However, Asynchronous communication as defined in this context is different from Non-Available communication: although the caller is not blocked, Asynchronous communication nevertheless requires the availability of the server or recipient module for the request to take place. Asynchronous behaviour is usually achieved via a polling mechanism at the requesting or client module. Certain distributed computing environments, for example Entera, offer both synchronous and asynchronous RPC capability.

- (Distributed) Transactional versus Non-Transactional
  A distributed transactional capability can coordinate and control several physical units of work possibly performed at application modules at different physical locations as a single logical unit of work, to be carried out in an all or nothing fashion. Products such as Encina, Tuxedo and CICS provide transactional capabilities.
- Static versus Dynamic
  In static invocation, the specification of the interface must be known at development time. In dynamic invocation, the exact specification of the called interface is "discovered" at runtime, built up by the calling program.

Communication Types and Coupling
Each pair of these characteristics can be compared for relative strength of coupling, using the coupling criteria we discussed earlier in this chapter. Figure 5.4 presents a summary comparison. Only some of the coupling criteria can be used as an effective discriminator for each pair, others only being relevant at the level of the product or the application.

The analysis in Figure 5.4 indicates the following:

- Available communication induces stronger coupling than Non-Available;
- Conversational communication induces stronger coupling than Non-Conversational;
- Synchronous communication induces stronger coupling than Asynchronous;
- Transactional communication induces stronger coupling than Non-Transactional;
- Static communication induces stronger coupling than Dynamic communication.

5.3 Coupling, Middleware and Systems Design

Using as a starting point Yourdon and Constantine's original classification, we have now developed a set of criteria with which to assess coupling in a distributed system. We can use this criteria to make coupling analyses of (a) middleware products – more specifically interface types provided by middleware products and (b) actual applications – either in architecting or designing new applications or in analyzing existing ones.

| | Type of information | | Administrative | Fragmentation | Interface complexity | Binding | | |
| | Control and data | | | | | | | |
	Data only?	Enable easy passage of control?	Application or infrastructure?		No. of different items	to Form	to Implementation	to Occurrence
Available	Application dependent	Difficult to very easy	Product dependent	Product dependent	Application dependent	Early	Product dependent	Product dependent
Non-Available	Application dependent	Very difficult	Product dependent	Product dependent	Application dependent	Late/ Not at all	Not at all	Late or not at all
Conversational	Application dependent	Very easy	Product dependent	Product dependent	Application dependent	Early	Product dependent early binding easier	Product dependent
CLRR	Application dependent	Difficult	Product dependent	Product dependent	Application dependent	Early	Product dependent	Product dependent
Synchronous	Application dependent	Easy	Product dependent	Product dependent	Application dependent	Early	Product dependent	Product dependent
Asynchronous	Application dependent	Difficult	Product dependent	Product dependent	Application dependent	Early	Product dependent	Product dependent
Transactional	Control and data	Easy	Product dependent	Product dependent	Application dependent	Early	Product dependent	Product dependent
Non-Transactional	Application Dependent	Difficult	Product dependent	Product dependent	Application dependent	Early	Product dependent	Product dependent
Static	Application dependent	Difficult	Product dependent	Product dependent	Application dependent	Early	Product dependent	Product dependent
Dynamic	Application dependent	Difficult	Product dependent	Product dependent	Application dependent	Late	Late	Typically late

Figure 5.4: Comparison of opposite communication types against coupling criteria

Default Coupling

Communication between application components in a distributed system is made possible by middleware. Each middleware product offers to the application one or more *interface types*. For example, a CORBA-compliant ORB will offer static object requests and dynamic object requests. DCE offers a synchronous RPC, as well as a conversational connection. Entera offers synchronous as well as asynchronous RPCs. Encina provides distributed transactions, and Tuxedo is capable of local and global (distributed) transactions. MQ Series provides asynchronous (non-available in our terminology) messaging.

Each interface type conditions the strength of possible interconnection between distributed modules and thereby prescribes the degree of freedom the designer has, in designing the actual interfaces of the application. The extent of this coupling can be determined using the criteria we have developed. Figure 5.5 shows the results of such an analysis. In performing this analysis, we have taken one step back from interface types provided by specific middleware products. We show a set of generic interface types – for example, rather than Encina's distributed transaction, we analyze generic distributed transactions, instead of Transact SQL or PL/SQL stored procedure we look at generic SQL stored procedures, etc. Some sharpness is lost, but we arrive at generally applicable results. Of course, the designer may carry out a product-based analysis, for example, in evaluating competing products.

On the basis of this analysis, we can rank the generic distributed interface types from high to low coupling as follows:

1. DTP transaction
2. SQL stored procedure
3. Synchronous RPC, object broker object request (static invocation)
4. Object broker object request (dynamic invocation)
5. Message-oriented middleware message (non-available message)

Assuming that the designer would strive equally hard to minimize coupling in both cases, an interface implemented with an SQL-based interface type will result in closer coupling than a synchronous RPC interface type. The coupling associated with each interface type of a middleware product can be regarded as a *standard or default level of coupling*, characteristic for that interface type. This is a convenient way of perceiving the coupling contribution a middleware interface type makes to the application, since (as we will see in the following section), for a specific application, application design and coding choices typically induce levels of coupling over and above this default level.

Application Induced Coupling

Even though the application designer's freedom is limited by the choice of middleware, he/she does add application related coupling through specific application design decisions. Take a synchronous RPC-based application as an example. There are five RPCs with seven arguments, six with ten arguments, and

	Type of information				Communication type	Interface complexity	Binding		
	Control and data		Administrative	Fragmentation		No. different items	to Form	to Implementation	to Occurrence
	Data only?	Enable easy passage of control?	Application or infrastructure?						
Distributed transaction	Control and data	Easy	Typically infrastructure	Typically no	Available, Synchronous, Non-Conversational, Transactional, Static	Application dependent	Early	Late	Late
SQL stored procedure	Application dependent	Average	Typically application and infrastructure	Product dependent; typically some	Available, Synchronous, Non-Conversational, Non-Transactional, Static	Application dependent	Early	Early	Early
Synchronous RPC	Application dependent	Average	Typically infrastructure	Product dependent; typically no	Available, Synchronous, Non-Conversational, Non-Transactional, Static	Application dependent	Early	Late	Late
Asynchronous RPC	Application dependent	Difficult	Typically infrastructure	Product dependent; typically no	Available, Asynchronous, Non-Conversational, Non-Transactional, Static	Application dependent	Early	Late	Late
Static object request	Application dependent	Average	Typically infrastructure	Product dependent; typically no	Available, Synchronous, Non-Conversational, Non-Transactional, Static	Application dependent	Early	Late	Late
Dynamic object request	Application dependent	Difficult	Typically infrastructure	Product dependent; typically no	Available, Synchronous, Non-Conversational, Non-Transactional, Dynamic	Application dependent	Late	Late	Late
(Non-available) message-oriented middleware message	Application dependent	Very difficult	Typically infrastructure	Product dependent; typically no	Non-Available	Application dependent	Late or none with self describing message	None	None

Figure 5.5: Comparison of interface types

three with eight arguments. Some RPCs are designed only to pass data as arguments. In some others control information, such as a flag to lock a database record, a key to determine the beginning of the next 20 records of a results list, or an indicator to show that the calling client is in edit mode (as opposed to add mode), is passed as a parameter. Based on our coupling criteria, for each implemented call, a certain amount of coupling is added to the default extent associated with the synchronous RPC. Moreover, we can imagine that given the same middleware product, and the same functional requirements, the application design decisions that two different teams make will result in different levels of coupling. Hence, application design decisions add a level of additional coupling, large or small depending on design decisions, to the default level associated with the interface type(s) of the middleware product. By examining the design of a yet to be developed distributed application or the design/code of an operational one, we make an assessment of application induced coupling.

5.4 Coupling Summary

In this chapter, we have extended the notion of coupling to a distributed environment. The consequences of coupling are well known and are no different in a distributed environment: the stronger the coupling, the lesser the modularity and consequently the greater the inflexibility of the system. The stronger the coupling, the more difficult and the more costly it is to maintain a system. The thread of reasoning in this chapter reveals several important features.

1. In a distributed setting, even though coupling arises out of the dispersion of application related knowledge, both the application and the infrastructure contribute to coupling. The infrastructure contributes to coupling in two major ways: first by being the repository of all or part of administrative information, and secondly by extending one or more specific programming interface types, each with a default level of coupling, to the application.
2. The choice of a middleware product for a distributed application brings with it one or more programming interface types, and with each interface type a characteristic level of default coupling. This default level of coupling can be compared with that of other types of middleware.
3. Since the type of middleware largely establishes the degree of certain dimensions of coupling, once the middleware is chosen the designer/developer's discretionary control over coupling becomes limited. However, through application and interface design choices, the designer introduces additional coupling. *Accordingly, the coupling that a particular distributed application exhibits is a combination of the natural coupling introduced by the middleware, and that introduced by the designer.*

It is important that the application architect or designer understands the coupling implications of middleware selection and application design decisions. The principles described in this chapter have many uses in this context. They can be employed:

- in the architectural level design of distributed systems and the detailed design of individual interfaces, to develop as well as review designs;
- in the analysis of middleware – for middleware products or interface types offered by a product – to compare middleware, and/or to match middleware capability against architectural or design needs.

Finally, we have seen that low coupling is an objective greatly to be desired in a distributed application. However, a moment's thought reveals that the same low amount of coupling cannot be sustained in *all* remote interfaces of an application. Rather, it is reasonable to expect *appropriate coupling* to be the goal in the design of distributed systems: that is, given a certain requirement, employing the lowest appropriate coupling to realize the requirement. We pursue this line of inquiry in the next chapter.

6. *Software Dependency*

6.1 Introduction

To repeat the closing words of the previous chapter, low coupling is an objective greatly to be desired in a distributed application. However, a moment's thought reveals that the same, low, amount of coupling cannot be sustained in *all* remote interfaces of an application. Rather, it is reasonable to expect *appropriate coupling* to be the goal in the design of distributed systems: that is, given a certain requirement, employing the lowest appropriate coupling to realize the requirement. What are these requirements? In the following pages, we introduce the notion of *dependency*.

Imagine that you are filling in your tax return. You get a tax deduction on some of the bank charges. You cannot recall the figures from memory. Therefore, you go to the filing cabinet, pull out the bank statements, copy the charges for the year. You then put the statements back, walk back to your desk, add up the charges and apply the tax deduction rule. You enter the resultant total in the tax return. You complete the return, and post it to the tax office, perhaps recorded or registered post to have some guarantee of delivery. You (may) receive an acknowledgment. You then go about your business. A month later, you receive a communication from the tax office, giving the results of their processing of your tax return.

There are two types of dependencies here. If we take the task as "filling in the tax return" then you cannot complete this task until you get the deduction information. So, temporarily stopping the main task, you performed a subsidiary activity that yielded the information you sought. You then resumed the task of filling in the return. Alternately, you may have asked your spouse to carry out this (bank charge totalling) activity on your behalf. This would leave you free to continue filling in other sections of the tax return. However, you still cannot finish – when you get the information from your spouse, you need to fill in the deductions column, and take account of this in your tax calculations. This is a *processing dependency*.

After you complete the tax return, your responsibility is to ensure that it is lodged with the tax office. You are not, in any shape or form, involved in what happens with the tax return at the tax office. Of course, the tax office's processing of your return will have some consequences for you (you may have to pay them or they you), but this is down the track. Essentially, after you complete the task of filling in the return, you place it with some agency that guarantees delivery to the tax office (the next destination in the work flow chain). You then go about your business. This is an *informational dependency*.

Here is a software example. You are taking an order. To complete the order, you need a discount calculation done. This is done on (a) items ordered, (b) volume of this purchase, (c) customer specific discounts negotiated annually between the company and their regular customers. This is not done locally, but at the host server. The local software supporting your task sends a request to the discount calculation component. This returns the result. You then complete the order and hit enter. The software supporting the order processing task places the order with a reliable delivery mechanism. You then take a coffee break.

The dependency between the software supporting your order entry task and the component providing the discount calculation is a processing dependency: the order entry task cannot be completed without that action being performed.

The Manufacturing and the Finance departments require the order, but you (specifically the order entry task) are not involved in any shape or form in what happens to the order within Manufacturing or Finance. You, the order entry task, are responsible for ensuring that the completed order is delivered to Manufacturing and Finance. This responsibility is discharged by you handing over the completed order to a competent agency. This agency is a message-oriented middleware "highway", which is designed to assure delivery. The order entry task is then ready for the next action, perhaps taking another order. Therefore the software supporting order entry has an informational dependency with the relevant Manufacturing and Finance software components. Indeed, we can design the system so that the task does not know or care about the recipients of the message. On completion, it simply hands over the message to a MOM-based "highway", associated with which is the intelligence to establish the recipients.

Types of Software Dependency

Processing Dependency
A processing dependency occurs when an application component needs, for its own processing, some remote work to be performed. There are two categories of processing dependency:

1. Simple Processing Dependency
Application component A needs, for its own processing, some work to be performed remotely by another application component B. That is, application component A cannot progress or complete its processing until application component B performs the requested action.

For example, the client software module for the "process order" task requires in order, the customer's credit status to be checked, an order header to be established, each order line to be accepted, the total discount to be calculated, all from different remote functions. Until one function in this sequence performs its work, the client software cannot progress to the next step of the task. Therefore, the client software module has processing dependencies with each of these remote modules.

Sometimes it is possible to manage processing dependencies so that a module can keep on working pending the results of a previous request. For example, the order processing module may be constructed so that it is possible for the clerk to take the order pending the results of the credit check, the creation of the header, etc. In order to complete the work though, all these items of work need to be performed successfully.

Sometimes a processing dependency may require a calling module to make a number of successive interactions with the same provider module; for example in making available the results list of a query, a block of 20 at a time.

2. Transactional Dependency

A transactional dependency is a more complex situation where application component A needs, for its own processing, some work to be performed remotely by other application components (for example B, C and D, in general at different physical locations in the network). Furthermore, to application component A, the separate work components that B, C and D perform is a single logical unit of work, to be carried out in an all or nothing fashion. Application component A cannot progress or complete its processing until this logical unit of work is completed (note that we define transactional dependencies in this specific sense – "transaction" in the sense of a single database storage operation is covered in processing dependency).

Informational Dependency

As a consequence of some event within its jurisdiction, application component A needs to convey some information to one or more remote components. With an informational dependency, there is no expectation of processing associated with a message, application component A needs to make known that some event has occurred, some new information has been generated, or some existing information has been changed.

Implementing Software Dependencies

We can regard a software dependency as a *requirement*. In implementing this requirement in a distributed setting, we will use a middleware product (DTP, RPC, ORB, MOM, etc.), and select an interface type provided by the middleware product (for example synchronous or asynchronous RPC, static or dynamic object request) upon which to design the application specific interface.

For example, in processing an order, we need to check the customer's credit balance. Since we cannot proceed with taking the order until the customer's credit balance is checked, this activity places a processing dependency between the calling – order processing client – module and the module that provides the balance.

We have a middleware product providing synchronous and asynchronous RPC-like interfaces. We select the synchronous interface, and implement a GetBal service:

GetBal (CustID, CustName, CreditBal, CreditLimit)

where CustID is the request argument and the rest, the reply arguments.

At each step in this process – in selecting the interface type and in designing the service – coupling is introduced into the system. The designer's burden is to minimize this coupling – that is, to ensure that the dependency is implemented with the lowest appropriate coupling.

There is one or a set of middleware interface types suitable for implementing each software dependency: simple processing, transactional, and informational.

Simple Processing Dependency
The defining characteristic of a simple processing dependency is the need for the recipient module to be available, for the calling module to proceed with or complete its task. Consequently, we need an interface type with the Available characteristic.

That is, SQL stored procedures, synchronous/asynchronous RPCs, and ORB-based static/dynamic object requests, or conversational interface types, fit the generic simple processing dependency bill; the particular case determining the exact requirement.

Transactional Dependency
The defining characteristic here is the transactional nature of the requirement. Consequently we need an interface with Available plus Transactional characteristics – that is, a middleware product with a transactional interface type.

Informational Dependency
In an informational dependency, there is no expectation of processing accompanying the message (the different consumers may process this information differently, and the manner in which this is done need not be specified by the producer), only a reliable delivery mechanism to which the sender can hand over the message is needed. The recipient need not be available for the sender to hand the message over to the delivery mechanism. Indeed, this is the defining characteristic of this dependency. Therefore, an interface with the Non-Available characteristic is indicated. This profile is consistent with the asynchronous (Non-Available) messaging capability provided by MOMs.

Dependencies and Appropriate Coupling

The concept of software dependency is very useful in addressing the question of appropriate coupling. Why appropriate coupling though? A moment's reflection shows that, since stronger coupling introduces higher maintenance costs to a system, a stronger than appropriate coupling introduces an avoidable cost. Conversely a lower than appropriate level of coupling is likely to introduce integrity problems: for example in implementing a simple processing dependency with an interface with the Non-Available characteristic, or in implementing a transactional dependency with an interface with an Available (but non-transactional) property can lead to serious problems with the application.

Thus far in this chapter, we have shown that some degree of coupling is *necessarily* introduced in implementing a distributed system. Therefore, rather than universally low coupling, the message for systems design is not lowest coupling, but *lowest appropriate* coupling.

- At the architectural level, good design amounts to identifying dependencies and selecting a middleware interface type providing the lowest possible default coupling *for those dependencies.*
- The designer must then design and build interfaces with the loosest possible coupling, by exercising control wisely over the discretionary elements of coupling.

6.2 Identifying Software Dependencies

In this scheme of things, we must first identify the requirement, the dependency. The dependency itself must be identified correctly; otherwise (as with implementing dependencies with appropriate coupling) we are in danger either of introducing an avoidable cost or introducing integrity problems into the system.

In certain instances, establishing the appropriate dependency is a trivial matter. For example, as we have seen, in taking an order actions such as performing a credit check or creating the order header imply processing dependencies: the calling module needs the results of the remotely performed credit check to proceed to the next step, creating the order header, and the result of this action for the following step, creating an order line, and so on. But in other situations the choice can be more difficult.

Sometimes informational dependencies masquerade as processing dependencies, sometimes simple processing and/or informational dependencies take the guise of transactional dependencies. In these situations, it is important that the discerning designer uncovers the actual underlying dependency.

Processing versus Informational Dependencies

Does the result of the work done remotely on behalf of application component X only return an acknowledgment?, and is the acknowledgment really necessary for component X to carry out or complete its task? If the answer to the first question is "Yes" and the answer to the second "No", then it is very likely that we are looking at an informational dependency. Because, if we only require the acknowledgment as an assurance of delivery, then the same effect is achieved if we "put" the necessary information in a MOM that provides guaranteed or assured delivery.

Imagine that the order entry task creates a sales order for some types of goods (items maintained in stock) and a manufacturing order for others (items manufactured to order). In the latter case, which is really a request to manufacture, the order entry software in the sales department currently updates the (remote) manufacturing system database as part of the order entry task. For successful completion, the order entry task software requires an acknowledgment of this update. However, we can reason that if the order entry module has access to a third party (middleware) that promises to deliver the manufacturing order to the manufacturing system, then its responsibility can be limited simply to making the manufacturing order available to the middleware. The order entry task need not rely on the results of any activity in the manufacturing system, since its responsibility is merely one of making the information available.

Therefore, typically where

- a piece of remote work returns an acknowledgment to the calling module, and
- the acknowledgment is not necessary for the calling module to carry out or complete its task

the apparent processing dependency can be resolved as an informational one.

Transactional versus Non-Transactional Dependencies

A common source of ambiguity occurs when we try to determine the dependencies between two data entities with some business relationship tying them together, for example, insurance policy and agent commission; order (order line) and inventory. Can this relationship be implemented in a transactional or non-transactional manner? Then there is the case of replicated data: when a local process updates local data, should the update of remote instances of replicated data impose a transactional or non-transactional dependency? Below, we examine these cases.

Dependencies between Different Entities

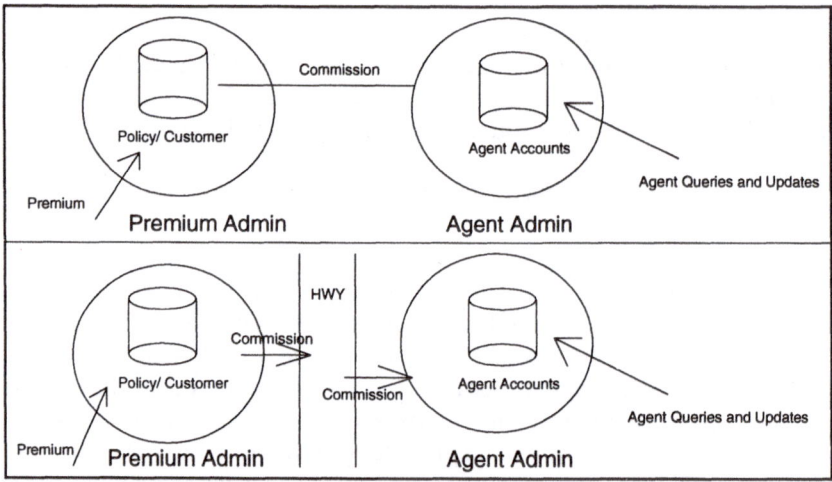

Figure 6.1: Resolving transactional dependencies – example 1

Consider an insurance premium administration task (Figure 6.1), which registers a premium payment by a policy holder against a policy. Each policy has an agent, who receives a commission from each premium payment. If applying the premium and applying the commission are not implemented together as a transactional unit of work, there will be a transient inconsistency in the system between the time of update of the premium and the update of the agent's commission. In general, *if this inconsistency can be tolerated*, then there is no impediment to implementing the functions in a non-transactional manner. One possible avenue is as follows.

The order processing task has a processing dependency only with the module responsible for premium registration. Once the premium is registered, then this information is publicized, and the agent administration system "picks up" this information to update the agent's commission.

The example of Figure 6.2 illustrates another situation of a dependency between two entities. Where crediting to the order and debiting from stock is not implemented as a single transactional unit of work, a transient inconsistency may occur between order and stock in processing an order (specifically an order line). In some circumstances, these inconsistencies may be tolerated, for example where a temporary stockout does not matter to the customer. Otherwise, a transactional dependency is indicated.

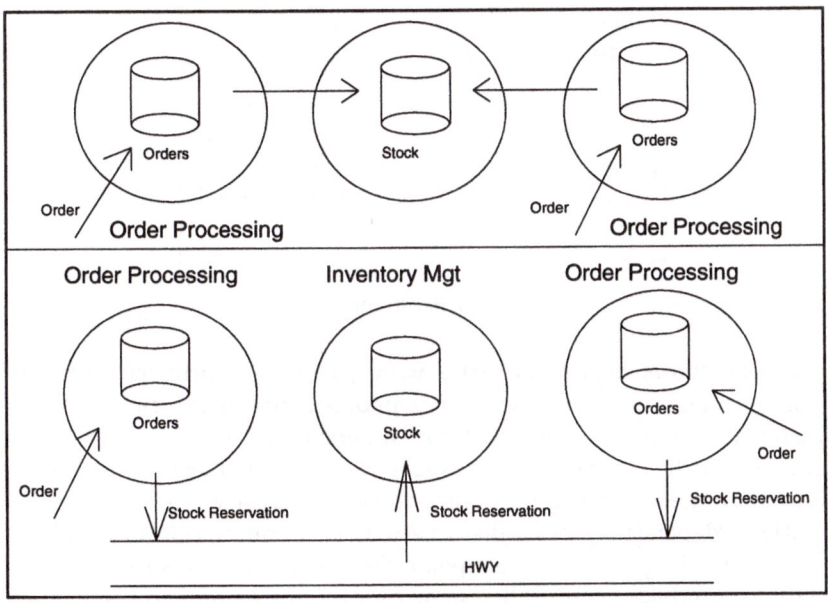

Figure 6.2: Resolving transactional dependencies – example 2

Accordingly, where there are dependencies between two or more entities or processes, a decision on transactional versus non-transactional dependency hinges upon *the degree of business tolerance to transient inconsistencies*. A transient inconsistency can be tolerated under two circumstances:

- an inquiry, processing, or update that entrenches or exacerbates the inconsistency cannot occur in the critical period, or
- the consequences of such an action during the period of transient inconsistency are relatively unimportant.

Under these conditions, an apparent transactional dependency between two entities can be resolved as a combination of simple processing and informational dependencies.

Dependencies with Partitioned or Replicated Data
Another common situation where there is a need to resolve the dependencies between distributed components is the case of replicated data. Here, when a local process updates local data, should the update of remote instances of replicated data impose a transactional dependency? Some of the scenarios are discussed below.

Figure 6.3 shows partitioned data: only one database gets updated as a result of an update action. Hence there is no issue here.

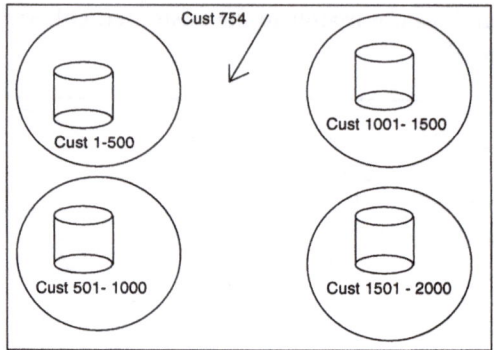

Figure 6.3: Partitioned data

Figure 6.4 shows replicated data, with partitioned primary data update responsibility. The relevant database gets updated first. If the ensuing transient inconsistency is tolerable, then that sub-system may "broadcast" the changed customer data, to be received by other sub-systems and update their copies. Under these circumstances, an apparent transactional dependency can be resolved as an informational dependency. Note that row-wise partitioning (illustrated above) as well as column-wise partitioning of update rights (e.g. sub-system 1 is responsible for creating a product record, sub-system 2 for pricing a product) is possible, and generally these considerations will apply in either case.

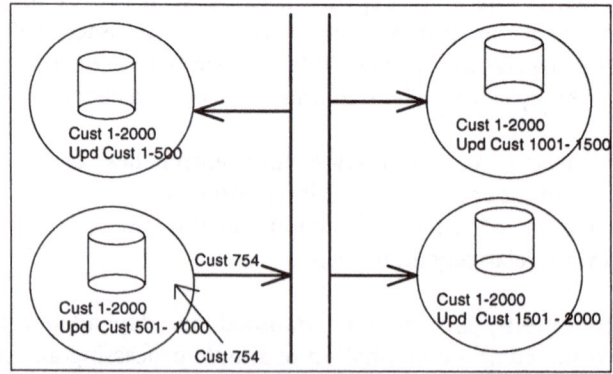

Figure 6.4: Replicated data, partitioned primary data update responsibility

Figure 6.5 depicts dynamic partitioning of update rights. One sub-system holds primary update rights until some event occurs. Thereafter, another sub-system holds primary update rights. For example, depots for a freight transport business is located in the cities of Melbourne, Sydney and Adelaide. A manifest contains details relating to each trip (vehicle, driver, details etc.) plus information on goods carried. Around the time trucks leave the Melbourne depot, the Melbourne originating manifests are broadcast and received by relevant sub-systems. Thereafter, all Melbourne originating manifests bound for Sydney are the responsibility of Sydney. All primary updates to these now occur in Sydney, and amended manifests are "broadcast" (those originally coming from Melbourne are picked up by Melbourne and the Melbourne copy updated). Again, if the transient inconstancies that occur can be tolerated, an apparent transactional dependency can be resolved as an information dependency.

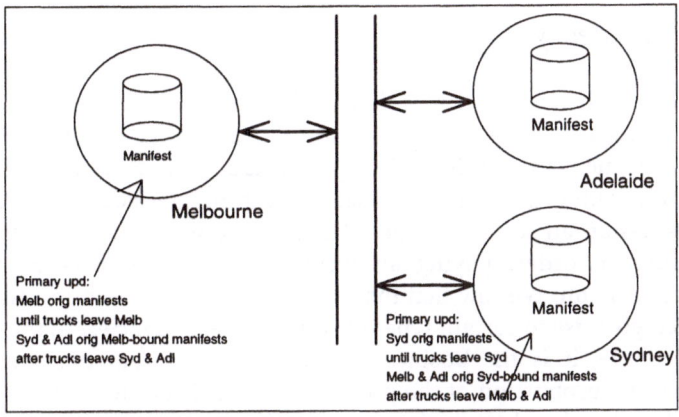

Figure 6.5: Dynamic partitioning of update rights

Figure 6.6 portrays a situation where data is replicated, but where primary update rights have not been allocated. The flight information is replicated. Each location has primary update access to the local copy of the same flight record. Under these circumstances it is unlikely that transient inconsistencies can be tolerated (unless the volume of update traffic is extremely low and it is possible to resolve inconsistencies periodically). Therefore, this type of relationship indicates a transactional dependency, each access to a record executing a distributed transaction that locks all three replicates and updates them in an all or nothing fashion.

Accordingly for replicated data, both the following criteria need to be satisfied:

1. Where replication of data exists, it should be possible for us to assign primary update responsibility to one copy of the data.
2. If this is possible, and if the transient inconsistencies in updating the other copies can be tolerated, then replication dependencies can be resolved as informational dependencies.

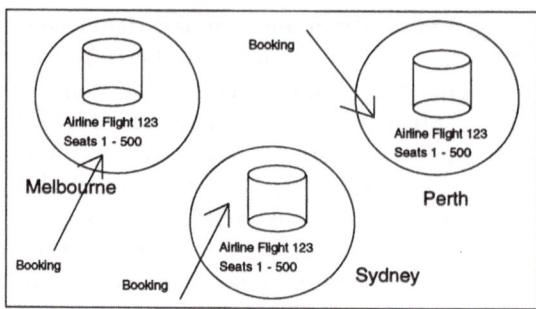

Figure 6.6: Replicated data, primary update rights not allocated

6.3   Origins of Software Dependency

Business Dependency

Dependencies can be regarded as being in the realm of the requirement, while coupling is a property of the implementation – in satisfying some dependency, you introduce some coupling through implementation, first via the interface type you select and secondly through the actual application interface you build.

In the discussion on software dependencies, we drew upon business activities such as taking an order, paying an insurance premium, making an airline reservation, and so on. We saw that the manner in which these business activities are performed give rise to certain types of software dependencies. In the insurance premium example, it is the business which lays down that the agent gets as commission some proportion of the premium. This rule has to be observed in the process of administering the premium, and its effect flows through to the design of the software components. Similarly with order entry, checking of the customer's credit, allocating stock on hand to the order, are dictated by the business and incorporated into the process of processing the order. However, these rules are not cast in stone. Different businesses choose to organize their processes in different ways. Consequently, the same business process, depending on the manner executed, can give rise to different software dependencies.

In order processing:

- Retail sales businesses, where the customers are casual and sales are typically cash, do not perform a credit check using their own debtors system; where appropriate (EFTPOS, credit card) the equivalent of the credit check is performed by an outside agency, the bank or the card vendor, at the time of payment.
- Some businesses may choose not to allocate stock on hand to the order at the time of taking the order. Businesses who do not sell stock on hand, but manufacture finished goods to order will typically not have this step at all in order processing. Other businesses, who have sufficient confidence in their inventory management process may choose to allocate stock to orders asynchronously of taking the order.

In premium processing:

- Some insurance companies do not employ agents to sell their products, using a sales force of their own employees who are not on commission. In the premium administration of such a business, there is no dependency at all on commission payment. Some other businesses may choose to calculate agent commissions half yearly on actual premiums paid, and yet others may calculate anticipated commissions half yearly and reconcile at the end of each period. In both these scenarios monthly premium administration can proceed without a processing dependency on commission payment.

Therefore the source of software dependencies is the business activities. The manner in which business activities are organized in a business ultimately result in software dependencies. In other words, *organizational or business dependencies* give rise to software dependencies. Let us loosely describe a business process as a set of business activities performed in some ordered manner. Business dependencies arise where one business activity needs to rely on another or others, or where one activity has responsibilities towards another (or others). This reliance or responsibility can occur in performing a single business process or in maintaining relationships between processes.

Earlier, when we devoted some space to the notion of appropriate dependencies, we stressed the importance of identifying software dependencies correctly. We stated that a higher than appropriate software dependency introduces an avoidable cost, whereas a lower than appropriate one will result in integrity problems. We can now restate this proposition: *software dependency needs to match the business dependency.*

Existing Systems and Software

In our experience, designers have not in the past paid adequate attention to matching software dependencies with the corresponding business dependencies. Either through ignorance of the consequences, lack of adequate tools for implementation, insufficient scope of responsibility/jurisdiction, or a combination of all these factors, designers have often worked in higher or lower software dependencies than are warranted.

- In an insurance company known to one of the authors, the general insurance business grew independently of the life and pensions (superannuation) business. Computer-based applications to support these businesses grew independently. This resulted in a customer of the general insurance business (i.e. a GI policy holder) and a life and/or pensions customer having no relationship to each other. Joseph Xavier Bloggs, possessor of a life insurance policy and a general insurance policy from this company was treated as two different customers by the two different Divisions of the company. There was no easy mechanism to capitalize on the opportunities afforded by their existing customer bases (which, for each Division was considerable) for example to sell products at a discount to existing customers, to reward customer loyalty, etc.

In other words, a dependency (an informational dependency) existed between the GI customer and the L&P customer. This was ignored by the designers who developed their initial systems, who assumed a situation of no dependency between the two types of customer.

- In another company, a company that has a number of retail outlets (each with its own warehouse) that function relatively autonomously, the product master files have grown independently of each other. Consequently, even though each outlet deals substantively in the same product lines, there is no easy way of cooperation between outlets, since the products were treated differently (e.g. with different product codes) in the different outlets. Here again, the (informational) dependency that exists between products at the different outlets was assumed not to exist.

- Currently in Company X, the dependency between the cash receipt and its application against existing invoices is implemented in a transactional manner. That is, a cash receipt and its application against open invoices are committed as a single unit of work; a receipt is not allowed in the system without also committing the distribution of the receipt amount against open invoices. However, the business can tolerate a transient inconsistency between the receipt of a payment from a customer, and the application of that payment to the open (as yet unpaid) invoices for that customer.

6.4 Managing the Implementation of Informational Dependencies

Thus far, we have examined ways of achieving a level of appropriate coupling, examining business dependencies and reflecting these upon software dependencies. We have observed how tighter than appropriate coupling can be resolved into looser variants. We noted that, under the appropriate organizational circumstances, informational dependencies can be a useful way forward. We have advocated the MOM as the preferred way of implementing informational dependencies.

Traditional centralized mainframe-based applications supporting the enterprise often communicate with each other via a (flat or database) file: Application A writes to a file; asynchronously, application B reads from it. This type of interaction, in our parlance, is an implementation of an informational dependency. Since these applications have typically evolved in a tactical fashion over the years, in spurts at different times, in response to different needs and initiatives – as opposed to following some grand blueprint – they can have compatibility problems: the format for the same data item is sometimes not consistent across the applications that use the data item. For example, applications A, B and C all deal with inventory items; each of them has their own format for the product code. In addition, applications interact in this manner via direct, customized, interfaces: application A, communicating with application B writes to a purpose-built file, which B reads. Application A communicating with application C writes to a purpose-built file, which C reads. Therefore, potentially, each communication channel between an application P and any other application can result in such a custom interface.

Therefore, even with asynchronous (non-available), data only interactions – in other words implementation of informational dependencies – we can engender relatively close coupling. There are two sources of this coupling:

- The first source of coupling is early binding to a form: application B, reading off the file to which application A wrote, needs to know the formats used by A and how they relate to the formats that it (i.e. B) uses. This is early (development time) binding. Any change to a format in application A, will now ripple through to the format translation module in B. This means that in response to a change in A, enhancement and testing needs to take place in B.
- With custom interfaces, each application interfaces directly to each of the other applications with which it communicates. These direct inter-application interfaces will grow geometrically in proportion to the number of applications in the entire environment. Since each interface induces a quantum of coupling, the total extent of coupling grows in proportion to the number of these inter-application interfaces. Obviously, this growth leads to high maintenance costs – each interface is one we need to maintain.

Therefore, we must be careful in managing the implementation of informational dependencies. For example, if our change is merely confined to replacing a flat file between applications A and B with a queue-based MOM, then there will be no resultant decrease in coupling. On the contrary, we must explicitly design the implementation of informational dependencies to minimize coupling.

- The first tactic is to uncouple application to application interfaces and to replace them with application to MOM interfaces.
- The second tactic is to loosen the customization: for example if application A writes much the same information to three flat files, for applications B, C and D to read, then we can replace them with a single common interface between A and the MOM; with the MOM delivering the messages to P, Q and R.

With these two mechanisms, we can reduce the geometric relationship between the number of applications and the number of interfaces to an arithmetic one, a very significant improvement. Figure 6.7 illustrates this point.

The third tactic is to quarantine the formatting information. First, we agree the message formats for all MOM-based traffic. Then, associated with each application we implement a piece of software that translates between the application's data formats and the agreed format for this message. Obviously, this format translation is only required for existing applications. Any new application can either choose to use the agreed standard for their data they need to "put to" or "get from" the MOM. Alternatively, they can use their own formats at the additional cost of a format translator module. Since we will uncouple custom interfaces, a MOM-based message that a certain application needs can nevertheless have items of information not of interest to that application. The format translation component can be given the additional responsibility of extracting from the MOM-based message, the data items of interest to the application. In this way, such a component can insulate the application from the outside world. We make extensive use of this type of component – which we call a "Gatekeeper" – later in the book, in the discussion on the Federation.

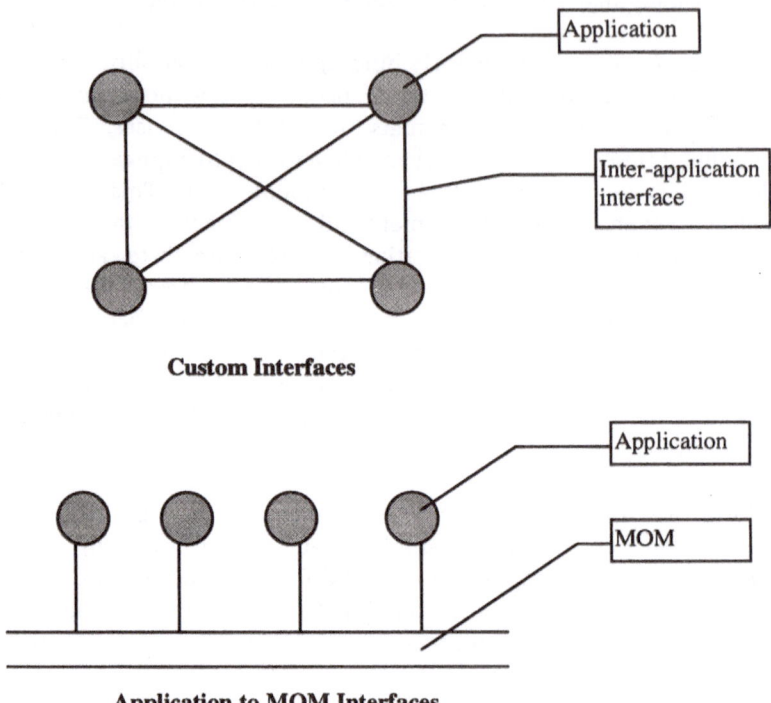

Figure 6.7: Loosening custom interfaces

6.5 Conclusion

We have examined the concept of dependency in this chapter, and observed the relationship between dependency and coupling. We have introduced the notion of appropriate coupling, and proposed some ways of loosening existing (or intended) coupling in order to achieve this aim. In summary, these are:

- the resolution of apparent transactional dependencies as a combination of informational and simple processing dependencies;
- the resolution of apparent processing dependencies as informational dependencies, and
- the management of implementation of informational dependencies.

Finally, in this chapter and the previous one, starting with concepts of coupling, and proceeding on to the notion of dependency, we have advanced a set of principles for the architecture and design of "good" applications, in the context of distributed systems or in using distributed computing middleware technologies. There are two domains of applicability of these principles.

- In the architecture and design of distributed client/server applications. Most of the principles elucidated in the discussions on the three-tier architecture, the nature of the interfaces between requester and request provider, the location of administrative and application information, the desirability of deferring deployment decisions, the need to minimize component proliferation can be derived from the principles of coupling and the aim of inducing minimum practicable coupling.
- In designing mechanisms for inter-application communication, where the applications involved may be legacy or client/server applications. Here, we make the leap into the stratum above the single application, focusing on the numbers of individual applications that support the enterprise. In the following three chapters, we lead the discussion into this arena; we examine enterprise-level application architectures and the "better" architectural forms suitable for this level.

Part 4

Distributed Computing and the Enterprise

7. *The Enterprise and the Distributed Application:*

Alternative Architectures

In this chapter, we use a scenario often found in industry – a centralized system that does not perform as required is to be replaced by a distributed client/server system – to illustrate the different forms of possible enterprise-level application architectures and their relative merits. We use the concepts of coupling and dependency introduced in the previous two chapters in the analysis of the different architectures.

7.1 Titanic Distributors Ltd

Let us consider a hypothetical business operation, Titanic Distributors Ltd, which buys, stores and sells goods to its customers throughout Australia. We look at Titanic's order fulfilment process.

Titanic has some degree of distribution in their operations. Order entry is centralized at the orders department in the head office in Sydney, with orders telephoned, faxed through or sent by mail directly by customers. The distribution of goods occurs via five branch offices, each servicing customers in a State, Victoria, New South Wales, South Australia, Queensland and Western Australia. There is also a head office in Sydney (NSW), which is distinct from the NSW branch office. Invoices are produced at each branch, and an invoice accompanies the goods. Customer payments are made to the head office Accounting Division. All branches hold the same stock items, but of course the stock levels are dependent on local demand. Pricing is done centrally at the head office, which establishes a standard price for each stock item. Individual customers negotiate with the head office, standing discounts on inventory items based on their purchase volumes and frequency. Typically, the time between the receipt of an order and its fulfilment is about three days.

7.2 The Current System

Currently, the business is serviced by an "integrated system" housed at the company head office. The system was purchased from Bovine Systems Ltd,

"Specialists in Systems Integration". They customized for Titanic's requirements a system that they had previously developed. The integrated nature of the system was marketed as an attractive feature of this system. "Note the integration of the order entry, inventory management and financial subsystems" was a common phrase used by the Bovine marketing staff, "a single action updates all the relevant files in the database". Titanic's IT Department now provides all support, maintaining and enhancing the system.

However, after using the system for some time several shortcomings have emerged.

1. A major source of complaints has been the order entry staff.
   - They have observed that some phoned through orders have been lost because the system had indicated stockouts at the time of taking the order.
   - They have also complained that they have to go through a screen where accounting information needs to be entered. Most of the time, it is a matter of saying "yes" to a series of default entries presented to them, but they are nervous that they (not knowing accounts) will not know when and how to override the defaults.
   - They are also concerned about the time it takes to enter each order. Often, there are delays for the computer to respond after the screen allocation of each order line and after accepting an order. This coupled with the accounting information screen that the staff have to go through, adds to the time to take an order.
   - There is another complaint that sometimes the customer changes the order, usually the amended order coming in within half a day of the original. Amending an order is a hassle, because by that time the system has allocated stock to the original order, the invoice produced and accounting entries have been made. However, the actual picking does not occur until the following day. Therefore, while the physical process can adapt, a great deal of work needs to be done in the administrative side of things to back out of the original set of entries and place the amendments in the system.
2. The inventory control manager complains about the reorder function of the system. It is kicked off completely automatically, based on the parameters set such as the reorder level and the quantity, and there is no scope at all for manual intervention. He needs to have the ability for his staff to monitor the computer-based reorder actions and to make adjustments when necessary.
3. The payment entry staff have similar complaints to the order entry personnel. They are frustrated that recording a payment is a long and involved process.
4. The IT staff are unhappy about the complexity of the system. They maintain that, typically, the impact of a change is extensive, and this affects their capacity to respond rapidly to user requests. Furthermore, because of real-time interactions between functions of different modules, the system cannot function without all its components. This is very serious because when something goes down the department is under big pressure to fix the problem immediately. They recall the time when a problem with invoicing meant that invoicing needed to be off-line for half a working day. This in itself would not have posed a major problem to Titanic's operations; they could have mailed

the affected invoices deviating from their standard practice of delivering them with the goods. However, the absence of a working invoicing module affected order entry, a much greater problem for Titanic, and one which brought the IT department into a great deal of disrepute. This type of problem occurs quite often and they feel powerless to take remedial action.

5. The staff in the distribution departments (the branches) have experienced that when the central computer goes down their operations are severely affected, often grinding to a halt. They do not see the need to involve the central system on something that is essentially a local operation. They want some degree of autonomy, where their own operations can be supported by some local computer-based resources, which they believe they can manage.

The system has been earmarked by management for re-engineering. But before we set out redesigning the system, let us examine the existing system and its shortcomings using the tools we introduced earlier.

7.3 Analysis of Dependency

We start our analysis by discussing the current status of the various system modules in the light of the dependency criteria of Chapter 6.

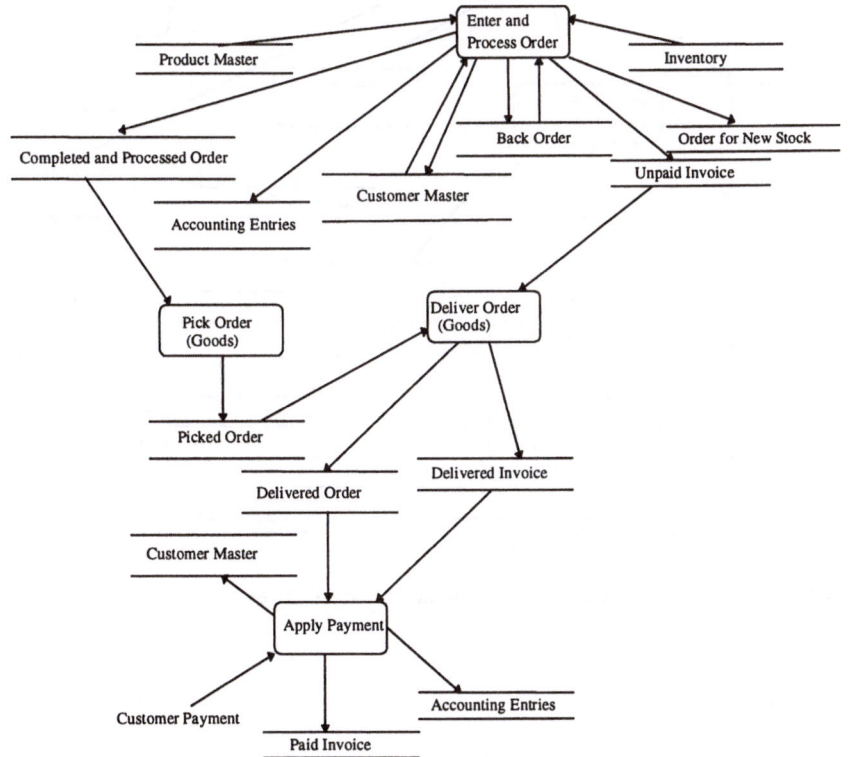

Figure 7.1: The "integrated" system

Figure 7.1 is a simple dataflow diagram of the system. Notice that the two tasks "Enter and Process Order" and "Apply Payment" each access a number of files. Let us expand on these tasks.

Enter and Process Order

Figure 7.2 shows that to complete the task "Enter and Process Order" the processes below also need to be completed; that is, in our terminology, the task "Enter and Process Order" has processing dependencies with all the following functions:

- Check Credit
- Manage Order Creation (which in turn has a processing dependency with the Process Order Line function)
- Manage Reorder
- Make Accounting Entries
- Produce Invoice

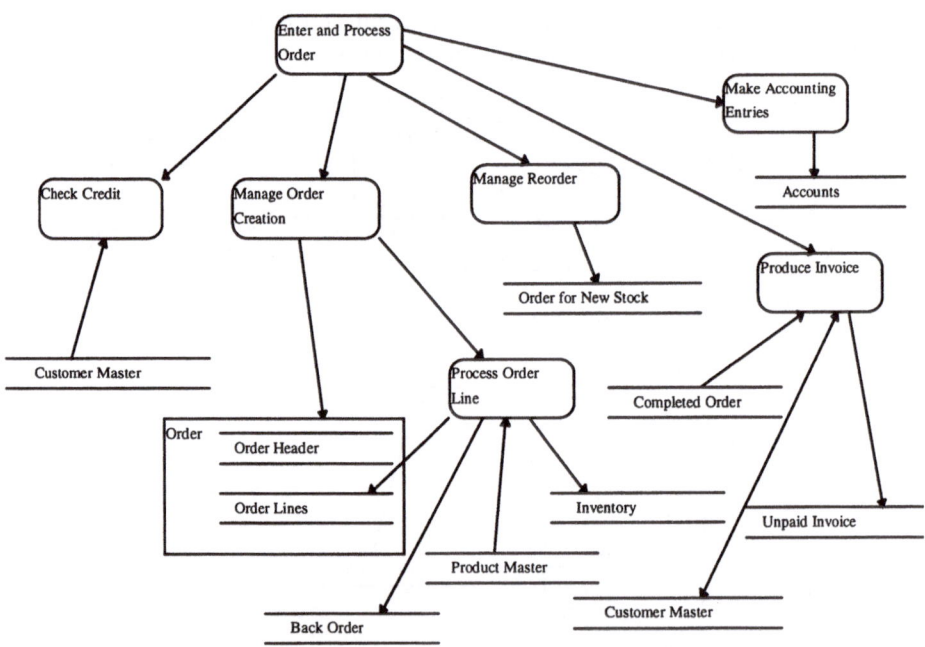

Figure 7.2: Enter and Process Order

Apply Payment

Similarly, Figure 7.3 shows that the task "Apply Payment" has the following processing dependencies:

- Apply Payment Against Open Invoices
- Update Customer Master (outstanding credit balance)
- Reconcile Payment Against Delivered Order
- Make Accounting Entries

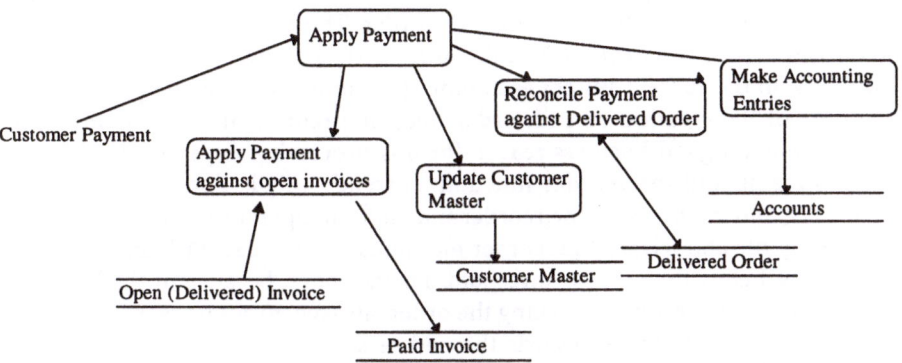

Figure 7.3: Apply Payment

It is important to note a couple of points from the foregoing discussion. First, a parent process with a number of processing dependencies will usually (though not always) require access to a number of data items during its execution, either by itself or by the other functions upon which it is dependent: see for example the chain Enter and Process Order → Manage Order Creation → Process Order Line. Therefore, even if processes are modelled at a high level (encapsulating the dependencies) as in the illustration in Figure 7.1, the large number of files shown as required for the process gives a clue that there may be a number of processing dependencies involved here.

Secondly, in a centralized system or in a process model that does not take account of distribution, an informational dependency between two or more processes is indicated by two or more processes whose sole means of interaction with each other is via a persistent structure such as a file. That is, for example, when process A writes to a file and asynchronously process B reads from the same file.

These processing dependencies that Bovine Systems created in their design reflect the real cost of "integration". The crucial question is, are these dependencies warranted? As we observed in the last chapter, a processing dependency induces a stronger degree of coupling than an informational dependency. Therefore, if these dependencies are not warranted, the module "integration" has been achieved at the expense of an avoidable cost – the consequences of stronger than necessary coupling.

Let us examine the processes of Titanic for the answer, since as we discussed previously, it is the business process that is the source of a dependency.

Order Processing

As we saw, order entry is done centrally, purchase orders from customers are received via fax or letter, or telephoned through. The turnaround time for an order is around three days, and usually the earliest an order is picked is a day after the receipt of the order. Therefore, there is no good business reason to allocate stock *at the time of taking the order*. Indeed, more harm than good results from allocating (or attempting to allocate stock) prematurely – the order entry staff have observed that some phoned through orders have been lost because the system had indicated stockouts at the time of taking the order. Therefore, the stock allocation function can occur asynchronously of the order entry activity.

Secondly, in the current system each time stock is allocated to an order (that is, at the time of the creation of each order line), the reorder function is invoked. Again, there is no good business reason for this processing dependency between order processing and the reorder function: currently this is done at least a day prematurely, and in any event the reorder function can operate asynchronously on the inventory file and trigger the reorder mechanism when a stock item's quantity on hand goes below the reorder threshold. Furthermore, because of the lag of at least a day between taking and picking the order, an asynchronous reorder process can sample the orders table towards the end of a working day, and deduce the actual demand on each item of inventory for the following day; this information can be factored into the reorder algorithm.

Thirdly, the actual accounts need not be updated at the time of taking the order. The account information can be contained as part of the order "transaction" and posted later, after the order is processed by allocating stock to the order. In addition (especially with this approach), the account information for the order can be built up behind the scenes as the order is taken, using defaults. This dispenses with the accounts screens that order entry staff are not comfortable with, speeds up order taking since no posting is done at the time an order is taken, and (until the time that the order is processed) obviates the need to make accounting reversals etc if the customer changes his/her mind.

Fourthly, the business constraint on invoice production is that the invoice is ready at the time the order is picked and is ready for delivery – the goods and the invoice are delivered together. This is at least a day after (may be up to three days after) the receipt of the order. The management is satisfied with the overall order turnaround time and the current method of invoice delivery. Accordingly, the invoice need not be produced at the time of taking the invoice, it only needs to be available when the order is ready for delivery. Thus the business process certainly does not warrant a processing dependency between processing the order and producing the invoice.

The business process favours these functions to occur asynchronously with taking the order. What then are the actions integral to taking the order? First, the customer's credit needs to be checked (there is a process for dealing with new customers, but we will not go into detail here). Secondly, we need to check the required order line item to ensure that it is a valid product marketed by Titanic. Thirdly, we need to determine the correct price for the customer. Therefore, the functions that provide these services will have a processing dependency with the "Enter Order" task. Note again that in another company with a somewhat different order entry process, a different set of processing dependencies may exist.

We now have the following scenario: the tasks Enter Order, Process Order, Manage Reorder, Make Accounting Entries and Produce Invoice, none of which are bound to each other by processing dependencies. The Enter Order task does have processing dependencies with Check Credit and Manage Order Creation functions (see Figure 7.4).

From the above discussion, it is clear that when a processing dependency has been re-engineered as an informational one, the exchange of information between interoperating modules changes from a synchronous mode to an asynchronous mode (that is, with the non-available characteristic). In a centralized environment, this communication takes place via a file of some sort to which one module writes and from which the other module reads. The read occurs independently and asynchronously of the write. Other schemes such as writing to a persistent structure such as a queue, stack, etc., are also possible, but as yet we are not concerned with the actual method.

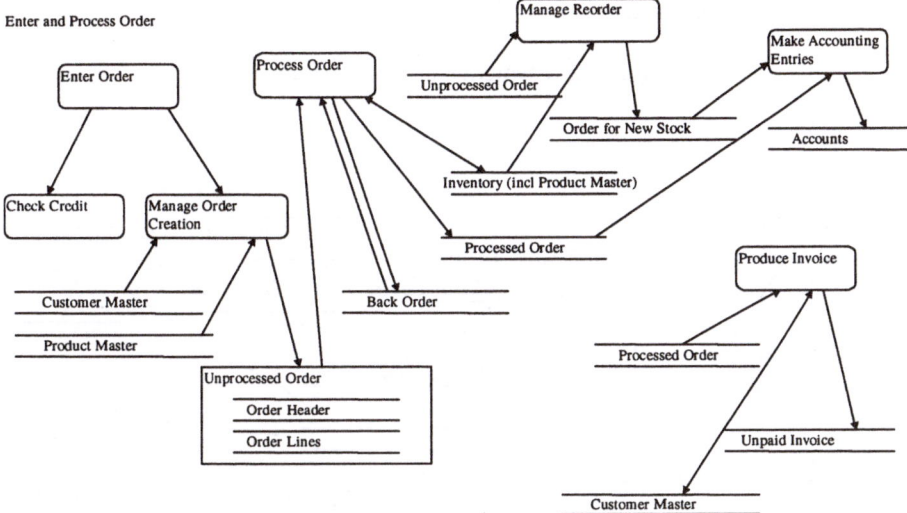

Figure 7.4: Enter and Process Order

Application of Payments

Figure 7.5 indicates a similar loosening of dependency in the application of payments. A similar analysis can be carried out here, and we leave it as an exercise for the reader. The outcome is that none of the following tasks are bound to any other by processing dependencies: Entering Payments, Application of Payment against Open Invoices, Updating Customer Credit, Reconciling Payment Against Invoices, and Making Accounting Entries.

Figure 7.6 shows the entire process, incorporating the new scenarios for Order Entry and Payment Application. None of the tasks Enter Order, Process Order, Manage Reorder, Pick Order, Produce Invoice, Deliver Order (Goods), Enter Payment, Apply Payment, Update Customer Master, are bound to any other by a processing dependency.

Apply Payment

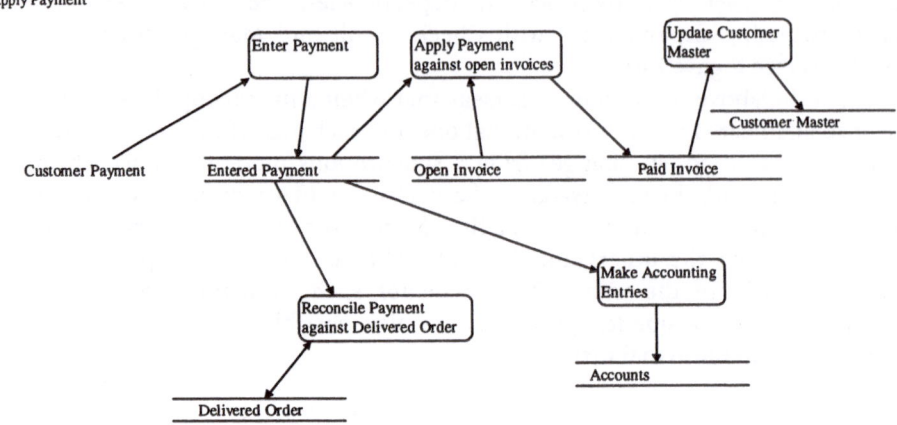

Figure 7.5: Payment Entry and Allocation

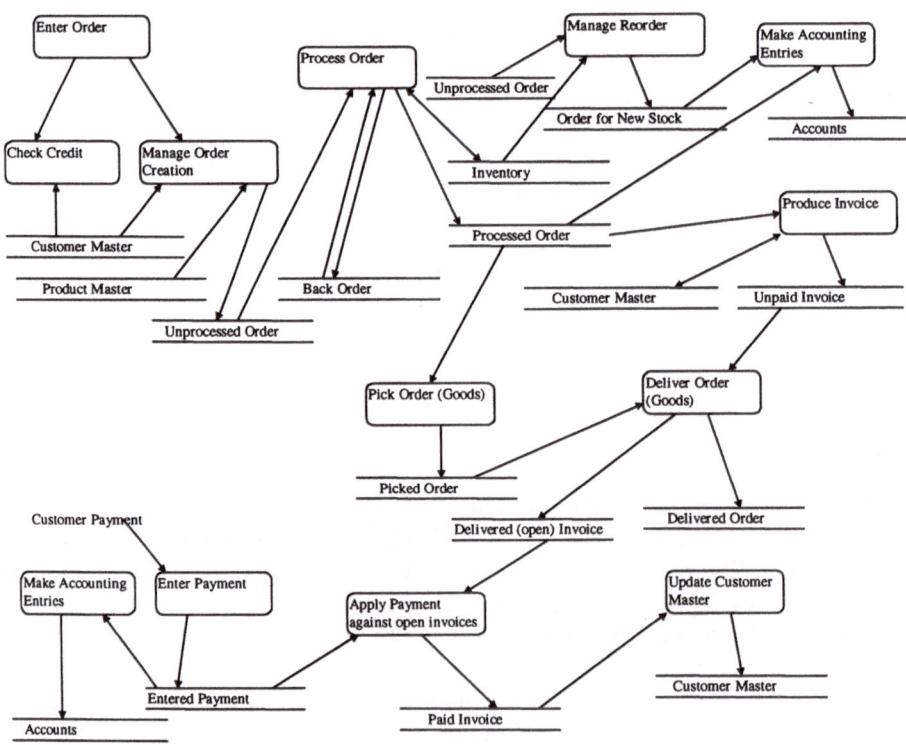

Figure 7.6: Order Fulfilment – loosely coupled systems

7.4 The New Distributed System

We have progressed the discussion thus far without taking account in any major way of distributing components of this application. We have examined the nature of the business dependencies between tasks of the business process, and attempted to match the software dependency with the business dependency. Through this exercise, we have come up with a set of tasks that possess no processing dependencies with each other. The question we want to answer now is: what are the alternatives for distribution, and their relative merits?

A Single Global Distributed System

Representatives of Bovine Systems have proposed a distributed system along the following lines: it uses the existing business rules and database design of the existing system, but "the existing system has been re-engineered to provide state of the art Graphical User Interfaces while preserving the richness of functionality and the instantaneous propagation of changes that characterizes the current system at Titanic".

We have illustrated a part (the order entry/processing task) of the new Bovine solution in Figure 7.7. All other tasks follow the same pattern. Application components are partitioned into three tiers. The server (2) tier houses the corporate data, and the data is centralized in the corporate server. Access to data is always via defined data access services (depicted as the rectangle/parallel line combination). Server (1) tier contains the logic for activities such as validation, processing, inquiry, and transaction management. This tier is always housed in a LAN or local department server.

The Bovine design contains several problems. First, the three tiers are machine based. That is, the deployment configuration is hard coded in the design. This design philosophy reduces the flexibility of the solution – for example, the order entry task could well manage without a separate LAN server, since it is carried out at the head office, local to the corporate server. Flexible deployment is an essential capability of a system like this since component deployment should be done to optimize performance, based upon geographic distribution, network capacity, local server capabilities, etc. Secondly, since the data is centralized the solution is vulnerable to central server/communication failure. In this respect this solution is no different to the existing character-based centralized system. Finally, this solution does not attempt to match its software dependencies with the organizational requirements: the close coupling we discovered in the original system still exists. For example, we see from Figure 7.7 that a task "Enter and Process Order" still exists, with the same processing dependencies as before. We have found that most problems of the existing system relate precisely to this closeness of coupling; therefore this distributed solution is very unlikely to improve the service level of the system.

Next, let us examine a solution, still a single global distributed system, but designed with greater attention to Titanic's requirements. As illustrated in Figure 7.8, the tasks have been partitioned along the lines suggested by our earlier analysis of dependency. This design uncouples some of the processing

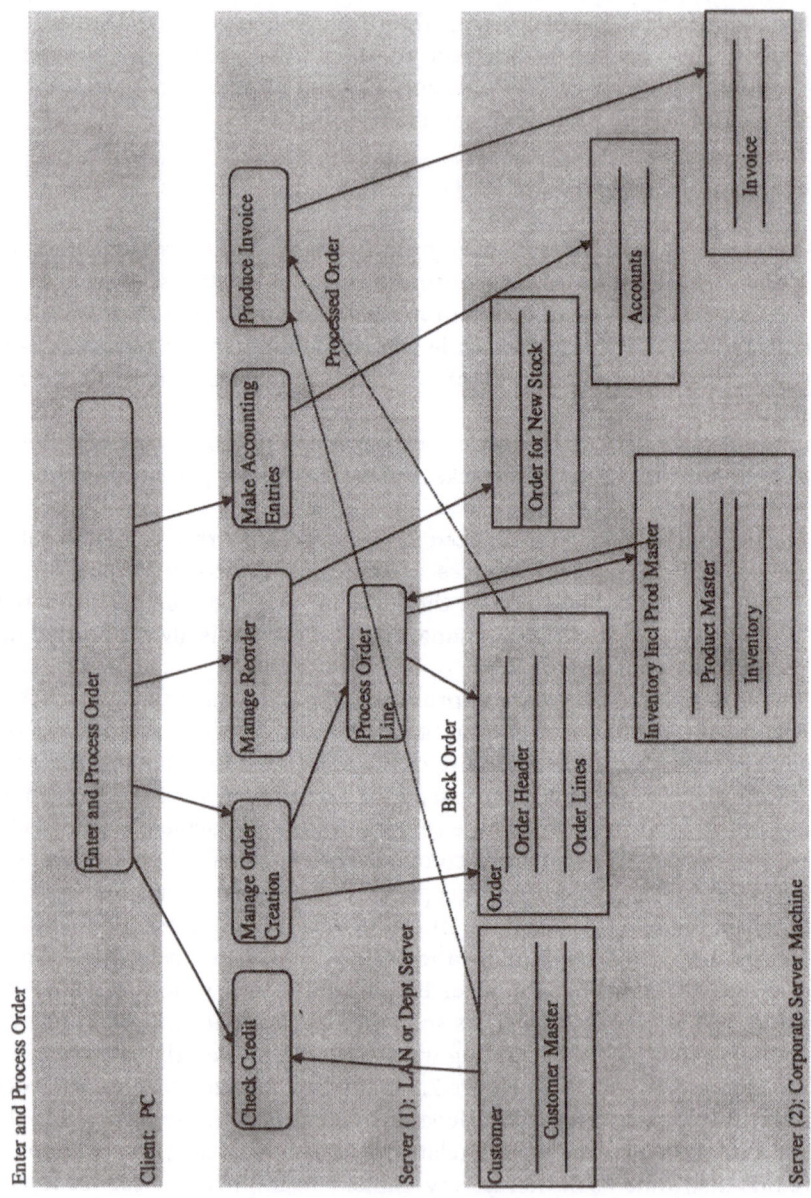

Figure 7.7: The Bovine Distributed System Solution

dependencies that existed in the centralized application and found its way unchanged to the Bovine solution. This design has separated out order entry, order processing, invoice production, and reordering into separate tasks that can be carried out asynchronously; similarly, entering a payment into the system and application of payment against open invoices are separate tasks. We further notice that the task user interfaces have now been distributed; that is, the tasks that are earmarked to be performed at the branches have components of their supporting software executing locally. Another attractive design feature is the flexible deployability of components: notice that components of the first server tier are earmarked to be deployed at the corporate server (local to the second server tier) as well as the branch server (remote to the second server tier).

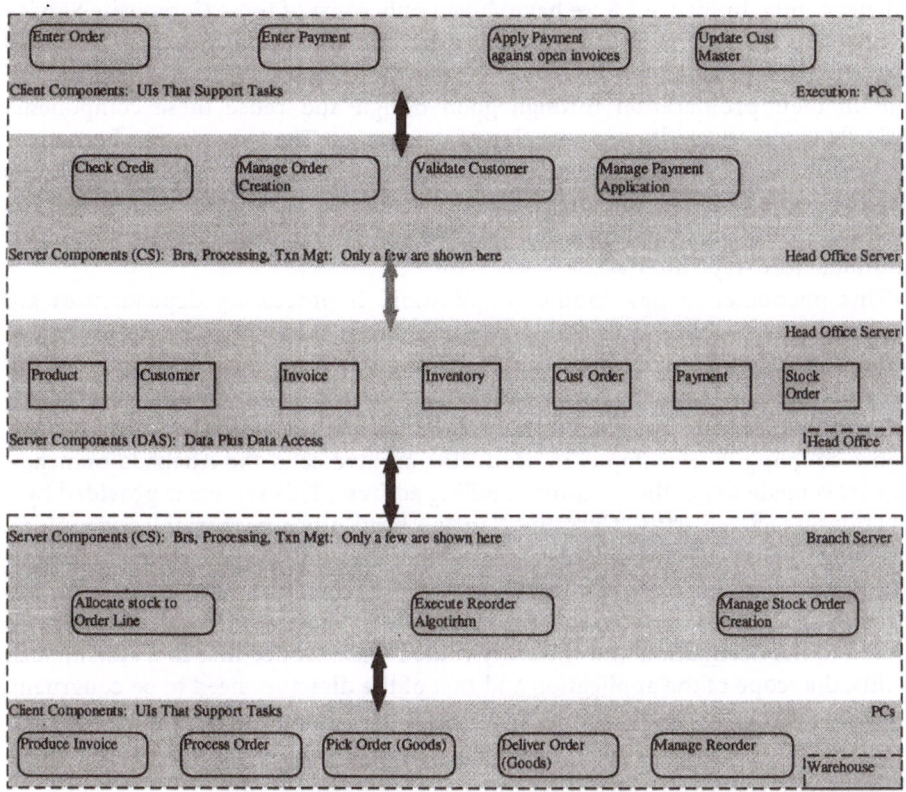

Figure 7.8: A three-tier distributed solution with task partitioning along dependency lines

What then are the weaknesses of this design? This design follows the three-tier model discussed earlier in this book. One of the features of this model is that every task-based UI and all its supporting components interact via processing dependencies. This has several consequences.

First, since all the data is centralized at the head office, we have a large number of processing dependencies being executed over a WAN – each task that is run from a branch will need remote (WAN based) access to server components responsible for maintaining corporate data. As is the case with the previous

design, this makes the system very sensitive to network and H/O server performance and reliability.

The second point is more subtle, but no less important. It has to do with the
coupling induced by administrative information.

System Growth and Coupling

As described in Chapter 3, a three-tier client/server system of this type contains, in
the second (CS) and third (DAS) tiers, request-providers (whether they be termed
server functions, methods or services). These services may be grouped together
(often together with data in an object-class type manner) or they may exist
independently. In Figure 7.8 we have shown only some of these Composite Service
components of the application – there is usually a large number of such functions
even in modest systems of this type. Furthermore, despite our best attempts to
contain their proliferation through good design and reuse these components
typically increase rapidly with the size of the system. The two system alternatives
for Titanic discussed thus far use RPC-like middleware. From Chapter 5, we know
that there is a characteristic default level of coupling associated with each RPC-
style interface. The coupling level for the total system will increase with each
additional RPC-type interface.

This phenomenon has another implication. If processing dependencies are
implemented via an RPC or RPC-like mechanism, then the location and usage
pertaining to each function needs to be registered at an infrastructure-level
directory/naming service. This arrangement induces the lowest coupling –
housing this information at application level (as we saw earlier) results in much
higher coupling. For example, in producing an invoice at the Adelaide branch, a
request is made to get the customer's billing address. This service is provided by a
function associated with "Customer" in the head office corporate server. Upon
receiving the request, the Adelaide components of the distributed systems
infrastructure makes a request to the directory, and (a) ascertains if the caller has
access rights to this service, and (b) its location. Thereafter, the request can be
routed to the destination and the reply routed back. Notice that in a system such
as this, the scope of the application and that of the directory need to be congruent.
Consequently, every service, every user and every location needs to be registered
in this directory. As the system grows and users, client, CS and DAS components
grow, the extent of coupling induced by this volume of administrative information
will also increase.

Therefore, as the application grows, we need to take measures to contain the
consequential growth in the magnitude of coupling.

Clustering is a very promising approach to distributed systems design. We
partition system components in clusters designed to support related (or
geographically grouped) tasks of the business process. Application components
that support some aspect of a business process are sited "close to where the action
is". A degree of local autonomy, such as that requested by Titanic's branches, is
enabled as is insulation from failures at the centre. Furthermore, we shall see that
certain types of clustering can contain coupling consequences of system growth to
an effective degree.

We look at two further design arrangements, a message-based clustered architecture and a request/reply-based clustered architecture.

A Message-Based Clustered Architecture

An Approach to Clustering

A major objective of distribution is to site application components that support some aspect of a business process "close to where the action is". This ensures that local groups have greater control over the system components that they use, and reduces their exposure to problems outside of their control. With this approach, when we distribute system components there will be clusters of application components, clusters that support related (or geographically grouped) tasks of the business process. Each cluster has some boundary, and the interaction of one cluster with others occurs exclusively via this boundary. Given the difficulty of implementing processing dependencies across this type of boundary (the need to minimize coupling between clusters is discussed later in this chapter and also in Chapter 8), the most desirable outcome will ensue if only informational dependencies flow across each boundary. That is, if we should be able to cluster application components such that there are no processing (either simple processing or transactional) dependencies flowing across boundaries. This indicates a MOM product for inter-cluster communication.

Remember that when there is an informational dependency, different software modules exchanged information through the use of a persistent structure such as a file. For example, when separated to take advantage of the informational dependency between them, the software supporting the tasks "Enter Order" and "Process Order" accessed and maintained the same "Unprocessed Order" file asynchronously. Clustering creates additional repositories of such data. Each cluster operates on data resident locally (i.e. within the same cluster). We therefore need to create local copies of data that more than one cluster will require. For example, if we assign "Enter Order" to one cluster and "Process Order" to another, then the "Unprocessed Order" data now needs to reside in both clusters. We can partition or replicate the data, depending on the specific requirement, so that it "lives" in each of the "Enter Order" and "Process Order" clusters.

- Partitioning: partition the data (based on say a key range) and allocate a single portion to each of the clusters.
- Replication: all records available in full to all the clusters.

The clusters are linked by message-oriented middleware, so the Enter Order cluster can put new/changed unprocessed order information in the MOM, and the Process Order Cluster can get these from the MOM. As we discussed in Chapter 6 and also earlier in this chapter, the asynchronous execution of Enter Order and Process Order tasks is possible because the consequent transient inconsistency (between unprocessed orders and processed orders) can be tolerated by the business process. However, now the physical distribution of the unprocessed orders data introduces an additional set of transient inconsistencies.

- First, if we have one order entry cluster and five (one each for a branch) process order clusters, then unprocessed orders now need to "live" in each of the six clusters. The centrally produced unprocessed orders can be partitioned for processing because there is no distribution overlap between branches. That is, the primary responsibility for processing can be partitioned among the branches according to the customer.
- Secondly, the Product and Customer information, which these clusters use as reference information, now need to "live" in each of the clusters. Since each branch must keep all products, the basis of apportioning Product is replication, while that of Customer is partitioning since each branch services a set of mutually exclusive customers. Since the primary update responsibility can be apportioned to the clusters, and since the ensuing transient inconsistencies are tolerable, these informational dependencies are feasible. This arrangement is shown in Figure 7.9.

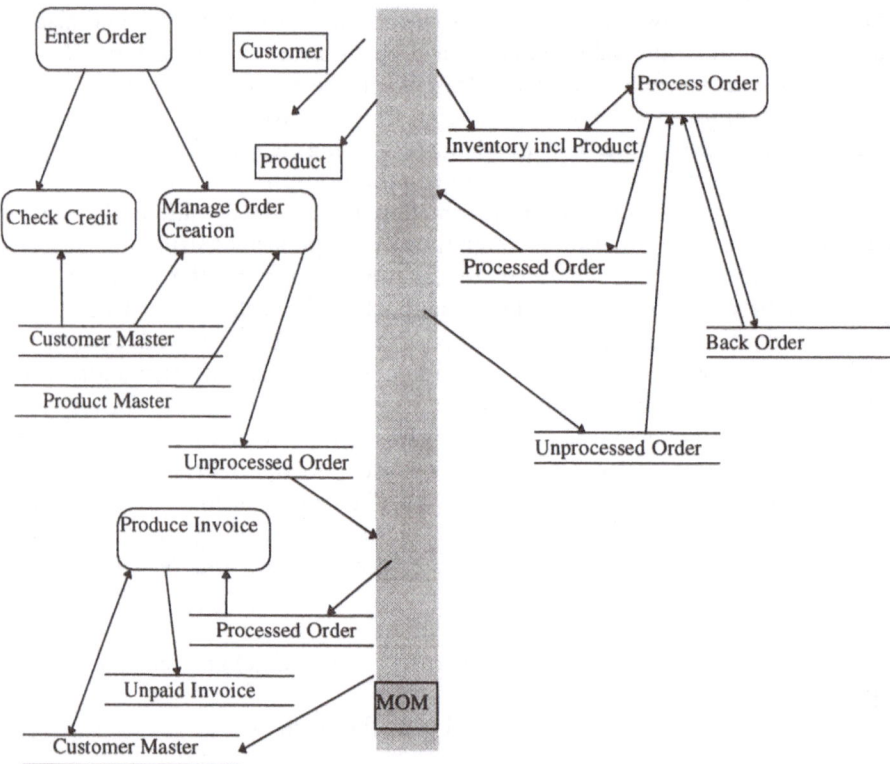

Figure 7.9: A Clustering Example: Note that the "Put" and "Get" activities to/from the MOM require some processing, not shown here

The number of different items of information maintained by the MOM system is an indication of the number of inter-cluster informational dependencies. This becomes an important design criterion that we need to monitor. That is, we need to establish cluster boundaries so that (a) we spawn only informational dependencies in the process, and (b) we are as parsimonious as possible with the additional number of informational dependencies we create. Next, we examine some clustering alternatives for Titanic with an eye to achieving these aims.

A Message-Based Clustered Design for Titanic

We first examine an arrangement where software components for each of the process components Order Entry, Inventory Management, Distribution, Invoice Production, and Payment Entry have been clustered together. Each illustration below (Figures 7.10 to 7.14) depicts the software components belonging to a cluster, the information that they have to read and write, and the information crossing each cluster boundary.

As we saw earlier in separating "Enter Order", Process Order" and "Produce Invoice" into clusters, clustering creates additional repositories of data. Each cluster operates on data resident locally, and this necessity creates local copies of data that more than one cluster will require; for example Product Master, Unprocessed Order, Processed Order, Customer, Picked Order, Order for New Stock, Unpaid Invoice, Delivered Invoice, Open (Paid) Invoice. In other words, information items will need to cross cluster boundaries and exist in at least two clusters. We have to (a) establish that the new dependencies we have created are in fact informational dependencies (that is, we have not created any processing dependencies), and (b) our cluster partitioning has not created a large number of unnecessary informational dependencies. We leave (a) as an exercise to the reader. As far as (b) is concerned, is this clustering appropriate? Or in a wider sense, while we now have some guidelines to define cluster boundaries:

- boundaries must be defined along existing information dependency boundaries
- the additional informational dependencies created must be kept to a minimum.

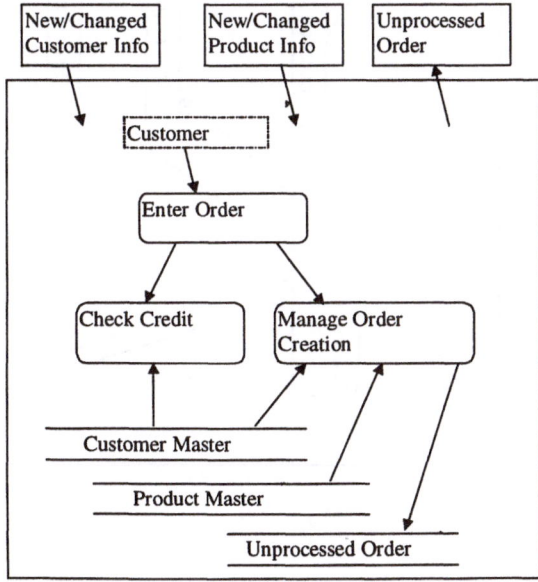

Figure 7.10: Order Entry

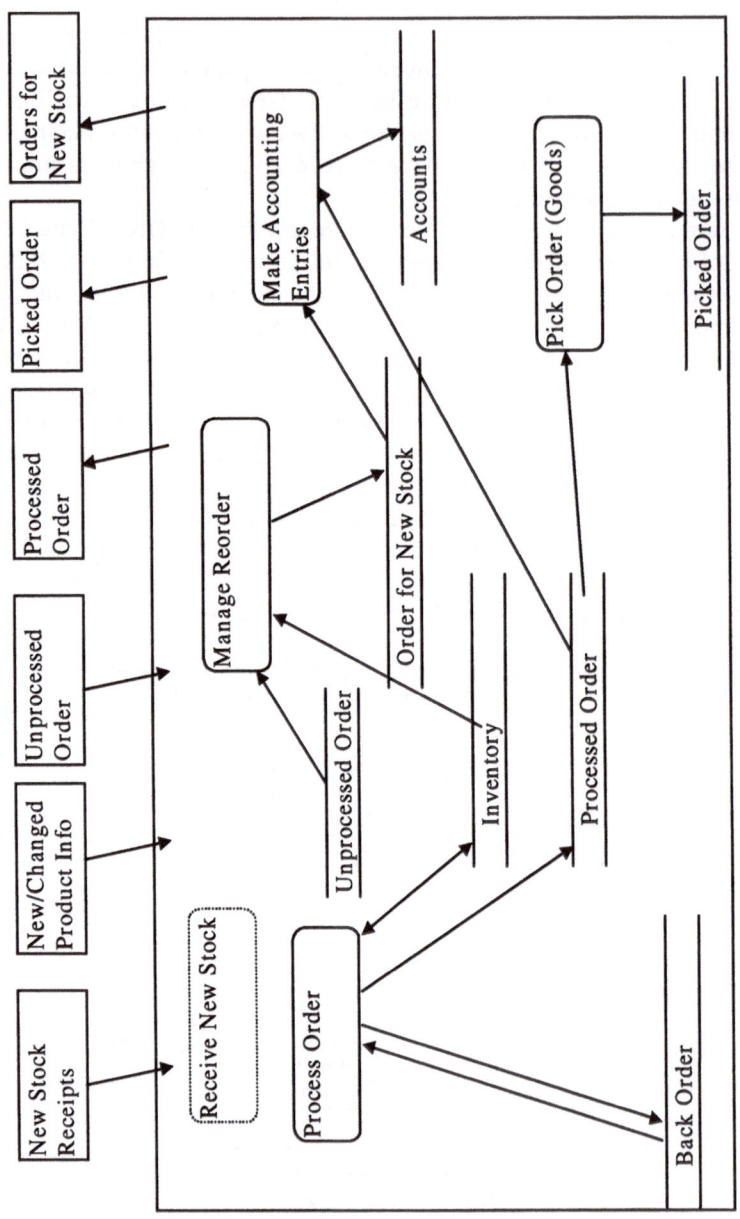

Figure 7.11: Inventory Management

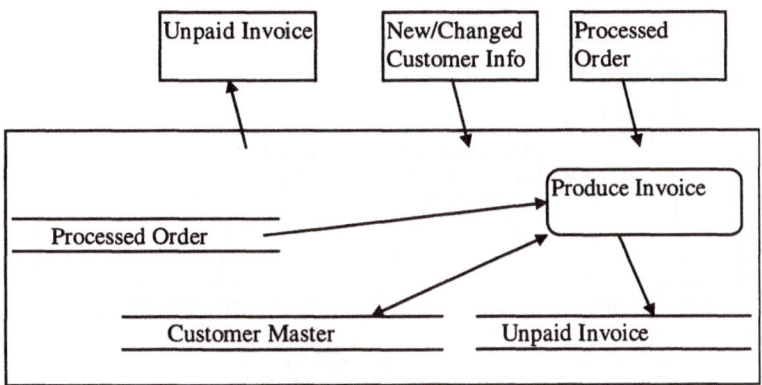

Figure 7.12: Invoice Production

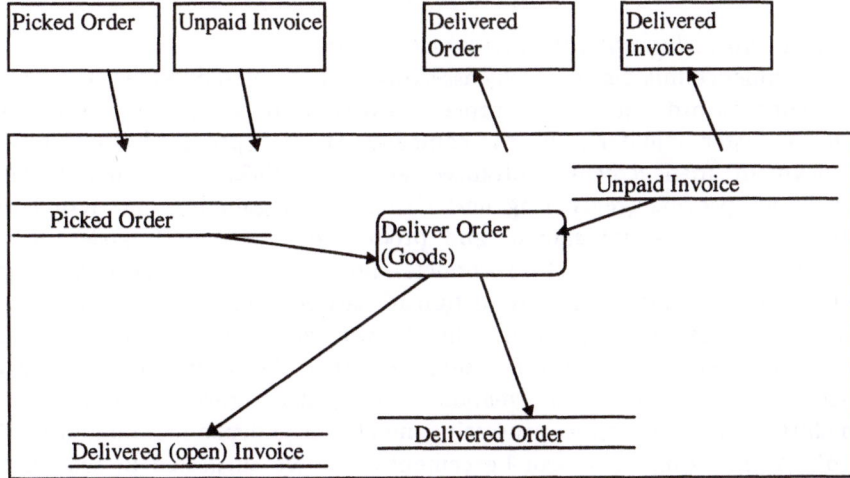

Figure 7.13: Delivery of Goods

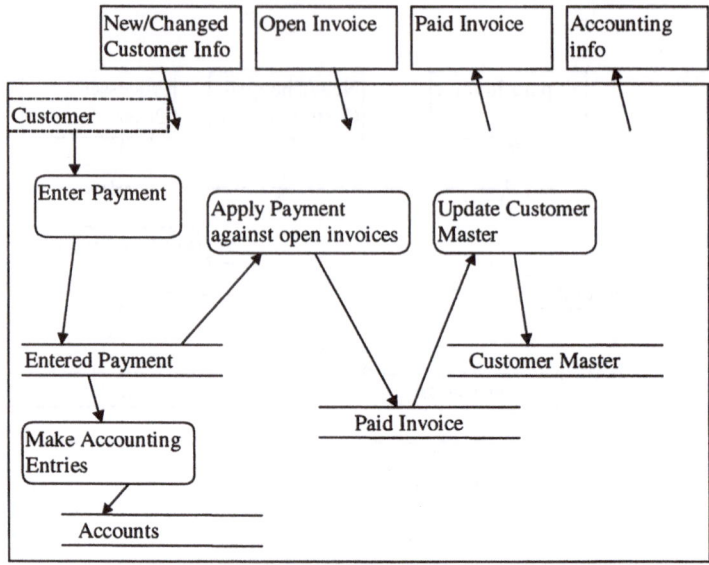

Figure 7.14: Customer Payments

Are there any other considerations in defining cluster boundaries, and indeed other benefits of clustering in this fashion?

Clustering: Processing and Administrative Isolation
Let us commence this discussion by asserting what we already know: The way in which Titanic's order fulfillment process is organized is a major driver of the design of cluster boundaries for the company. Titanic's process has order entry and payment management centralized at head office, as is the customer maintenance process (registering new customers, negotiating new terms with existing ones etc. – not shown) and product management (registering new products and pricing new/existing products – not shown). Inventory management, order distribution, and invoice production are carried out at each branch.

Properly done clustering can achieve two types of isolation: *processing isolation*, as well as *administrative isolation*. Processing isolation is an obvious consequence of having only informational dependencies cross cluster boundaries: each cluster carries out *all* its processing, no cluster is dependent on another for any of its processing. This can be cemented (as we suggested in section 6.4, "Managing the Implementation of Informational Dependencies") by confining knowledge of formats used in a cluster to that cluster.

Administrative isolation is somewhat more subtle. Implementing processing dependencies requires a number of administrative information items: For instance, for each RPC or RPC-like function we need the location of the RPC provider and the authorized users for this function. Because of its manageable size, within a cluster it is possible to comfortably maintain this type of information, which we may call application administration information. Assume that we have RPC style communication crossing cluster boundaries – we will need, at runtime, an inter-cluster request to be validated and authorized. Therefore, we need to maintain in respect of each service that is provided, information on authorized users in all clusters. Furthermore, in respect of each service that is provided by another cluster, we need to maintain in this cluster, the information on the exact location of that service – and a cluster typically can contain several server machines where these services are located. In short, where processing dependencies cross cluster boundaries, we have very little (if any) isolation of application administration information, since we need to maintain for inter-cluster communication a level of detail of location and usage information similar to that for intra-cluster communication. However, if we isolate clusters on the basis of informational dependencies, then for an information item it produces and sends out, a cluster need not know or care about *the individual users within another cluster consuming that information item.* For example, the Sydney Order Entry cluster need not know or care about the fact that in the Melbourne branch clerks Smith, Jones and Grey are authorized to process the order. It is sufficient for control over this authorization to be confined to the Melbourne branch. What Sydney needs to be concerned with is that each order it "puts" into the middleware link will be reliably delivered to its destination. This confinement of the detail of individual consumers of information to a cluster is one aspect of application administrative isolation. Furthermore, with informational dependencies, it is easy to confine location knowledge – for each cluster, it is easy to have a single location as the focal point for inter-cluster communication (we term this the "Gatekeeper', see Chapter 8). Therefore, the maximum location knowledge that one cluster needs to know of another is the location of this Gatekeeper. In implementing this concept, we can relieve clusters of the burden of maintaining this knowledge altogether. The management of inter-cluster communication (which clusters produce or need to consume what data items) can be accomplished by structures outside the applications running within a cluster (this aspect will be discussed in Chapter 9).

Therefore, we can say that the isolation of application administration has been accomplished when one cluster is isolated from knowledge of another cluster's location and usage information.

- A cluster need not know what other clusters consume the information it puts out.
- A cluster need not know what users within another cluster consume an information item.

Therefore, a consequence of processing isolation is that a cluster can achieve a large degree of isolation of application administration.

Allied with application administration are such items of general systems administration information as login authority, access to system resources like printers and disk storage, monitoring/accounting of resource usage, scheduling of background jobs etc. If our goal is to achieve isolation of application administration, then as a practical matter we should aim for isolation of this general systems administrative information as well.

For Titanic, for example, Invoice Production and Inventory Management occurs at a branch. Titanic's five branches are large, each situated at an Australian capital city. It is intended that each branch be a single systems administration area. All computing resources in each branch are connected via a LAN. In this scenario, we will not gain anything by creating a cluster boundary between Order Processing and Inventory Management and thus implementing application processing isolation between the two activities: the users' logins, their access to printers, to the job scheduler, will be managed centrally for the branch. Therefore, although purely application/business process logic may make it appear so, other considerations militate against splitting Order Processing and Inventory Management into their own clusters. The most sensible course is to designate each branch as a single cluster. *Therefore it is very desirable to make a cluster's boundaries coincide with a systems administration boundary.*

A similar argument holds for Titanic's head office; the head office is designated a single cluster.

Following this logic we end up with six clusters, one each for the branches, and one for the head office. The tasks or process fragments in each cluster are shown in Figure 7.15.

Location	Tasks/Process Fragments
Head Office	Order Entry
	Management of Customer Payments
	Customer Maintenance (not shown)
	Product Maintenance (not shown)
Branch	Inventory Management
	Invoice Production
	Distribution
	Associated Accounting

Figure 7.15: Clusters

All the data and processing for a cluster is contained within the cluster. Physically, each cluster needs a local server. Furthermore, as we discussed earlier, a cluster is managed as a single systems administration unit. Within a cluster, we can implement a three-tier architecture; for example, Inventory Management and Invoice Production tasks each will have its task-based UI, and the relevant server components; the CS and DAS components associated with these tasks are all housed within the same cluster as the UI. Within a cluster, informational dependencies between tasks can be implemented using asynchronous access to the same file or database table. The same software components are replicated at each branch.

Since message-oriented middleware provides the communication between clusters, the MOM infrastructure needs to have access to information about each message type, its source cluster, and its destination cluster(s). As we discussed earlier, the middleware domain need not require any information about the individual producers and consumers of information within a cluster. We notice that the number of additional informational dependencies created is now less than that with the earlier cluster boundaries. The informational dependencies created by having multiple instances of the data items – shown in Figure 7.16 entering and leaving the MOM highway – are feasible because (a) primary update responsibility can be rationally apportioned and (b) the ensuing informational dependencies can be tolerated by the business process. Again, we leave it to the reader to carry out the analysis.

Figure 7.16 shows the clustering arrangement schematically. Information items that each cluster "puts" in and "gets" from the MOM middleware "highway" are depicted in the figure.

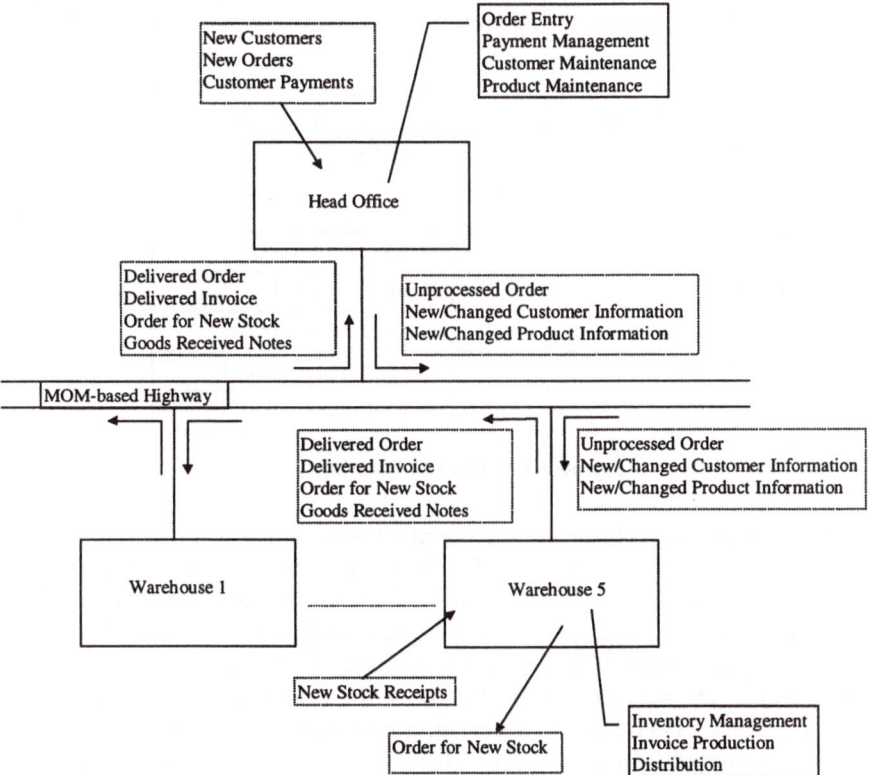

Figure 7.16: The message-based clustered solution

Administratively, we have seven distinct areas: the six clusters plus the MOM. Each cluster maintains its own administrative information: the application administration information such as location and usage of each application component, general administration information such as login authority, access to printers, monitoring/accounting of resource usage, scheduling of background jobs, management of desktop applications, etc. Each cluster is completely autonomous in this respect. The linking MOM administrative region needs to maintain information about each data item (unprocessed order, processed order, invoice, customer, etc.), its origin cluster, and destination clusters. For each piece of inter cluster information, no details of individual users is maintained at the MOM administrative region. The division of the whole into autonomous, separately administered clusters, and the fact that the linking domain need not track usage by individual combines to make a significant saving over other schemes.

Finally, note that this autonomy need not prevent, say, a head office user from logging in from the Brisbane depot. It would be possible to provide the H/O user with remote access to the head office domain from the Brisbane branch.

A Request/Reply-Based Clustered Architecture

As a contrast, let us briefly compare the message-based clustering architecture with a request/reply-based clustering architecture, assuming a similar distribution of tasks.

In common with the previous clustering arrangement shown in Figure 7.15, we now maintain locally the major files we use. As before, this approach creates multiple instances of the relevant files. For example, Figure 7.17 shows some of the files we now maintain and their locations.

File	Location
Orders	Head office, each branch
Product Master	Head office, each branch
Customer	Head office, each branch
Invoice	Head office, each branch

Figure 7.17: Files and Locations

Unlike in the previous clustering arrangement though, we now treat the update of each instance of replicated data as a distributed transaction. For example, when a new order destined to be fulfilled at the Adelaide branch is entered at the head office, the new orders record is inserted simultaneously into the Adelaide Orders file and the head office orders file; when a new customer is entered into the system from head office, all instances of the customer file are updated simultaneously; when a price change is effected to an existing inventory item, all product master records are updated simultaneously. However, since we found that the informational dependencies arising out of distributing these data can be tolerated by the business, we are unnecessarily implementing a series of informational dependencies as processing dependencies. This, as we have said before introduces an avoidable cost in terms of additional coupling.

Let us revisit some of the sources of this additional coupling. Processing isolation is not possible. In addition, for example, it will not be possible to complete an order targeted for Brisbane, if the Brisbane server happens to be down at the time of taking the order at head office. Furthermore, if the Brisbane server were down, then the head office staff will have very little control over its coming on-line again, since the Brisbane server (as are all servers) is managed out of the Brisbane branch.

Administrative isolation is not possible either. The simultaneous updates of certain items of information at different clusters mean that application administration information at the level of granularity of individual functions and individual users need to be maintained across clusters. This indicates either a global directory or some close linkage of cluster-based directories, impinging on local autonomy.

7.5 Distributed Application Alternatives: Discussion

In our experience, most designers rely exclusively upon the request/reply mechanism, their designs falling either into the request/reply based global or request/reply based clustered categories that we have discussed in this chapter. Designers often do not adequately exploit opportunities to implement systems based upon non-processing interactions. It is true, for example, that distributed transaction processing technologies provide many attractive features, in hiding TP management detail from the programmer, in scheduling and load balancing capabilities, etc. However the costs of additional coupling – in terms of additional complexity and maintenance effort – introduced in implementing a non-transactional dependency as a transactional interaction, though very significant, are often overlooked.

In this chapter we saw different approaches to the design of a distributed system, a system whose scope encompassed a significant part of the enterprise. We have discussed three-tier client/server systems at some length earlier in this book. We saw in this chapter that as an enterprise-level solution, a single three-tier system has significant drawbacks. In the main, these are as follows. First, what we labelled a global three-tier system earlier in this chapter contains distributed software components, which use conversational, RPC-like, or DTP middleware for their interaction, and which access a single central database. This type of application architecture typically does not provide the most efficient means of supporting a large, geographically distributed business operation.

- Communication across a WAN: while a three-tier application structure allows distribution of software components to satisfy performance/efficiency needs, being constrained to conduct most of the interactions of substance via a WAN nevertheless introduces a performance penalty.
- There is no scope for local autonomy. Local autonomy is desirable from a technical/operational perspective because it gives a degree of insulation from failures to other parts of the network or system; this arrangement is vulnerable to failure at a single point – the central host or a network link to it. It is also desirable from a political perspective, since providing or enhancing local control sits well with the flow of power and authority – especially in geographically distributed operations.

- The growth of software component numbers. We observed the tendency for the growth of CS and DAS components with system size. There are two related issues here:
    - The growth of the number of actual (CS and DAS) software components;
    - The growth and complexity of the administrative environment: for a global three-tier system we need global administration.

    Both these tendencies increase the complexity of the system, and introduce heavy penalties for systems upkeep and further evolution.

The obvious solution is to cluster the system, that is to group data and software components such that some local operations are supported by local software. Clustering has the possible penalty of data partitioning or replication, because we now have to distribute data that previously resided in a central location. A clustered solution that exclusively uses conversational, RPC-like, or DTP middleware for interaction between application components was also shown to be wanting in certain respects. With data replication comes component replication. Some of the replicated components and interactions are likely to be superfluous: for example, simultaneous update of all replicated data may not be required by the business process. Moreover, we will require some significant global elements in the distributed directory structure that manage this type of system, exposing us to similar penalties with growth.

We found that properly designed clustering with message-oriented middleware as the mechanism of communication between clusters has the best potential to weather these problems.

In designing such a system, establishing cluster boundaries is of prime importance. Drawing cluster boundaries along lines of informational dependencies enable clusters to enjoy processing isolation and application administrative isolation; selecting an appropriate administrative domain for cluster boundaries enables us to achieve general administrative isolation. At divisional, enterprise, or even inter-enterprise level, processing and administrative isolation are goals greatly to be desired, since they enable us to "divide and conquer": to break a large, complex, and unwieldy whole into smaller and more easily manageable parts. With processing isolation, we can potentially manage the maintenance of software components within a cluster independently of any other, so long as we fulfil our obligations to the larger system by putting the required information in the appropriate format, and getting the required information, to/from the inter-cluster MOM. With administrative isolation, we can independently carry out all systems administration activities within a cluster. We call such an arrangement a *Federated Application Architecture*. Such a cluster we term a *domain*, and the linking MOM, the *Federal Highway*. The federated architecture is a very promising basis to design applications for the enterprise, and we discuss this concept further in the next chapter.

Finally, we cannot stress too highly that the fundamental driver of the form of the application is the business process(es) that the application(s) aims to support. Obviously, there is a class of applications – for example airline reservations, banking systems managing deposits/withdrawals – where large centralized applications of extensive geographic scope using transaction processing capabilities are essential. However, the business processes of the enterprise require several individual applications, and our objective here is their integration in the most appropriate manner. It is possible to segment business processes so that informational dependencies are tolerated between them (see, for example, Chapter 10). The designer needs to scrutinize the (existing or intended) business processes to uncover possibilities for clustering: tightly coupled aspects of business processes require tightly coupled software solutions and vice versa.

8. *The Federation*

8.1 Overview

In the previous chapter, we examined different distributed application architectures and observed the potential of the MOM-based clustered approach, which we subsequently named the Federated Application Architecture. We saw that with a properly designed Federation, we can achieve both processing and administrative isolation of domains. Here we elaborate on the notion of the Federation and we establish the parameters for the design, implementation and deployment of enterprise-wide federated applications.

We introduced a Federation as a collection of domains, each responsible for its own data and processes, joined via a *"Federal Highway"*. Domains communicate via messages, with the Federal Highway being responsible for delivery. A domain interacts with the Federal Highway by "handing over" to, and "picking up" from, the highway, relevant messages. Since the intention is to isolate each domain as much as possible in terms of processing and administration from the rest of the Federation, we postulate the existence of a *"Gatekeeper"* software module to handle all interactions of a domain with the Federal Highway. Sitting at the domain's boundary the Gatekeeper places outgoing messages for consumption by the Federation and picks up relevant messages from inter-domain traffic and delivers them to an appropriate destination within the domain.

A domain has specific obligations to the Federation, for example:

- complying with the agreed type and format of the messages the domain puts onto the highway;
- complying with the periodicity of the placement (i.e. within a certain time of the triggering event);
- behaving according to an agreed strategy when recovery is necessary.

Because of its processing and administrative isolation, a domain is free to organize itself and evolve in any manner it sees fit, so long as its obligations to the Federation are preserved. Figure 8.1 displays a schematic of a Federation. The sections that follow describe the individual components of the Federation in more detail.

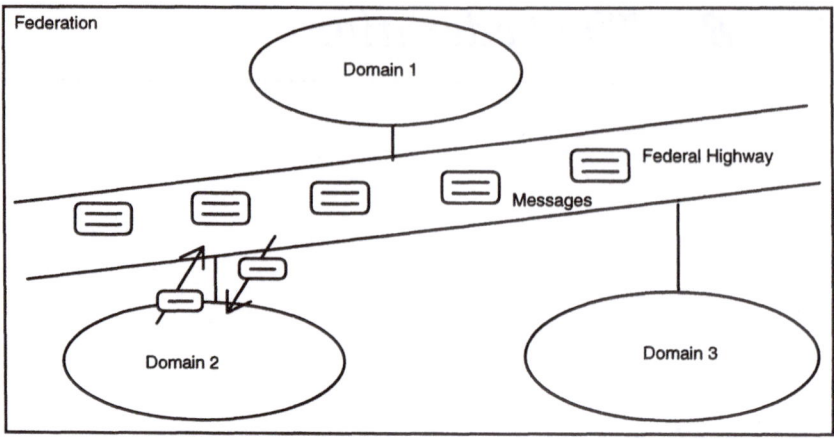

Figure 8.1: The Federation

8.2 The Domain

A domain is a cluster of applications and supporting technology. When discussing Titanic's problems we found that there could be several alternatives to clustering, and therefore domain boundaries can be established along several different lines. A domain may:

- contain applications or application components supporting an organizational process or closely related parts of a process;
- support the operations of some organizational unit – a section, division, or department;
- support the business functions of the enterprise at some a geographic location;
- be organized around some hardware/software platform(s) (Unix, Windows clients, and TCP/IP; MVS mainframe and terminals etc.).

Demarcating Domain Boundaries

Due to the importance of the consequences, demarcating domain boundaries is a central issue when designing a Federation. In the previous chapter we formulated the following guidelines:

- Only informational dependencies cross domain boundaries; processing dependencies do not span domain boundaries (recall that informational dependencies are only possible where the business can tolerate the resulting transient inconsistency, and where primary update responsibility can be apportioned unambiguously for the data elements involved).
- The principle of parsimony must be observed in the informational dependencies that the highway needs to manage; that is, boundaries must be established to minimize these dependencies; in particular to minimize the

additional informational dependencies created by the establishment of domains.
- Domain boundaries should be drawn with the aim of ensuring not only processing isolation but also administrative isolation.

The way domains are partitioned depends on the individual circumstances of the enterprise, and this determination has to follow a careful analysis of the business of the enterprise. The complexity of the business processes and the information technology infrastructure of a modern enterprise makes the demarcation of domains a challenging task.

Since the major partitioning objective is to confine closer dependencies within a domain, the architect should be guided by:

- the structure and layout of the enterprise and its processes;
- the structure and layout of the existing information systems and technology.

From the perspective of the enterprise and its processes, the dominant form of organizational grouping provides us with a starting point for candidate domains: partition along process lines in situations with a predominantly process orientation, along functional lines where the dominant structure is a functional organization, or on a geographic basis for enterprises structured in this fashion.

From the IT perspective, you may find candidate domains where a form of communication appropriate to the dependencies between them has been implemented, but in our experience this is a rare phenomenon. You typically find coupling that is too loose, for example legacy systems in incompatible platforms with either paper-based communication or some rudimentary file transfers between them. Alternatively you may find implementations exhibiting too close a coupling, for example the use of a TP monitor to couple relatively unrelated software components. Consequently, the partitioning approach needs to be tempered by the structure of existing systems, which may contain closely coupled interactions across these boundaries. Where coupling that is either too close or too loose has been implemented (in existing systems) across candidate domain boundaries, then we should redesign these links to be informational ones. This exercise will involve some re-engineering of existing systems, but in our opinion the associated costs (indeed all transitional costs) will be more than justified by the medium to long term advantages of the federated architectural form.

Thus far, we have talked about moulding the domains with the existing organizational structure and process. The alternative, of designing the domains in the context of a business process redesign, is also possible. This approach will be more expensive, but where the existing processes are seen not to deliver desired results and outcomes, is certainly an option worth considering. Consider: both in this chapter and the previous one, we have observed how a close mapping is possible between the organizational processes and the form of the systems supporting these processes. With the federated architecture, we aim to cement this mapping, to leverage off a close synergy between the organizational processes and their distribution on the one hand and the form of the enterprise systems on the other. It is evident that if we are to succeed in this endeavour, the organizational processes ought to be in good shape – information systems exhibiting close synergy with poor organizational processes are not likely to deliver positive outcomes for the enterprise! If we take this route, then the re-engineering of the business process should be the driving force – the boundary demarcation and the re-engineering of the software components should follow suit.

Inside the Domain

A domain's internal structure and organization need not be visible to other domains, because of its processing and administrative insulation: apart from its obligations to the Federation, the domain can remain opaque to the Federation – its internal structure, technology, implementation, etc., need not be visible to the outside world. Furthermore, provided its obligations to the Federation are fulfilled, a domain is free to organize itself and evolve in any manner it sees fit. Furthermore, because of the relative autonomy that domains possess, different domains within a Federation can be very different: they may be different in size, their basis of organization may be different (e.g. a business function, business process, geographic location, or some technology platform). A domain will possess its own data and process model, and possibly its own technology platforms and management structures.

The information dependencies and the "data only" messaging mechanism with the Federation has the consequence that there will be no procedures waiting for the return of a RPC, or a module in a domain left "hanging" because a process involving another domain fails to return in time. Operationally, a domain is insulated to a large degree from the vagaries of the rest of the Federation.

Within a domain, all dependencies (processing – simple and transactional, plus informational) are permitted. Inside a domain it is possible to have a mix of a number of applications of different types:

- entirely distributed client/server applications or application components;
- a mix of legacy and distributed applications;
- entirely legacy applications.

Where a domain contains distributed applications, it may choose any of the prevailing types of middleware – SQL, DTP monitor, object broker, MOM, an RPC product, or an Intranet – for intra-domain communication.

In some cases, a hierarchy of domains can be envisaged. For example a Federation covering an enterprise, with domains based on branches or divisions of the enterprise. At the next level, a Federation covering the group of enterprises, with domains based on the individual enterprises.

8.3   The Federal Highway

The Federal Highway is implemented using message-oriented middleware, with each domain having a connection to it through its Gatekeeper. The Federal Highway:

- offers federal message services to all domains within the Federation;
- guarantees delivery to the desired destination (s) of a message "put" into it;
- administratively, has access to information on data items it carries – type, origin, destination(s), authorization and usage information;
- never uses authorization/usage information at the level of individuals within a domain: producers and consumers are always domains.

The MOM implementation of the highway enables delivery protocols to be looked after at the infrastructure level rather than the application level (at the application we "put" or "get" messages). As we maintained previously, this reduces coupling, simplifies the application logic and produces safer and more easily maintainable code. These protocols are notoriously difficult to implement, requiring programming skills not always readily available within a development team. Also, the MOM infrastructure software is usually extensively tried and tested, and reliable. With this approach it is only necessary to provide a backup/recovery procedure in case a domain becomes unavailable for an extended period of time.

Because different MOMs implement their capabilities differently, we deliberately have been vague about the actual mechanism of interaction between domain and Federation. Depending on the type of MOM used, a domain may broadcast, publish, or alternatively write to a queue or set of queues. Conversely, a domain may subscribe to published information, or read from a queue or set of queues. The Federal Highway, however, is most comfortable with the notion of domains as information producers and consumers: an information item produced at one domain may have one or more consumers of that item in the Federation. Most MOMs can be adapted to suit this communication requirement. Later in this book describe two implementations of the Federal Highway, one using a MOM product with publish/subscribe capability and another with a queue-based MOM. We use terms such as "get", "put", "publish", "subscribe" in a generic sense, and not to favour any MOM implementation over another.

The Federal Directory Services

Regardless of the technology used, point to point contact of any kind between domains should be kept to a minimum (preferably zero!) in order to reduce inter-domain coupling and ensure consistent, easily maintainable, and secure mechanisms for provision of inter-domain services. A domain should not be required to contact another to find out about its published information or data format, but the interaction should be implemented at the Federation level. A federal directory service should be provided to insulate domains from each other and provide an intermediate layer where the necessary information to publish and subscribe is readily available. Domains willing to publish or subscribe to a data item should do that by contacting the directory to find the necessary information. Depending on the required operation, this can include the data that a domain publishes, who subscribes to a data item, data and message formats, etc. This approach reduces coupling, and enforces the correct protocols for interoperation.

The directory contains the necessary administrative information – at the level of the domain.

For each information item carried on the highway it contains:

- formatting information for the message;
- location information: source domain, authorized destination domain(s).

For each domain in the Federation it contains:

- any rules of consumption of individual pieces of information of an information item (if read-only, otherwise which specific pieces are permitted to be changed: for example, for a Manifest a consumer can only change the received date and time plus received quantity);
- service levels for produced information;
- type of recovery behaviour.

Self-describing messages, messages that precede the data with a section describing it, involve an even looser degree of coupling. The semantic content of each message type still needs to be agreed upon; but the domain will have discretion on the order, length and type of the data in a message. For example, a new customer message still needs to contain the id, name, delivery address, contact name, contact address, and contact telephone number, but the order of this information and the field lengths can be described in the metadata at the front of the message. If this approach were adopted, then message formats need not be directory-defined. This simplifies the role of the directory service.

Message Delivery Mechanisms

Using a message-oriented middleware product for the implementation of the Federal Highway has definite advantages: the complexity of ensuring message delivery is taken out of the hands of in-house programs and transferred to a tried and tested infrastructure. Among other services, MOMs provide an Applications Programming Interface to a programmer, typically through a set of commands that can be embedded in a host language. MOMs provide different message semantics – different ways to provide different grades of message delivery services.

A major plank of our reasoning behind implementation of informational dependencies via MOM middleware is its capacity for assured or guaranteed delivery. Therefore, we may ignore the different message semantics and implement the Federation based on assured or guaranteed level of message delivery service. In such a case, subscribers to a data item are guaranteed to receive the message, and to receive it exactly once. They are free to ignore it or screen it out. To guarantee delivery, messages are saved by the middleware on a permanent medium such as disk before transmission, but the application programmer is oblivious to this arrangement.

This level of delivery is typically the highest service level offered by MOMs, and comes at a cost. Therefore, as a practical implementation decision, we may well choose to allocate different delivery service levels to different messages, based on their importance. Some of the grades of service offered by MOMs are:

- A message is delivered exactly once: messages are guaranteed to be delivered once, despite failures and avoiding repetitions.
- A message is delivered at least once: messages are guaranteed to be delivered at least once; the messages are repeated until an acknowledgment is received.
- A message is delivered at most once: there is an attempt to deliver the message, but in case of failure there is no attempt to repeat it.

If we wish to allocate different grades of service to different messages, we should bear in mind that the intended consumption of the message is at least as important as the kind of information the message is carrying. As an illustration, consider the information item <New policy number, value, details etc.; cumulative total of policies issued>, in the following two scenarios:

- The message is consumed to update a daily totalizer Web page for publicity purposes. The total is updated every hour. The failure of a message to reach its destination is relatively unimportant, it probably will not matter if a message is simply skipped and the total updated in the next period. At most once semantics should be adequate for this purpose.
- The message is consumed by the domain that invests the premium income. The failure of a message to reach this destination could mean that the premium income received cannot be reconciled with the monies available for investment. Guaranteed delivery (exactly once semantics) is indicated in this case.

8.4 The Gatekeeper

The Gatekeeper is the interface between the domain and the Federal Highway, and is responsible for the domain's interaction with the highway. The Gatekeeper:

- traps events of global significance within the domain and messages intended for inter-domain travel, and ensures that these messages are correctly prepared and placed for routing by the highway;
- from inter-domain traffic, selects those messages relevant to its domain and passes them on to the appropriate application component within the domain;
- under abnormal conditions such as recovery from failure, behaves in a pre-specified manner that is understood by the Federation;
- handles any format translations that may be necessary, and possibly screens out from incoming messages items of data not relevant to the domain, and from outgoing messages any information the domain is not contracted to supply.

Additionally, the Gatekeeper can play a significant role in ensuring that the domain's wider responsibilities are carried out properly. For example, for all information produced by the domain, the Gatekeeper can establish that the update rules assigned to the domain are not violated; it can also monitor the service levels agreed to by the domain, and notify the appropriate staff should there be non-compliance.

The Gatekeeper responsibilities may be carried out by either one or more application components within the domain, or be spread among domain application and infrastructure levels. It is useful, however, to have one interfacing software component handling interactions between a domain and the Highway. The actual implementation of Gatekeeper functionality is contingent upon the MOM chosen for the Federal Highway, the intra-domain middleware, and their capabilities.

8.5 The Contract: A Domain's Obligations to the Federation

The responsibilities and obligations that a domain has to the Federation have to be established so that they are properly specified and understood. We call this a "contract". A contract guarantees the cooperation of a domain in the Federation in much the same fashion as a legal contract binds two contracting parties. A contract establishes, and therefore limits, the domain's level of exposure at federal level to a well specified set. Since the contract determines what is to be shared and when and how, a domain will know its obligations both in terms of quality and quantity. The contract performs two different but complementary functions:

- to a consumer, it guarantees the delivery of the necessary information in a timely manner, in the agreed format and to the appropriate place;
- to a producer, it controls the extent of, and the effort required for, its role in the Federation.

A contract specifies:

- what a domain is committed to do, and under what circumstances – domains participating in a Federation must, for example, commit themselves to publish the contracted information in the times and manner specified;
- what domains are allowed to do, or are restrained from doing. For example, if a domain is interested in a data item being published, and the contract allows its access to it, the domain is authorized to subscribe to the item and it has the right to receive the item when published. The same domain is authorized to stop subscribing to the item if it is not required anymore.

Accordingly, the contract contains the following types of metadata:

- data (and the formats) originating in the domain that are of more than local interest; data (and formats) originating elsewhere that are of interest to the domain;
- rules associated with the above categories of data: there will in general be rules about the treatment of inter-domain data. For example, a domain A picking up

order information from inter-domain traffic needs to know that, for domain A the orders are read-only;

- behaviour under abnormal conditions such as recovery from failure, to avoid threatening the integrity of the Federation;
- security mechanisms such as authentication and encryption: since sender-receiver anonymity at domain level is desirable (i.e., middleware maintaining such information), the authentication of messages that a domain picks up from the Federal Highway is a very important issue;
- performance and service-level guarantees: may be appropriate in some designs. For example, for message type X, the originating domain undertakes to put a new message into the highway within time T of the event that generates the message.

The contract may be organized as follows:

- A general section that applies to all domains. The general section describes rules, protocols, formats, standards and other items or procedures of general application.
- An individual section that specifies particular domain obligations. The individual section establishes the parameters for interaction with the domain, such as terms, conditions and periods for publishing information, authorization provisions for messages consumed by the domain, private protocols, etc.

Quite apart from its role in the realm of the Federation's software, the contract performs some important roles in the realm of the enterprise and its actors. The terms of the contracts are to be determined by the enterprise, specifically by the people representing the domains and those responsible for the overall implementation. Managers of business units can have considerable power within an organization, and it would be unwise to assume their complete cooperation without them having control of the extent of their involvement. The proposition that an organizational unit will be prepared to expose its data or processes with no prescribed limits does not take account of elements of organizational reality such as politics and power. Therefore, the conception of domains that limits a domain's exposure to the "outside", and their cooperation via a contract arrived at by common agreement rather than imposition, sit far more comfortably with the realities of the organization – in contrast with a naive model of unstinting cooperation between different foci of organizational power.

A domain X wishing to consume an information item never applies directly to the producing domain, but to the level of the management of the Directory Service. If authorized, then X will become a consumer of that item of information in the format with which it is generally available to the Federation. This pattern of behavior brings to the fore the notions of mediation and standardization: access is mediated by a third party, and access is provided under standardized conditions.

Similarly, a domain cannot unilaterally suspend the publication of information that other domains consume; neither can a domain unilaterally change its format or update rules: consuming domains have to be guaranteed by the contract framework that they can reliably get the data. However, the scheme should provide protocols (that is, the method of negotiation and arbitration with other domains of the Federation) that should be followed by a domain wishing to suspend or stop the publication of certain data.

Furthermore, a contract can include, by agreement, sanctions in case of failure to fulfill an obligation – for instance what measures should be adopted if a domain fails to measure up to the agreed service levels.

In summary then, the contract specifies the manner in which the integrity of the Federation is maintained through its operational life. As such, formulating the elements of the contract is a fundamental part of the overall design of a Federation; its negotiation and ratification by stakeholders to the Federation is a crucial step to be performed prior to the implementation of the Federation. The degree of formality of the organization process that is involved in these steps is contingent on the enterprise. Once the contract is finalized, then the software components that reflect the contract will live within the Highway infrastructure, such as the Directory Service, and within the Gatekeepers to each domain. Of course, the contract is not cast in stone, but organizational mechanisms to cope with change and evolution do need to exist. Indeed, the loose coupling of this federated form is intended to make change and evolution easier.

8.6 Processing and Administrative Isolation

We introduced the notions of processing and administrative isolation in the previous chapter. Domain boundaries, if drawn sensibly, can achieve both processing isolation, as well as administrative isolation.

Since each domain carries out all of its own processing, no domain is dependent on any other for any of its processing. What would happen if there were processing dependencies between domains? If, for example, the inter-domain interfaces were processing dependencies (implemented perhaps with RPC type interactions), then using our coupling analysis techniques, we can relatively easily deduce (as we did in Chapter 7) that a greater degree of coupling would exist than the case where there were only informational dependencies implemented via MOM middleware. Some of the adverse consequences of the coupling introduced by inter-domain processing dependencies are:

- one domain's resources being utilized at the behest of another – this has consequences for (a) privacy, (b) security, and (c) resource utilization/costing and chargeout;
- the requesting domain needs to wait upon response by another (over which it has little or no control) to progress its work;
- the need to contrive a polling mechanism to implement event-driven information flows (for example, the manufacturing domain polling the order processing domain for new orders) resulting in unnecessary network traffic and waste of cycles;
- for each RPC interface provided by Domain Y, the calling module in Domain X needs to know not only the interface specification, but also needs an

understanding of what the called module does. This constraint has considerable impact on the independent evolution of the two domains.

With processing isolation none of these issues is likely to surface.

The other desirable goal is achieving administrative isolation. The point about administrative isolation in this context is that *it is very difficult, (if not impossible), to have administrative isolation without processing isolation.* For each RPC or RPC like function, we need the location of the RPC provider and the authorized users for this function; and in practice it will not be sufficient to register an authorized user of an RPC in domain Y as "Domain X" – in effect allowing access to all users in domain X. It will be necessary to register the individual users in domain X who are allowed to access domain Y's RPC. This too has adverse consequences for maintenance; your location and access maintenance now spans domains.

On the other hand, if we isolate domains on the basis of informational dependencies, one domain need not know or care about who (which user) in another domain consumes an item of information. Each domain is able to manage access as an internal matter. If application administration isolation is possible, then it is feasible to go a step further and achieve general systems administration isolation; i.e. the management of such items of general systems administration information as login authority, access to system resources like printers and disk storage, monitoring/accounting of resource usage, scheduling of background jobs etc. within a domain.

With processing and administrative isolation, the Federation will be in a very good position to weather the effects of growth and change. Each domain can be managed separately; because there is no requirement to maintain administrative (location/usage) information at any lower granularity than a domain, the administration of the Federal Highway too will be able to weather the effects of growth. Hence as a consequence of this looser coupling, as the enterprise-wide system grows this architectural form imposes less administrative and maintenance overhead when compared with other types of dependency between domains, and therefore will be easier to operate and maintain.

The authors have experience of attempts in the industry, for example in large enterprises, to quarantine systems from the effects of other systems. These generally have been ad-hoc, employing no generic underlying principles. ANSA (1993) specifies a useful software model for "Trading and Federation" that recommends:

- a context-relative naming scheme, rather than a global hierarchical one;
- traders (components who specialize in knowledge of services provided by other components); and
- autonomy for members of the Federation.

However, this model still uses the processing interaction paradigm for communication, with the consequence (as argued earlier) of tighter coupling than the Federation proposed here.

8.7   Transition to the Federation

The concept of isolation also has important consequences for the implementation of the Federation. One of the most commonly reported problems in industry is that of the difficulties encountered when designing and implementing systems in a monolithic fashion. Such projects often stall due to their sheer size and complexity: there is a large initial investment of time and money, but the project often loses steam after a time period and finally is all but abandoned. Projects take too long, running into trouble through cost and schedule overruns engendered by optimistic early estimates, changing scope and requirements, turnover of key project staff, and perhaps even more seriously turnover of the sponsors and champions of the project. The consequences for the enterprise of such a failure are often very serious, in terms of money and human effort, and the loss of staff morale, the credibility of the IT department, and in shaping the company attitude to this type of endeavour in the future.

The transition to the Federation will be a major exercise, but it need not be a monolithic one. One of the major attractions of the Federation is its capacity to be implemented in a gradual fashion. A suggested sequence is outlined below.

First, analyze and determine the candidate domains. Specify the informational dependencies: the messages and their characteristics.   Then agree on the technology for the Federal Highway. Thereafter, specify the infrastructure: the directory services and generic Gatekeeper capabilities. Up until this juncture, the process has been enterprise-wide in scope, but confined to analysis and paper specification only. We could now take a decision to proceed further, based on the detailed costs and benefits, which would now be possible to establish.

Once the middleware and the supporting infrastructure is ready to go, we can bring domains into the Federation fold in a gradual manner. We can induct a new domain X into the Federation as follows: once a domain is joined to the Federation, to successfully "put" and "get" required messages from the highway (and for domains already in the Federation to successfully receive messages originating from this domain). Once this routine is established, the existing links of domain X with domains already in the Federation can be broken. The experience of the initial domains can be applied to the implementation of the oncoming ones, learning from any initial mistakes and, where possible, reusing software (for example, the Gatekeeper software).

There is also a comfort factor with this approach: business unit managers typically have considerable power, and more often than not control the purse strings of the IT department. They will have to be convinced of the benefits of the new developments before they commit their resources to the cause. Observing successful implementations of Federation components can assuage many fears and highlight the advantages of joining the overall scheme. With a gradual approach, the scope of each project can be confined to a manageable size, with there being several such projects following an overall plan.

Moreover, it may well be possible to manage even the incorporation of a single domain into Federation in a gradual manner. The Gatekeeper is the crucial piece of software for this stage: Typically, when the Gatekeeper traps a message from the highway it delivers it to a target application within a domain. It is possible to select an application with which to start the development and incorporate the domain, iron out the problems that could arise, and then uncouple its existing links with other members of the Federation. Then, we may bring other applications of the domain into the Federation gradually via the Gatekeeper.

8.8   Federated Architecture and Organizational Structure

As we discussed earlier in this chapter, in partitioning the domains, three competing types of boundaries have to be considered as candidates for domain boundaries:

- Organizational boundaries: these could be existing boundaries, or intended ones where the software architecture is built to support an anticipated organizational change. The likely boundaries may be based on:
  - organizational units such as departments, divisions, cost centres, etc.;
  - organizational functions or processes, (which may or may not coincide with the above demarcation).
- Geographical boundaries: physical sites where parts of the enterprise are located.
- Technology boundaries: demarcated by existing platforms/application groups.

There is (Davenport *et al.*, 1992) reason to believe that a model that admits politics and conflict may better reflect reality than a model of unstinting cooperation and unfettered exchange of information. Davenport *et al.* (1992) suggest federalism, a model where potentially competing or non cooperating parties are brought together by negotiation, as a preferred archetype. The proposed Federated architecture is well placed to support this type of behaviour. First, no process belonging to another domain will exert control over a local process or resource (e.g. locking records during a distributed transaction), since processing and transactional dependencies are excluded from the inter-domain arena. Secondly, location and user information pertaining to a domain is confined to that domain. In short, apart from the window into it represented by the contract (determining the domain's runtime behaviour vis-à-vis the Federation), a domain can be made opaque the Federation. The nature and extent of the domain's dealings with the Federation can be negotiated, the outcome being the contract; and the internal workings of the domain may be exposed to the Federation only to the extent that the organizational owners of the domain are comfortable.

The term "architectural mismatch" was originally proposed by Garlan *et al.* (1995) over assumptions in the technical domain that conflict with the reality, such as a service that a given software product is supposed to provide and upon which architectural decisions have been made falling short of expectations in terms of flexibility or performance. We can now extend the concept into the organizational domain to also take account of mismatches between software architecture and the assumptions it makes about organizational reality. This Federated architecture aims to minimize architectural mismatch in this extended sense of the term. With the domains mirroring important organizational boundaries, and its behaviour able to support a variety of organizational behaviours, the *Federation can become the software counterpart of the enterprise.*

8.9 Example: An Australian Transport Company

Transco is a freight services company with an Australia-wide operation involved in inter-state movement of freight. The company has been serviced by a centralized system that only partially supported their operations, and was operating near the threshold of its scalability. They required a system that would better support their operations, and because of these limitations, were amenable to a complete replacement of their current applications and platform.

A major requirement of their new system was the ability to effectively support their operations, which are distributed. The depots are distributed centres of control, each of which manages the movement of freight in its locality, and cooperates with other depots to progress the business process. The system was required to provide localized control, to secure a significant degree of insulation for local operations from failure of remote systems, and to respond rapidly to local events that have a bearing on operations.

In the new system design, each depot was supported by a separate domain, containing applications and data to support its operations. The major applications supporting a depot were:

- customer maintenance;
- order processing;
- local vehicle scheduling and management;
- consignment processing;
- long haul vehicle management including manifest management.

Data and processing local to each domain was organized so as to eliminate processing and transactional dependencies across depots – confining inter-depot dependencies to informational dependencies. To preserve these dependencies, an accompanying set of rules on primary responsibility for the data in each inter-domain message was formulated. For example, each manifest has certain data items whose primary responsibility lies with the originating domain (depot) – such as destination, consignment ids, vehicle configuration, etc. – and certain items whose primary responsibility lies with the destination domain – such as arrival time. Also, proof of delivery (POD) for a consignment is the responsibility of the destination domain.

In addition to these operational domains based on geographical divisional lines, a head office administration domain was created. This latter domain supports a central head office function and contains the main administrative applications of Transco such as billing, accounting, payroll and fleet administration. Again, this decision followed an analysis of the operational and administrative systems, which established that only informational dependencies existed between them.

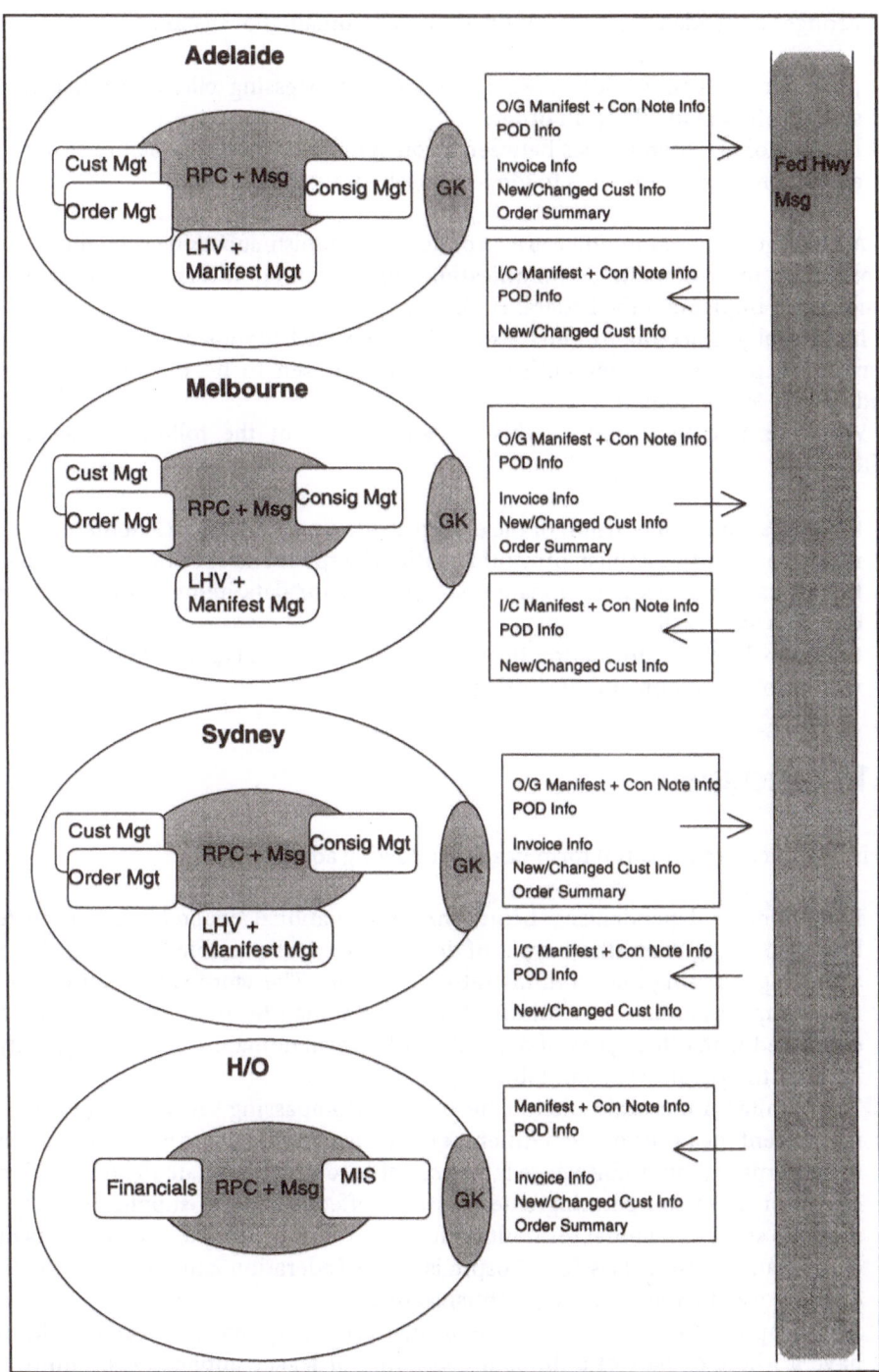

Figure 8.2: Transco – domains and inter-domain messages

Notes: GK = Gatekeeper; LHV = long haul vehicle; Mgt = management; Msg = message; POD = Proof of delivery

Stronger dependencies were confined to each domain. For instance,

- processing dependencies between the order processing client software and server software in taking an order;
- transactional dependencies between a consignment note and a manifest in the allocation of consignments to long-haul vehicles.

A message-oriented middleware product with publish/subscribe capability was chosen for inter-domain communication implementing informational dependencies – to implement the Federal Highway.

Incidentally, since the product also delivered asynchronous request/reply plus transaction processing capabilities, it was also chosen to be the intra-domain middleware for all domains.

We were able to formulate this design because of the following enabling criteria:

- there was a natural division of the enterprise-wide operation into domains;
- it was possible to establish only informational dependencies between domains;
- the allocation of primary update responsibility for data items to the different domains was feasible;
- the inter-domain information flow was of the broadcast type, from the domain with primary responsibility to others.

8.10 Conclusion

This federated architectural form has the following advantages:

- Inter-domain dependencies, being only informational dependencies, require looser coupling than others types of dependency. It is possible for a domain to achieve processing and administrative isolation. Therefore this architectural form imposes much less administrative and maintenance overhead when compared with other types of dependency between domains, and consequently is easier to operate and maintain.
- The architecture is scaleable to enterprises encompassing several remote sites, in different locations or even different countries. Although we have focused on the enterprise, this architecture is also suitable to accommodate the interaction of two or more co-operating enterprises: to effect customer-supplier relationships, to serve as a model for multinationals, groups of companies, networks of co-operating enterprises (e.g. hospitals). The Federation can also provide an effective way forward for merged businesses.
- Legacy applications can be integrated relatively easily into this framework, to have a whole or part of a domain consisting of legacy applications. Limiting inter-domain dependencies to informational dependencies means that the scope of effect of legacy applications can be contained within a domain. Furthermore, in general, message-oriented middleware offers the easiest connectivity to legacy applications.

- With informational dependencies/MOMs, synchrony of sender and receiver does not matter. Therefore, messages can be sent as the events occur, or as consolidated information at designated times. Messages can be read as they arrive or at convenient designated times, thus providing a great deal of flexibility in the timing/scheduling of inter-domain communications.
- A great deal of congruence is possible between the architecture on the one hand and the organizational structure, as well as the politics of organizational behaviour on the other. This is the preferred paradigm, given that the development and upkeep of enterprise-wide distributed applications usually involves disparate parties at all stages of the software life cycle. The concept of domains embodies the idea of independent organizational units brought together by cooperation and negotiation.

Finally, remember that the Federation is an architectural form or style. As befitting an architectural style (Chapter 2) the Federation has a distinctive form, and a set of architectural principles. We can implement instances (i.e. individual designs) that comply with this style. Indeed, in practice we would be likely to design or encounter designs with different *degrees of compliance*.

9. *Implementing the Federation*

This chapter discusses an implementation of the proposed Federated architecture based on IBM's MQ Series middleware. We centre the discussion on how the MOM infrastructure can be used to manage the required interactions within the Federation, and we specify protocols that could be followed in such an implementation. We focus on the development of a Federal Directory Service, and the necessary protocols and procedures for the various Federated activities – to allow domains to enter and leave the Federation, publish and subscribe to data items, find published information, request an item for publication, etc – are introduced and their implementation using the middleware is suggested. In order to achieve this capability, we have constructed a publish/subscribe mechanism over the queue-based MOM capability provided by MQ Series. Sections 9.1 and 9.2 discuss our general approach and proposed Federation protocols, but the detailed queue information is deferred to Appendix 2. Details such as security and recovery procedures that were outside of the objectives for this chapter and would have obscured the discussion have been purposely left out.

Work is progressing on the development of a generic, reusable architecture for Gatekeepers, the other major superstructure component of the Federation. This implementation is part of the Federated Application Architecture (FAAR) Project at the Royal Melbourne Institute of Technology (Australia).

9.1 Introduction

Overview

The enterprise-wide Federation requires the implementation of a "Highway" where domains place messages as a response to internal events. This amounts to the deployment of an "information bus" that carries the messages between communicating domains. This "Federal Highway" is actually a figure of speech, an image representing the real medium carrying data among domains. When we say that a domain puts a message "on the bus" or "on the Highway', we mean that there is a purposely dedicated infrastructure where the message is placed that is in charge of the message delivery. The medium chosen for this implementation is the MQ Series middleware product from IBM that manages a set of queues where applications can place and retrieve messages. Since domains are able to join or leave the Federation, establish communication for the first time, and in the most common case simply exchange information, a set of protocols is necessary so that their interoperation via the "information bus" is assured. This in particular requires maintaining the necessary administrative information including publications, domains, queues, formats, frequencies and a set of procedures to be followed when federal activities are taking place.

Our implementation relies on establishing a Federal Directory Service to mediate the communication between domains when some of their contractual obligations are to be effected. The Directory manages a database that maintains records for entities such as domains participating in the Federation, publisher-subscriber relations, data items available for subscription and publication, and their frequencies, but only at the level of a whole domain – no internal domain information is reflected on the Directory structures. The Directory also keeps the necessary queue information for publishers and subscribers to be able to communicate. Domains interact in specified ways with the Directory when they want to join or leave the Federation, when they want to become publishers or subscribers, when they want to change the parameters of a publication, etc. That is, domains use the services of the Directory when trying to set up or change the conditions of their operation within the Federation. To ensure consistency, the conditions of all interactions between publishers and subscribers have to be agreed upon through the Directory.

After being registered, publisher domains are allowed to offer information generated locally, either because it has been requested or is likely to be of global interest. Once a publication is made available, the publisher is bound by its contract to comply with the parameters of the publication, such as name and format of the items and periodicity of the broadcast. Subscriber domains are entitled to locate in the Directory available items of their interest, and to subscribe to their transmission by using a subscription protocol and specifying the required parameters. Once such an agreement is incorporated in the Directory service, the contractual obligations ensure that the originating domain is to publish the required information at the agreed times. Recalling our example in Chapter 7, if a customer places an order through the Enter Order module, the originating domain (its Gatekeeper to be precise) must broadcast to subscribers the Unprocessed Order data items by compiling appropriate messages and placing them on the queue(s) previously agreed upon via the Directory. These (for the publisher) remote queues are under the control of the subscriber, and are to be managed only by the subscriber Gatekeeper.

Subscribers – their Gatekeepers – retrieve messages from the relevant queues and deliver them to the corresponding applications within the domain. In the example above the Process Order module was a subscriber to the Unprocessed Order information; this is therefore retrieved from the relevant queue by the Gatekeeper and forwarded to the Process Order application for processing. After taking care of the order, the Process Order module puts into the Highway the Processed Order information to which the Produce Invoice module is subscribed.

With regards to when messages are broadcast, recall that there are two different possibilities:

- messages are published as a response to a triggering event: a new policy is issued, a new order is taken, an order is processed, etc.;
- messages are collated and published with an agreed frequency.

The following sections describe in detail how the queuing middleware is used, the responsibilities of a Gatekeeper, and the different protocols to be followed within the federated organization.

MQSeries Queuing Middleware

MQSeries is a message-oriented middleware that runs on dissimilar computers, operating systems and locations. In general terms, when two applications need to communicate, one application places a message on a queue, and the other application gets it, asynchronously, from the same queue. Applications are written using the Message Queue Interface (MQI), MQSeries' application programming interface, which includes facilities for setting up and managing queues. MQSeries simplifies the connection between heterogeneous environments by offering:

- MQI, a high level program interface that shelters programmers from differences in operating systems and underlying networks.
- Guaranteed message delivery and uniqueness. The infrastructure guarantees message delivery by writing the message first to non-volatile memory and then placing it into the corresponding queue. If a receiver is not available, the message is kept for a later delivery upon the receiver's availability. Messages that definitely cannot be delivered are placed in special dead letter queues, from where an application can take corrective action.
- A main server component, the Queue Manager, is in charge of providing applications with messaging services and processing the MQI calls issued by the applications. The Queue Manager makes sure that messages are put on the appropriate queues and routed correctly to other queue managers.
- Tools to create and delete queues, start and stop queues, browse through queues' contents, sight, view information on and reply to messages and other administrative tasks.

The Directory Services Domain

A main component of the Directory Services is a database storing the required information for domains to interoperate. The structure of the data is depicted in Figure 9.1.

The Directory also stores the information needed to fulfil the contracts between domains participating in the Federation – in particular to describe the roles that they perform in relation to an item. With respect to an item under publication, the Directory database includes:

- publisher identification;
- subscriber identification;
- publication identification;

- item(s) identification (multivalued);
- format of the items;
- periodicity of item publication;
- name of the subscriber's destination queue where the item is to be placed;
- name of the queue manager that administers the subscriber's destination queue.

Directory database tables and their content

Domains	Publication	Subscriptions
Domain_Id Name Description	Publication_Id * Publisher_id * Item_Ids (multivalued) Description Format Size Publication frequency	Subscriber_Id Publication_Id Queue manager name Queue name

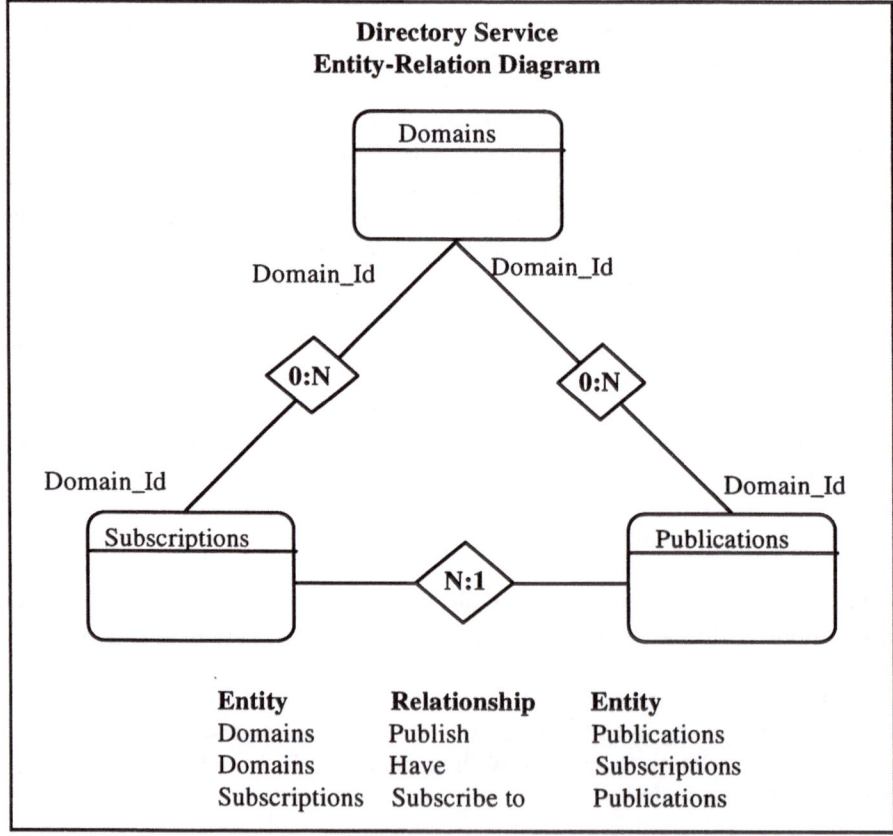

Entity	Relationship	Entity
Domains	Publish	Publications
Domains	Have	Subscriptions
Subscriptions	Subscribe to	Publications

Figure 9.1: Directory database structure

For example, consider a simple Federated scheme consisting of Sales, Head Office and Warehouse domains (see Figure 9.2). The Sales domain receives customer requests via the Enter Order module. From these requests, Sales broadcasts to the Federation the product codes, customer details, quantity required and due date for delivery. The Warehouse domain subscribes to that information since it is all relevant to the delivery. Also the product codes, total amount of the sale and the salesperson's name is published by Sales because it has been subscribed to by Head Office. The time of the sale is available but it has no subscribers so it is not published at this stage.

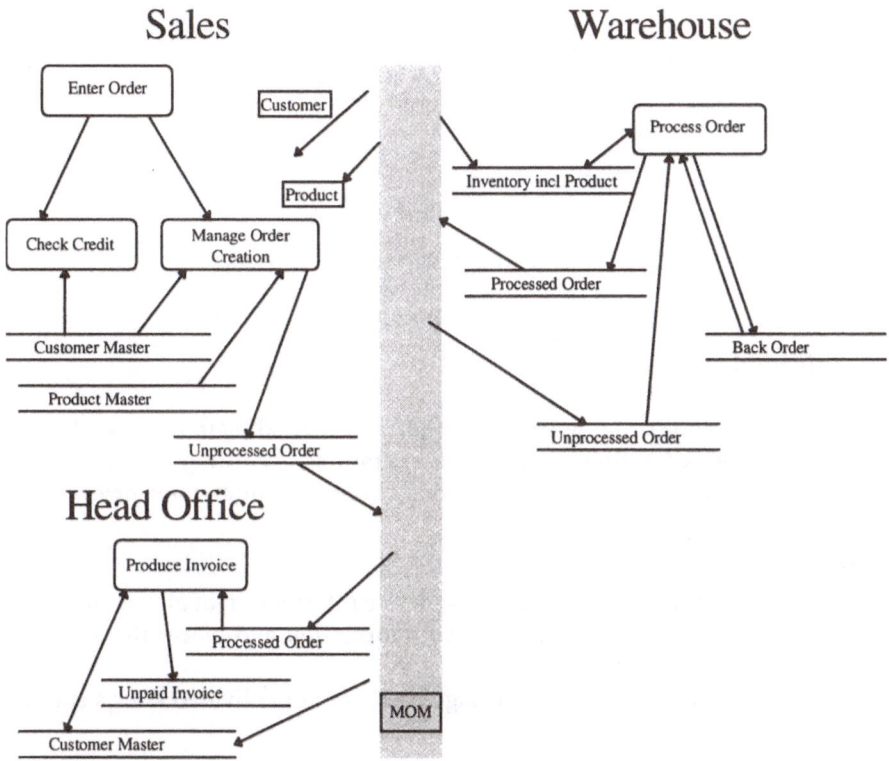

Figure 9.2: A simple Federated scheme

The module "Process Order" within Warehouse processes the order, determines what is to be delivered, when and to whom, and puts the delivery information in the Highway. Head Office subscribes to this information for its Produce Invoice module, which issues the corresponding invoice and publishes the invoice number, order number and total of the invoice. Both Sales and Warehouse subscribe to this information to reconcile the totals of orders and delivery dockets against total of invoices. The information is published in response to a triggering event, such as a sale being made, a delivery docket being produced, or an invoice being issued.

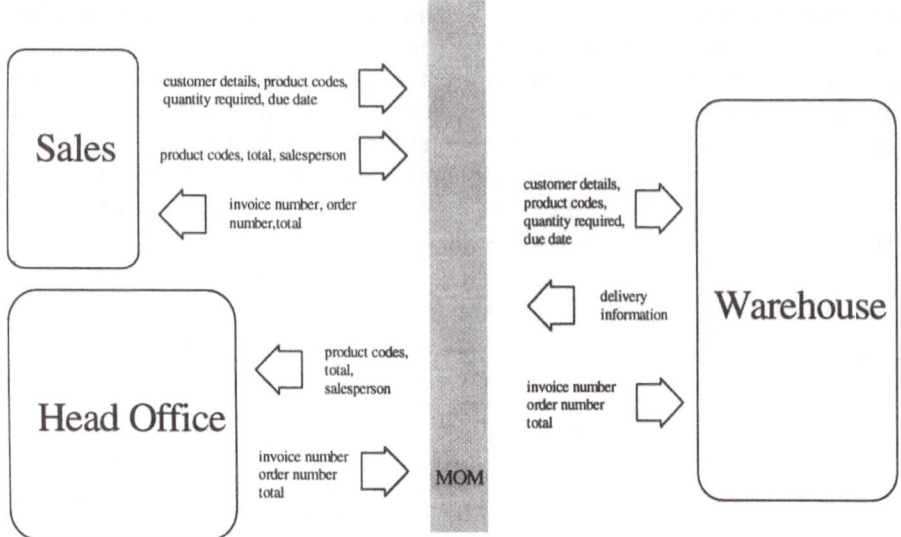

Figure 9.3: A simple Federated scheme – messages

The Gatekeeper

The Gatekeeper is one or more software applications residing in the boundary of a domain with the Federation. It performs operations according to the domain's contract specifications. Gatekeepers' responsibilities are enumerated below:

Publisher's Gatekeeper

- Traps events within the domain that generate information of global interest.
- Prepares messages with the subscribed information and places them onto the appropriate subscribers' queues.
- Deals with "dead messages" – messages that are not delivered after a specified period of time.

Subscriber's Gatekeeper

- Retrieves messages sent by publishers and delivers them to the corresponding applications within the domain.
- Deals with format translation and frequency considerations.
- Manages the local queues, to delete messages once they are retrieved, create new queues when required, etc.

Of course, when domains are both publishers and subscribers, Gatekeepers are responsible for all the operations described above.

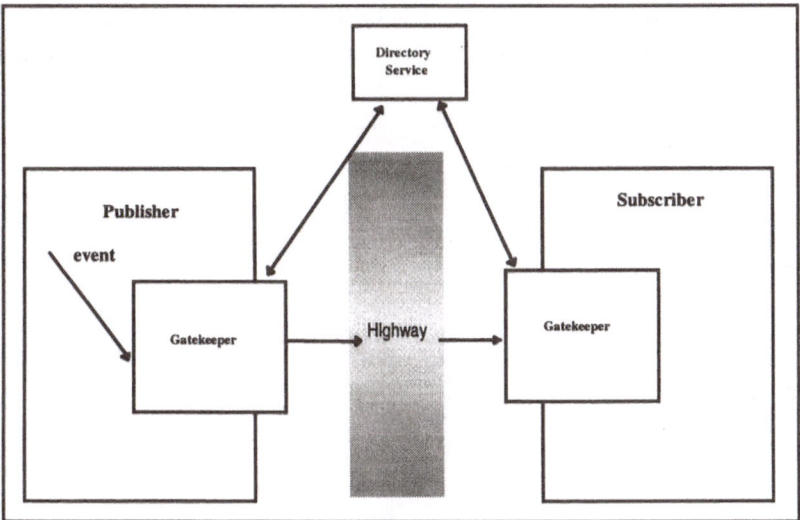

Figure 9.4: Message transmission among domains

9.2 Federation Protocols

The functioning of the Federation is based on a number of procedures that determine the maintenance of the directory service database, the domains operations and the publication of subscribed information. These procedures specify the steps to be followed when domains need to interact within the Federation. The following section discusses these procedures at the level of the interaction between domains and between domains and Directory. It describes how messages are exchanged between publishers, subscribers and the Directory, without including queue information. A queue level description of how these exchanges can be implemented using standard queues is included in Appendix 2.

Initiate a New Publication

The Directory contains information about items under publication or available for publication. New publications are data items not included in either of the two categories. Three situations can initiate a new publication:

- A domain has found an item or items of interest currently being published, but bundled together with other items or being broadcast with an inadequate frequency. The prospective subscriber can request the item(s) to be set up for a new publication.
- A domain is searching for the publisher of a certain information. The domain sends a request message to the Directory, which in turn broadcasts a request message to all other domains. The message contains a description of the required information and details to make the subscription effective if the publisher is found.

- In the second situation a domain decides to offer a new item for publication. The domain sends a message to the Directory advising the availability of a new item.

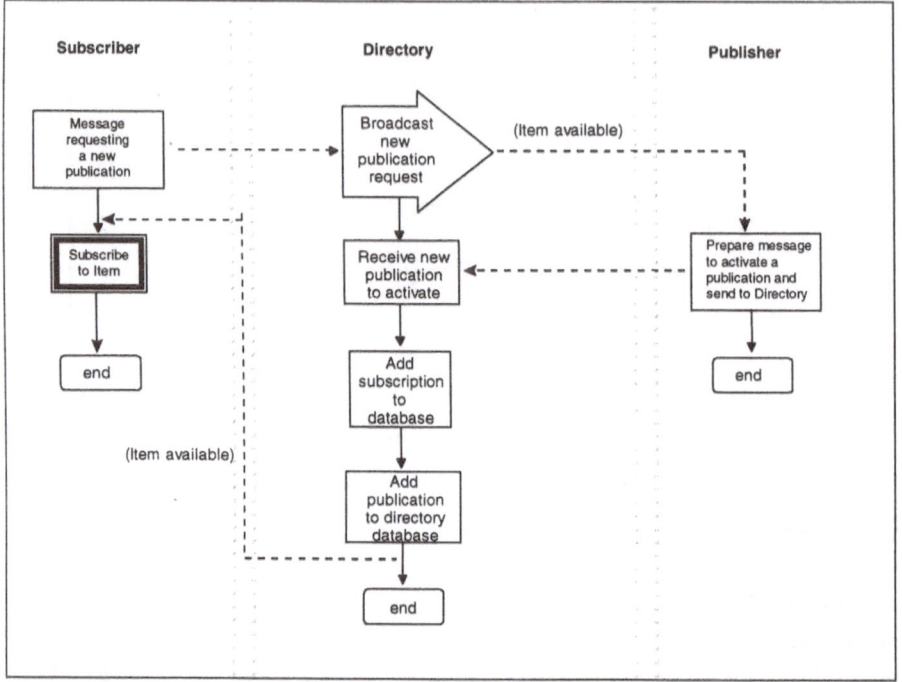

Figure 9.5: Initiate a new publication

If the broadcast finds a publisher, the publisher initiates the new publication and the Directory advises the prospective subscriber of the item's availability. The subscriber then uses the "Subscribe to a Publication" protocol to initiate the subscription.

Subscribing to a Publication

According to the contract framework, a domain has the right to subscribe to any publication present in the Directory database. The prospective subscriber prepares and sends a message to the Directory specifying the publication to which it is interested in subscribing (the publication must be available already). The directory updates its database with the new subscriber information. (See Figure 9.6.) The directory also prepares and sends a message to the publisher, for it to update its local database publication information. The publisher then starts to publish according to the "Publish" protocol.

Note that since the publication is available, according to the contractual agreements discussed in Chapter 8 no acknowledgments are necessary in the above protocol.

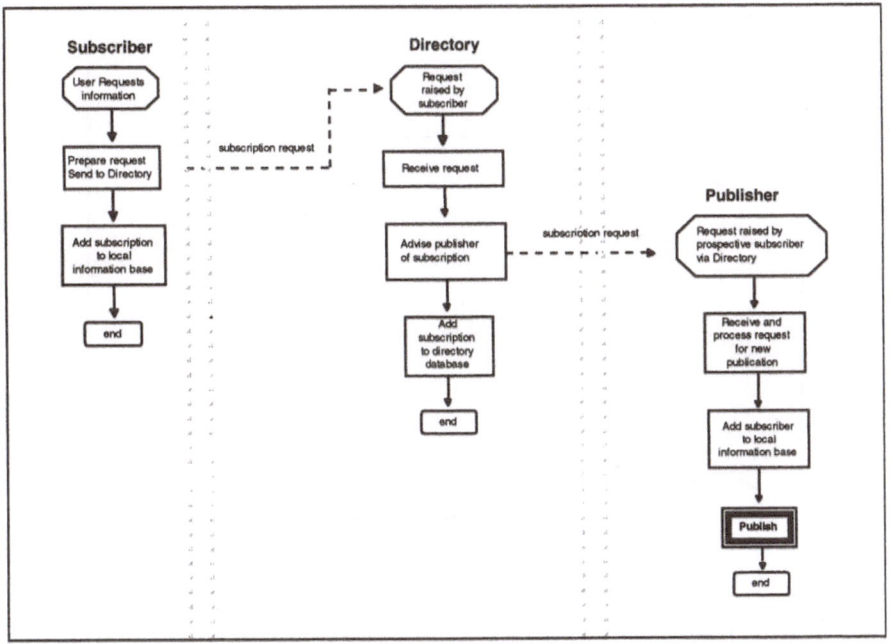

Figure 9.6: Subscribing to an item

Start a Publication

When a domain is to start publishing an item for the first time, it prepares a message for the Directory advising on the starting of the publication. The message includes details such as the publisher identification, item identification, and publication characteristics such as the format, size and frequency of the publication (see Figure 9.7).

Publishing

The publication of information can happen once a contractual arrangement between a publisher and a subscriber has been established (Figure 9.8). The publication starts with the event that generates the information containing subscribed items, or with the timing event indicated in the contract. The publisher's Gatekeeper prepares and delivers the appropriate messages to each of the subscribers by placing them in the corresponding queues under control of the subscribers' queue managers.

Delete Subscription to a Publication

A subscriber can unilaterally stop its subscription to a publication at any time. To do so, it prepares and sends a message to the Directory requesting the deletion of the specified subscription (Figure 9.9). The message contains the publication identification.

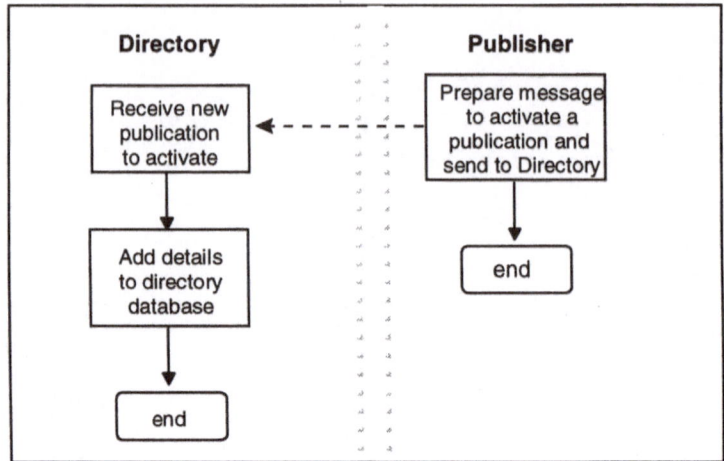

Figure 9.7: Start publication of an item

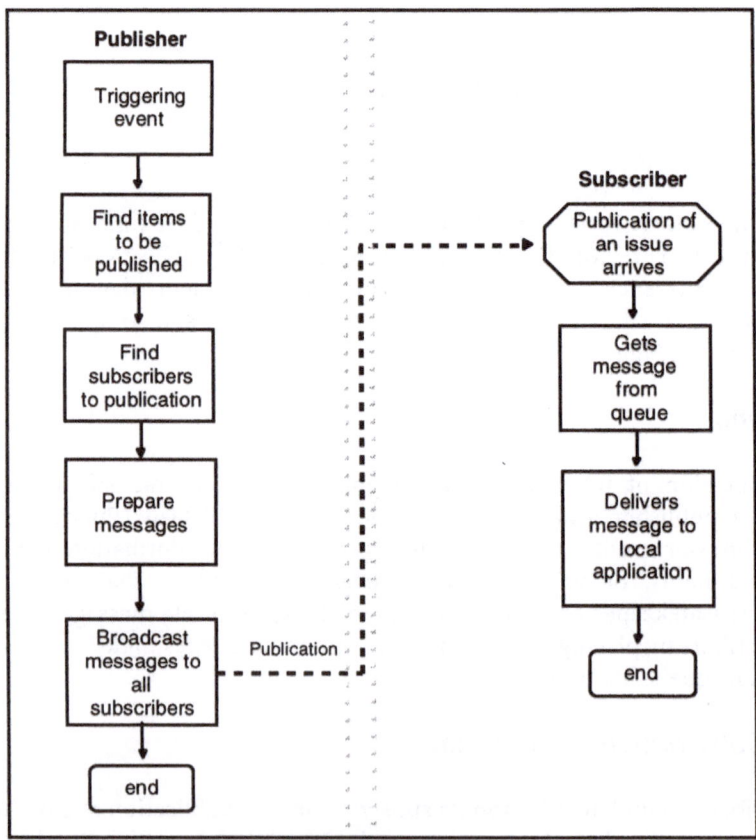

Figure 9.8: Publish a publication

To perform the deletion the Directory prepares and sends a message to the publisher to allow the update of the publisher's publications information base. The Directory also updates its internal database. Again, given the contract framework there is no need for acknowledgments between the intervening parties.

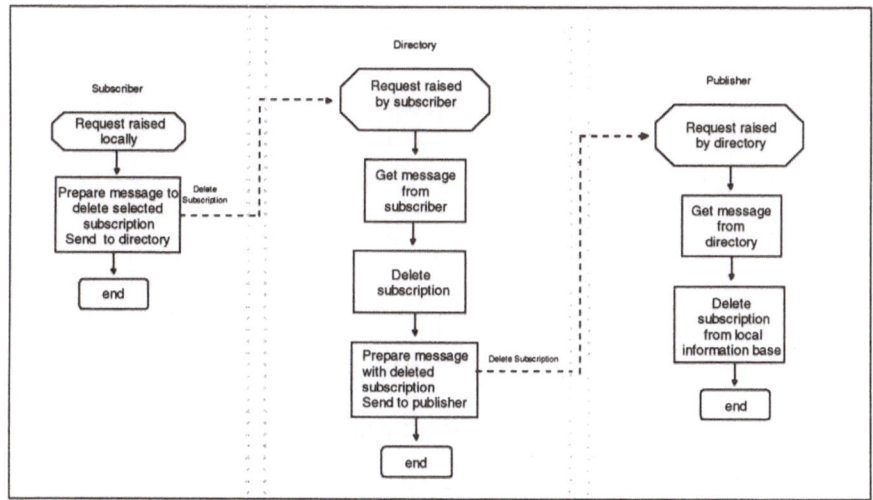

Figure 9.9: Delete subscription to a publication

Delete a Publication

A publisher domain cannot unilaterally decide to stop one of its publications. For the domain to be able to stop the publication, there cannot be any domains subscribed to it. When a publisher domain intends to stop publication, it prepares and sends a message to that effect to the Directory (Figure 9.10). The Directory checks whether there are any subscribers, and if it finds one or more subscribers to the item, the directory sends a message to each affected subscriber asking to free up the subscription to the publication. Depending on the subscribers' replies the Directory will proceed with the deletion of the publication, or it will advise the publisher of the impossibility of stopping the publication. According to the contract semantics discussed in Chapter 8, the deletion can proceed only if all subscribers agree to it.

Delete Domain

A domain participating in the Federation may decide to leave it at any time. The only prerequisite is to have previously stopped any publication and/or subscription in which it was involved. The domain proceeds with the protocol "Delete a Publication" for all its publications, and "Delete a Subscription" for all the items to which it has been subscribed. If the protocols execute successfully, the Directory proceeds with the deletion of the domain from the Federation by erasing it from its internal data structures (Figure 9.11).

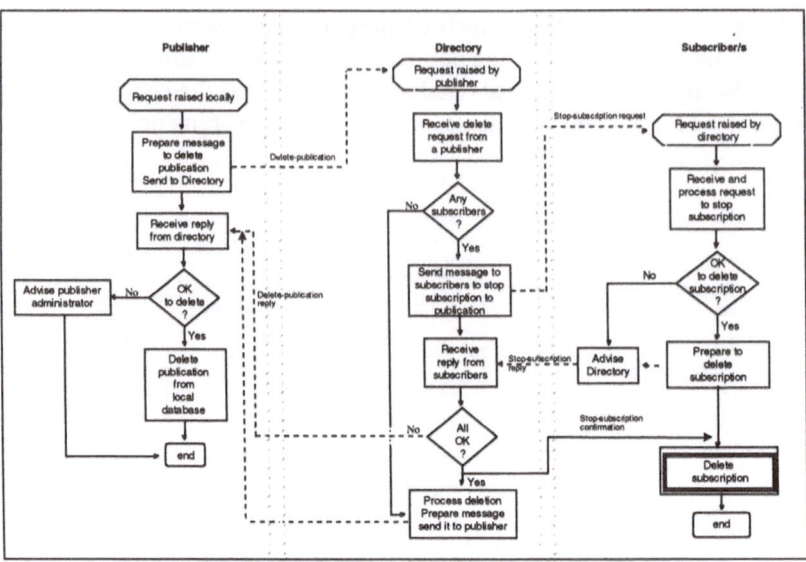

Figure 9.10: Delete a publication

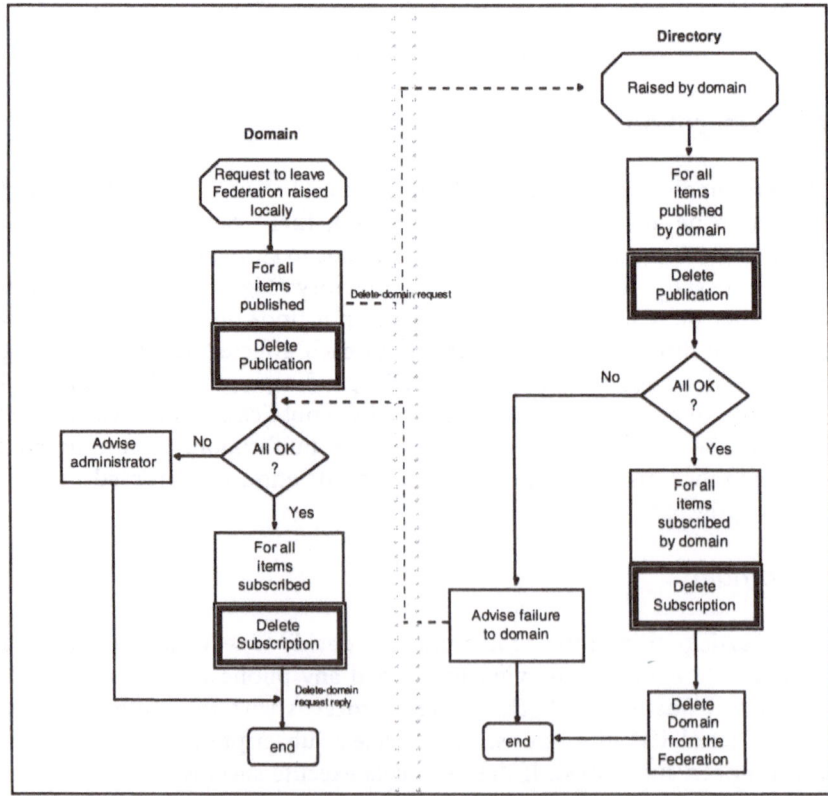

Figure 9.11: Delete domain

Modify a Publication

A publication can be modified by a request raised by a subscriber or by its publisher (Figure 9.12). From the protocol point of view, a modification is equivalent to a deletion of the existing publication, and a subsequent initiation of the new modified one.

- The subscriber raises the request by preparing and sending a message to the Directory, which checks for the existence of other subscribers affected by the proposed modification. If there are such subscribers, the Directory sends them a request asking for the acceptance of the change. If the request is accepted by all the domains involved, or if there are no such subscribers, the Directory prepares and sends a message to the publisher to proceed with the change.
- The publisher raises the requests by preparing and sending a request message to the Directory, which checks for subscribers and consults the affected ones on the acceptance of the modification. If the request is accepted by all the domains involved, the Directory prepares and sends a message to the publisher to proceed with the change.

In any case, if the modification is accepted, the current publication is deleted and the new modified one is introduced.

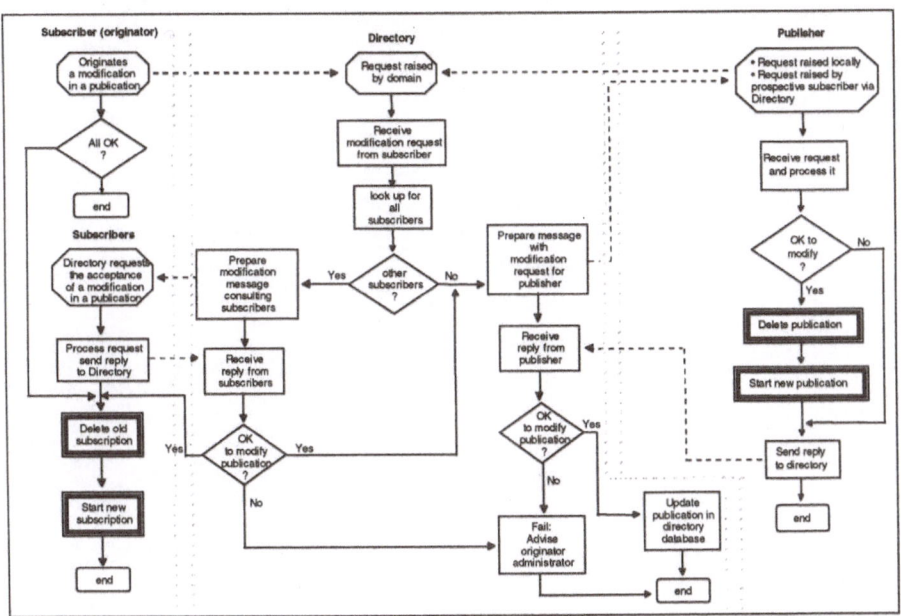

Figure 9.12: Modify a publication

10. Experiences in a Financial Institution

10.1 Motivation

Time: Early 1990s
Place: An Australian Financial Institution

"The Bank" is a major Australian-based financial institution. As more and more procedures have been automated in order to meet the increasing complexity and sophistication of its business, the Bank's information systems have grown to include a very large number of applications. The Bank's applications today are numerous and run on many different platforms, including MVS, OS/400, AIX, HP/UX, OS/2 and Guardian.

A large number of the current applications interact with one another to exchange data and services (Figure 10.1) – these interactions are necessary to meet the business requirements of the Bank. As a result, the inter-relationship of interoperating applications has become very complex, and the effort required to comprehend and implement these inter-relationships has become progressively greater. The nature of these interactions make the introduction of new applications, or changes to the functionality of existing applications, a very complex matter. Application interfacing, making changes in one application as a result of changes in another application or the introduction of a new application, is a significant burden for the Bank. The major contributors to these interfacing costs are:

- the need to map data between the formats required by the various applications;
- the balancing and control activities associated with ensuring that transactions are correctly posted to the various subsidiary ledgers and to the general ledger;
- the significant amount of development effort that goes into building and maintaining duplicate functions – functions in one application that are provided by, and probably logically belong to, another application. Most of the time duplication of functions is seen as a simpler solution than connecting the individual components of various applications.

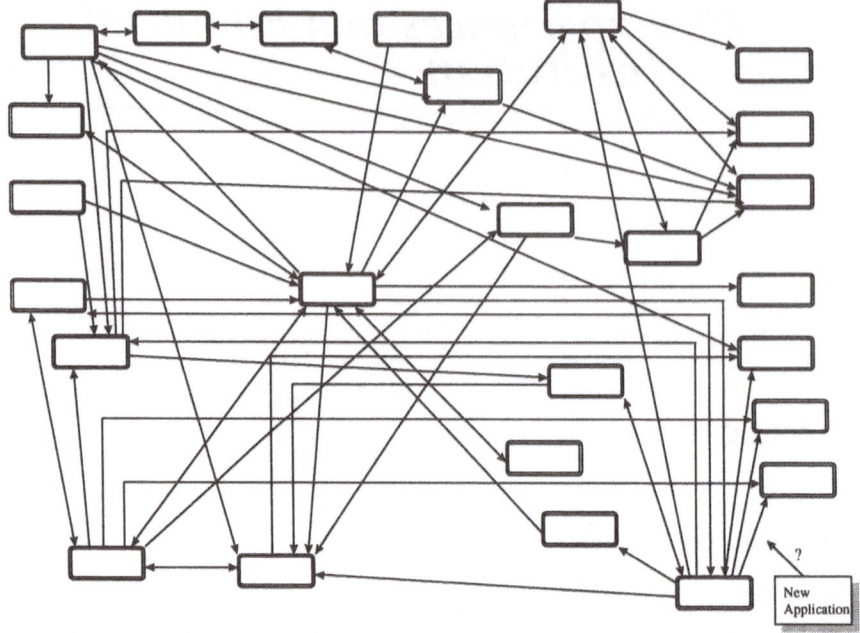

Figure 10.1: Major systems, their relationships and interfacing (names of individual applications have been withheld)

In short, there is knowledge of one application's processes and formats in other applications. For example, the duplication of validation functions, with one application carrying out validations on behalf of another after which the validation process is repeated at the second application; a format translation component that directly translates the format of application 1 to that which is required by application 2 embedded in application 1, all increase this knowledge, *hence the very tight coupling.*

An important aspect of this situation is the flow-on effect that requires modifications to several applications as a result of a single change. Of course, with these modifications there is a need for end-to-end testing. Therefore, a single change results in a "round of spending" through many applications.

The Bank estimates that as much as 15 per cent of the cost of IT development is taken up by these application interfacing costs. On some applications, the costs have been even higher. If the Bank continues with the present approach of directly linking new applications to existing ones, with time the situation will worsen, and the integration costs will rise still further. Because of these costs, it has been predicted that the replacement of a major application or the development of a system supporting new business opportunities may well become cost prohibitive. The effort required to integrate them with the other systems in the Bank, combined with the development costs, could outweigh the prospective benefits of the business opportunity.

In order to reduce the risk, cost and time to market for new systems, there is a clear need to reduce the complexity of systems integration. This need is all the more important because current business directions indicate that the interactions among systems will increase – the current method of directly linking new applications into the old applications, is not sustainable.

- The current thinking within the Bank is to promote shared use of common functions using the client/server style for interactions between systems in order to promote reuse and derive economic and time reduction benefits. This will also cause the interactions among systems to increase.
- There is a strategic decision to promote a higher exchange of information, in particular data, between applications.
- It is intended that new application packages be put in a position to be integrated with the overall infrastructure.

Therefore, there is a strong business need for an efficient, consistent, location independent and transportable interfacing architecture to reduce the complexity of systems integration. Implementing such a scheme will mean reduced risk and cost and reduced time to market for new/changed application systems.

Application Data Interchange (ADI)

Objectives
The Bank has defined the Application Data Interchange architecture as the means to reduce the complexity and associated cost of systems integration. The objectives of this architecture are to:

- Facilitate a seamless design of business solutions by using the most appropriate components from multiple application systems. The architecture must overcome the technical difficulties imposed by the variety of hardware platforms, legacy systems and application design standards.
- Simplify the integration of application systems. The architecture must provide an isolating layer of robust highly functional structures to act as interoperation middleware.
- Reduce the complexity of infrastructure design needed in individual applications by providing a consistent interface for the use of the ADI infrastructure. The architecture must isolate the common technical services, such as network security and inter-application controls, from the application systems.
- Improve the application system development process. The architecture must improve development process quality and reduce the time to market of the developed applications.
- Encourage consistency in application architectures. The architecture must provide the basis of a development framework that enables development of application systems in a consistently architected manner.

The ADI framework has been designed to encapsulate data and functions where they are most aptly housed, and to provide methods to access these services by other applications. At a high level, if application A requires a service that is already provided by application B, then ADI should avoid duplication by providing a path for A requesting that service. As a basic design philosophy, it is postulated that application A need not be aware of B's architecture or internal data structures.

To achieve these objectives, applications are isolated, hidden "behind" Intelligent Gateways (IGs). The purpose of the Intelligent Gateway is to provide generic services for data translation and end-to-end balancing of transaction movements. Both of these services are more alike than different for the integration of different applications into the Bank's system environment, so productivity benefits are expected to flow from the disciplined use of these gateways. Figure 10.2 illustrates this basic ADI principle.

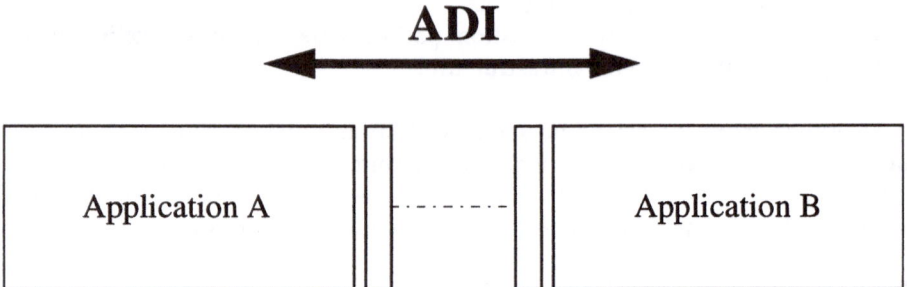

Figure 10.2: Application isolation behind gateways

10.2 The Approach to ADI

Following the discussion above, four key concepts underpinned the architecture of ADI. These concepts were:

1. Balancing and control;
2. Intelligent gateways and message formats;
3. Routers and domains;
4. Multiple platforms.

Balancing and Control

Transactions that are processed in the Bank's systems must satisfy stringent end-to-end balancing criteria. From their initial entry into the Bank, through all processing and handling until their final entry into the general ledger, the control and enforcement of these conditions must be undertaken by each application involved in the operation. This implies that when a new application is developed in house, or a new application is purchased, specific code must be inserted to handle end-to-end balancing, resulting in a major driver of higher integration costs. The location of these functions depends on the Bank's environment, and often their implementation must be duplicated to house them in each application. Duplication is wasteful, it makes software difficult to maintain, and the insertion of this code into purchased systems decreases the Bank's ability to upgrade to new versions of the applications.

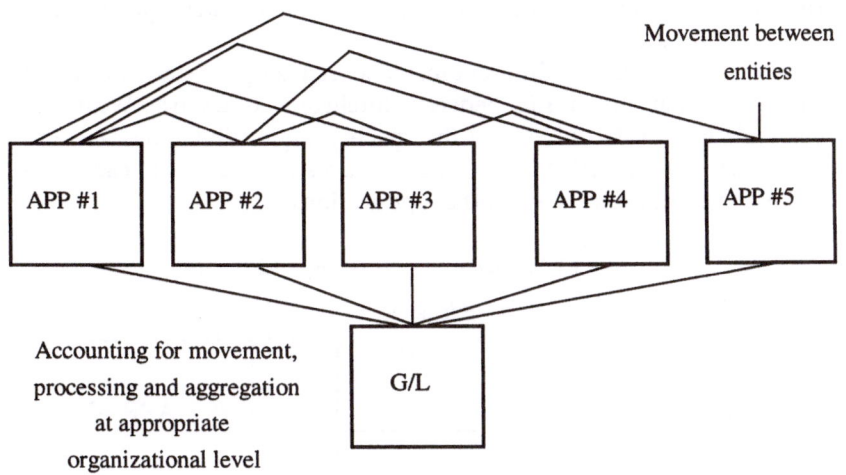

Figure 10.3: The old approach to systems balancing and control

With ADI, individual applications do not provide this capability; rather the Intelligent Gateways generate control account entries, with other, non-ADI, processes responsible for ensuring balance and correcting processing errors.

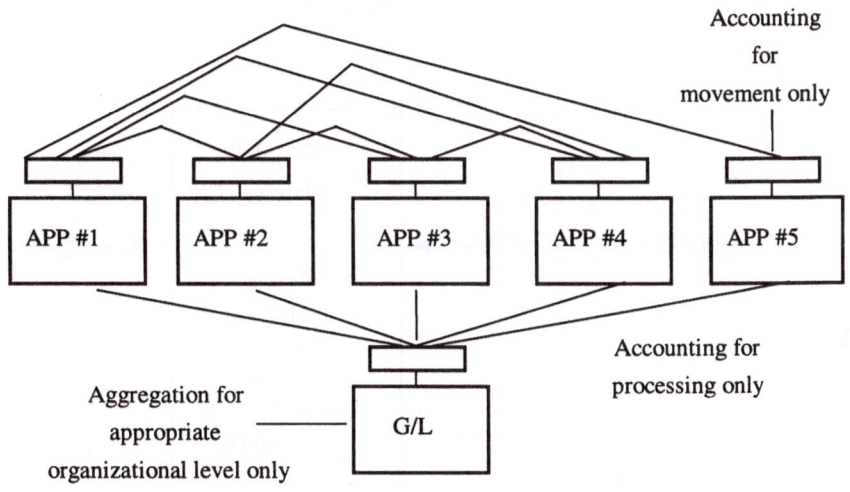

Figure 10.4: Simplification of systems balancing and control through layering

Intelligent Gateway and Message Formats

Each of the applications purchased or previously developed by the Bank has its own transaction and message formats. Amendment and extension of each application interfacing to other applications to handle different transaction and message formats increases the cost, complexity and interdependencies of the Bank's IT environment.

To tackle the problem of different formats, ADI adopts a standard message and transaction format for traffic between Intelligent Gateways. With ADI each application's IG translates between the specific application's message and trans-action format and the ADI standard. This reduces the changes to each application to enable it to communicate with other applications.

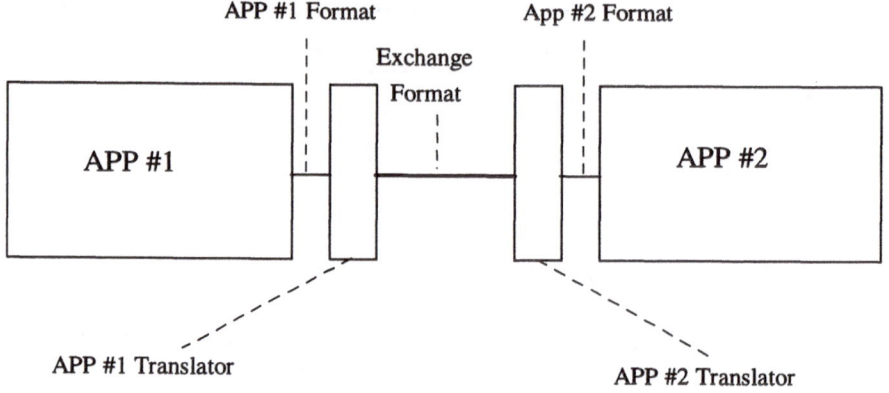

Figure 10.5: Message transformation

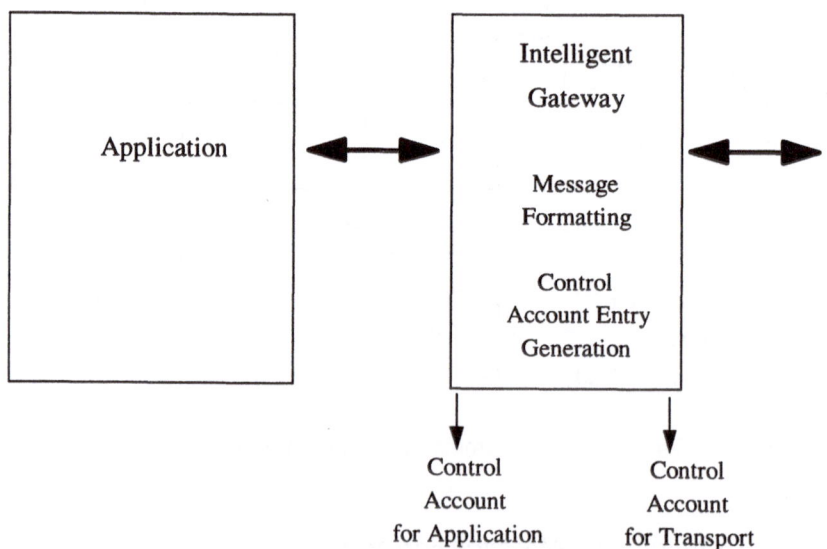

Figure 10.6: Key concept: intelligent gateways

Applications developed in-house after ADI is implemented would use ADI standard message formats. Therefore, for these applications, no transformation of incoming and outgoing messages is required.

Routers and Domains

Routers were conceived to move messages from one Intelligent Gateway to another, based on some straightforward directory functions. However, the notion that the messaging chaos prevailing in the Bank could be reduced to a single messaging "uni-speak" was regarded as "too much too soon". The solution was to adopt a hierarchical approach, which included a number of interacting domains at the top of the hierarchy. Each of these domains supports a consistent internal messaging structure, and it is connected only to other domains by inter-domain gateways. These gateways are the inter-domain version of the Intelligent Gateways within a domain.

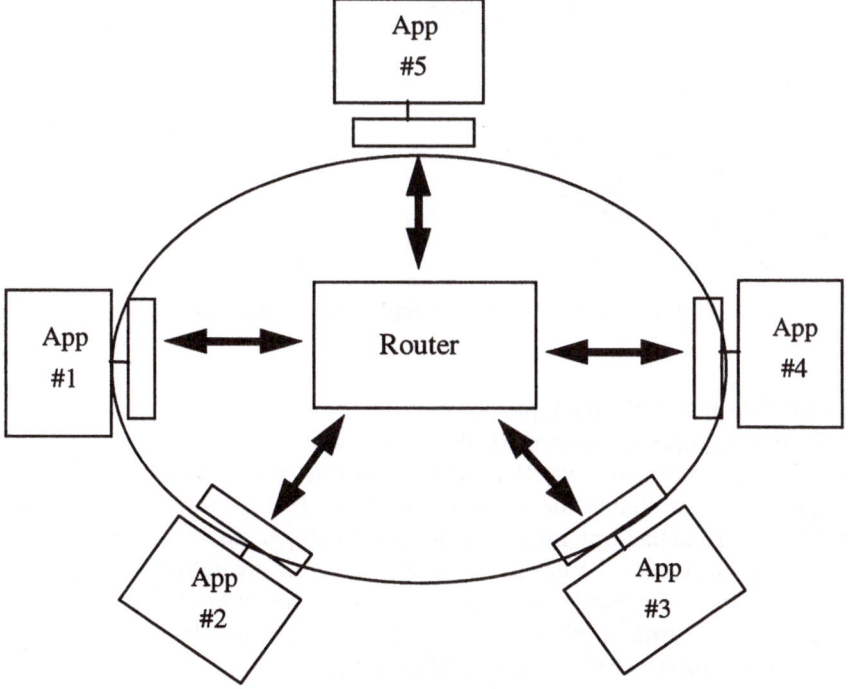

Figure 10.7: Key concept: router

Underpinning Design Principles and Requirements

In order to gain the benefits of ADI, it was necessary to introduce some clear design principles for all systems developers to follow. At a high level, these principles are:

- minimize change to existing applications;
- no application specific logic to be contained in ADI;
- based on Messaging and Queuing Model;
- based on a Client/Server Model;
- time out is the responsibility of each application;
- applications only handle their own errors.

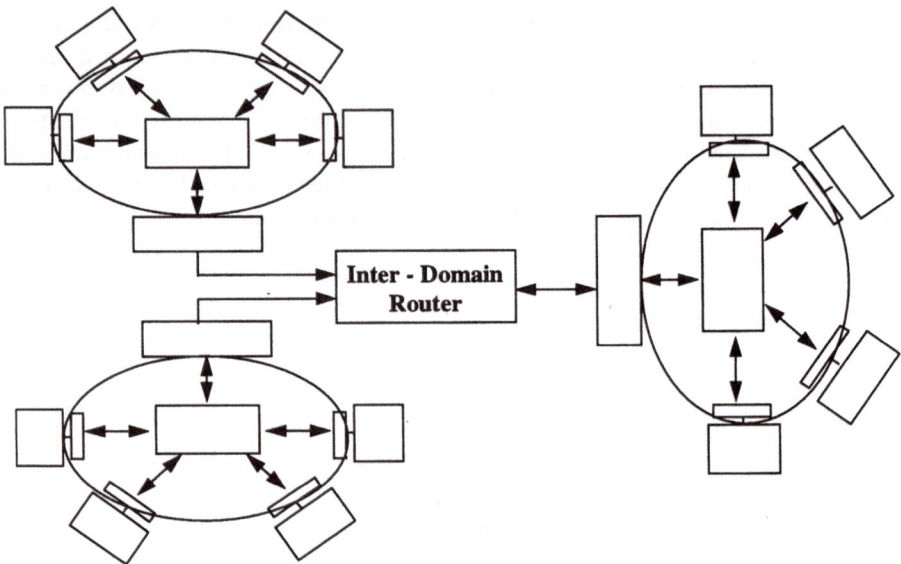

Figure 10.8: Key concept: multiple interacting domains

Minimize Change to Existing Applications
In order to minimize upgrade risks, difficulties and costs during the implementation of ADI, a central aim was to remove, or at least reduce as much as possible, the dependency on change between applications. In this way it is possible to ensure that ADI can be implemented with minimal impact to existing applications, so the migration path to the use of ADI can be more easily defined to require less effort and provoke the least disruption. The bulk of the effort will be required to consolidate an existing application's many interfaces and balancing and control requirements to interface to a single intelligent gateway.

No Application Specific Logic
The duplication of functions discussed above was conceived at the time as the simplest solution to the problem of readily providing the services required by the different applications. This resulted in the distribution amongst many applications, in a non-structured way, of logic related to other applications. This approach has undesirable consequences for maintenance, and is one of the main constraints hampering application enhancement. The strategy of ADI is to enforce the localization of a unit of processing logic within an individual application. This will contain changes to a single piece of processing logic to a single application

thereby reducing overall maintenance costs. By isolating an individual business function within a single application, it is also possible to "plug-in" a new application, or replace an existing one, with minimal disruption. Note that it is extremely important that ADI remain ignorant of application processing. If ADI is to communicate with many systems, it is very tempting, and may be perceived at times as highly expedient, to include application specific logic within ADI. This must be avoided if the goals of ADI are to be achieved.

The concept of housing and containing application logic where it should naturally belong also has consequences for the Intelligent Gateways. Application logic should not be housed at the IGs, but within the relevant applications. Examples of application logic that must not be built into an IG are:

- processing decisions based on the validity of application data;
- processing decisions based on timeliness of another applications response.

Based on Messaging and Queuing Model
Key to the implementation of the ADI and IG concepts is the role and function of the data transportation infrastructure, which must support synchronous and asynchronous communication between applications on a variety of platforms. IBM's MQSeries middleware provides support to handle these transport requirements. MQSeries can be deployed across a variety of platforms and make the total environment appear as a single-platform cluster.

Client/Server Model
ADI should implement a client/server model enabling bi-directional data flows. Both batch and on-line services are to be supported transparently to the client and the server.

Time Out
Handling of time out is the responsibility of each application. As part of ADI's isolation from application function, ADI does not monitor the performance of any transaction. If an application sends a message that must be processed within a certain time then the application must monitor this. If the message times out then the sending application must carry out the processing required to inform interested parties or to undo any relevant application processing.

Error Handling
An application does not handle errors created or propagated by other applications. A key objective of ADI is to isolate applications from each other's functions. This isolation includes all error processing. If an application handles errors on behalf of another application then the former application needs to know details and some processing requirements of the error generating application, and hence the two are not isolated from each other.

10.3   ADI Conceptual Design

Time: Mid 1990s
Place: The Same Australian Financial Institution

ADI Components

Intelligent Gateways and Data Transportation
ADI proposes the implementation of Intelligent Gateways (IGs) to insulate each application from the implementation details of others. Through the relevant IGs data is relayed from one application to the downstream applications.

Figure 10.8 illustrated the complete ADI environment. In the ADI scheme, a set of IGs served by a common data transport mechanism constitutes a domain. IGs residing in separate domains communicate to each other via inter-domain IGs, or, depending on the choice and complexity of the data transport mechanism, from one IG to another regardless of physical machine boundaries.

An application can interface in two different ways with its ADI IG:

1. Tight Coupling. Application changes are limited to satisfying interface requirements with the IG. Application-specific hooks are required within the IG to map application transaction formats and contents to ADI services. This approach is the most likely implementation option for existing applications.
2. Loose Coupling. By using ADI components or standards within the application, application specific exits are no longer required within the IG. This is the preferred approach for new applications.

Flow Through an Intelligent Gateway
The Intelligent Gateway is a multi-layered structure that processes input and output information step by step, one layer relaying to the next once its processing has finished. When a message is routed to an application, it is intercepted by the IG and processed as follows:

- Edit for Services Provided – the Intelligent Gateway determines if the application supports the services requested in the transaction (this check is not if the data is correct but if the domain standard request for services is actually supported by this application).
- Decompose Routing Information – the Intelligent Gateway removes the routing information associated with the transaction.
- Issue Systems Balancing and Control (SBAC) Entry - the Intelligent Gateway issues the SBAC entries to enable end-to-end balancing by the application.
- Format for Application – the transaction is reformatted from the Domain Format to that required internally by the application.

The flow of the output process is as follows:

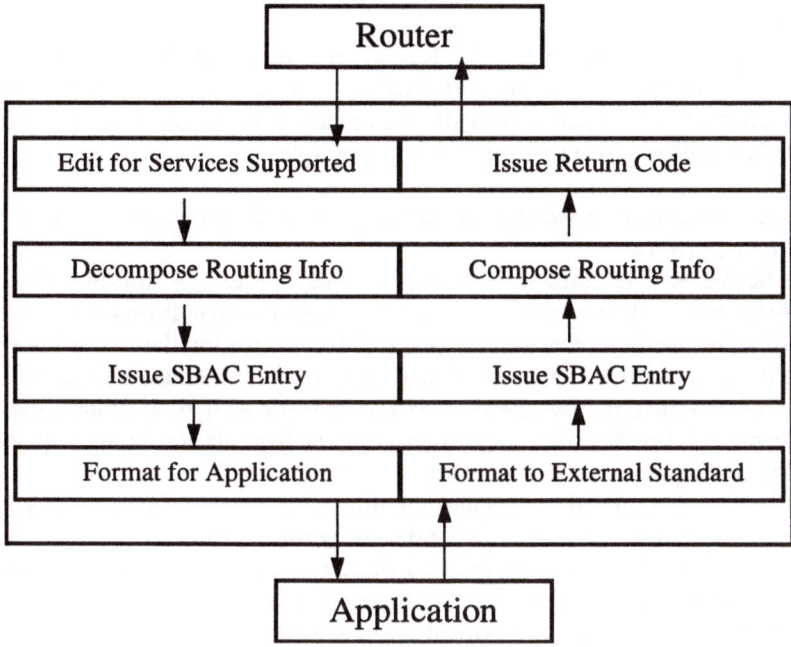

Figure 10.9: Intelligent Gateway functional overview

- Format to Domain Standard – the response (operation or transaction) from the application is reformatted from the application's internal format to comply with the Domain Format.
- Issue SBAC Entry – the Intelligent Gateway issues the Systems Balancing And Control entries to enable end-to-end balancing by the application.
- Compose Routing Information – the Intelligent Gateway determines and adds the routing information to be associated with the response. This information is the only information used by the router(s) to process transactions/responses.
- Issue Return Code – the Intelligent Gateway returns to the router the resultant success or failure of the operation/transaction that the router passed to it.

"Horizontal" movements as well as "vertical" are allowed at any "layer" within the Intelligent Gateway. For example, if an error is detected at any point in the message processing within the Intelligent Gateway no further processing is done to the message. Rather, the message is immediately rejected, passed across to the corresponding same-level layer, and an outgoing error message is prepared and output back to the sending application or router.

ADI Functions and Support Features

Several features and capabilities are required for ADI to be effectively developed and deployed. This section describes the conceptual design for those functions and support features.

Data Format Standards

The introduction of message/data format standards, at least between ADI Intelligent Gateways, was considered critical to the success of ADI. During the analysis phase, the decision was made to implement messages with self-defining formats. The following are perceived as key principles:

- The data format standard consists of two parts, an ADI header and an application data portion.
- The header will contain information to enable message interpretation and decomposition (hence the term self-defining message format). It remains possible for the data record definition and decomposition data to reside on the ADI directory. There is a trade-off between directory management and access, and communications overhead. It is possible for ADI to support both self-defining and directory defined formats, or even formats consisting of part self-defining and part directory defined.
- The header is standard across all domains, and contains the necessary information required to effect gateway and routing functions.
- Format standards within the data portion, and mechanisms to maintain and look-up documentation of existing formats were agreed upon and implemented. While these are not critical to the success of ADI, the introduction of standard formats would decrease the record translation effort within ADI, thereby decreasing opportunities for application logic errors, improving performance and enabling reuse of data already moving between applications. This makes possible the introduction of common formats and exchange information between applications without the need to build new non-ADI interfaces.
- Definition of formats on a dictionary to support software development discipline, and improve application integration and maintenance activities.
- The format standard should be consistent with the approach of Australian (AS2805) and International (ISO8583) standards. This allows suppliers to provide applications consistent with ADI data format standards.

Router/Data Transport Mechanism

The Router is an architectural component that physically manages the exchange of data between ADI Intelligent Gateways. It is designed to be a reliable transport layer, responsible not only for delivery but also for the integrity of data records. To this end, the Router is the primary manager of routing data records and error recovery. The decision was made to provide this data transport facility through MQSeries middleware; it contains *no* application logic or knowledge.

ADI Directory

The directory service is the hub of ADI. It records all valid requests and the routing information for the application servicing each request. The directory also contains:

- definitions of applications and intelligent gateways;
- what messages are processed by this intelligent gateway;

- routing information;
- balancing information;
- data format definition (including application or ADI format indicator);
- encryption and compression requirements;
- field definitions (picture, length).

The ADI directory is perceived as a component of enterprise dictionary information describing applications, services and messages. This function includes facilities to maintain and use the directory. These facilities include:

- directory maintenance;
- directory look-up;
- directory listing (selective and full-dump capabilities).

System Utilities
A set of utilities is required for use by applications and intelligent gateways. These sub-functions are:

- encryption services (including key management and storage);
- compression services;
- collect diagnostics/statistics;
- log utility.

Recovery
This function provides for the regular recording of system status, and the subsequent ability to recover the system in the event of a gateway or system failure. This recovery should be managed in such a way that data in progress through the gateway network can be recovered, and the required processing restarted without loss of system integrity.

10.4   ADI Architecture: Summary and Discussion

Summary

The ADI architecture (Figures 10.10 and 10.11) provides a robust and highly functional middleware using messaging and queuing principles. Although the message is the basic unit of communication between application system components, ADI is more than just a manager of messages. ADI consists of the following:

- It is a formally stated design architecture consisting of message routers and application gateways. The message router manages the receipt, transmission and logging of messages within the ADI environment. The application gateways provide the application interface to ADI.
- There are design rules and conventions with respect to the ADI. These rules and conventions address availability, application system processing cycles,

commitment to message delivery, security, system balancing and controls, data independence, and development and testing support.

- ADI operational software will perform key processes, such as gateway processing, directory management, data translation, availability management, security processing.

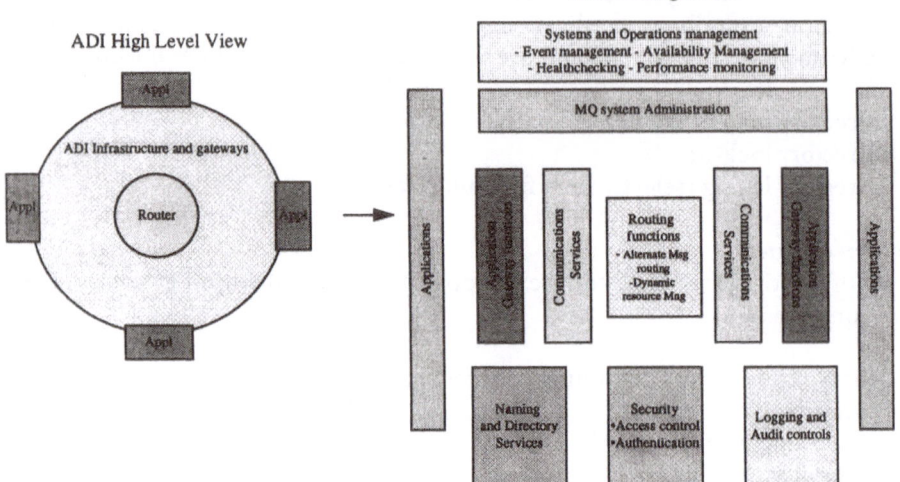

Figure 10.10: ADI components

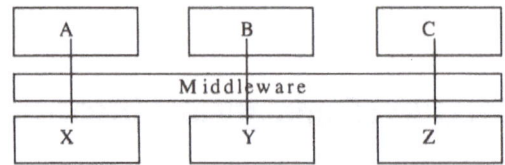

Figure 10.11: Schematic ADI architecture

The high level requirements of ADI are summarized below.

- The ADI architecture provides the technical means by which one application can request the service of another application, even in an on-line environment. To do so, the client application develop an ADI interface to request the service of another application. If the service is not already established through ADI the server application will also need to develop an ADI interface. Client applications are unaware of the location of the server application.
- The ADI must be available 24 hours per day and seven days per week. Applications using the ADI can set their own availability requirements. To support strict response time applications, the availability of the target

application must be visible to the source application through the ADI infra-structure availability service routine.

- The ADI has no regular processing cycles.
- The ADI handles two classes of messages: those that must be delivered and those that can be discarded in the event of system failure. Application designers must be aware of the impact of the failure on the messages originating from their application, and cater for this eventuality
- Applications using the ADI must individually arrange their balancing between themselves and the ADI.
- There is no requirement for the data items used in more than one application using the ADI to be consistent.
- Gateway processing: A gateway is the interface between the ADI and the application system logic. The gateway provides the means by which an application passes a message to ADI for routing and the means by which an application receives a message. Gateways will execute on many different environments: MVS (CICS, IMS and Batch), AS/400, OS/2 and UNIX (AIX, HP/UX etc.), and NT.
- Dictionary: It plays a vital role in the operation of the ADI. It contains the definition of all application system processes and their messages.
- Directory Management: ADI manages the interaction between components of a large number of application systems using a directory. The directory will record all applications using the ADI, the messages passing between them, and the data carried by each message. The directory will be built from a dictionary external to the ADI.
- Data Translation: The gateway of the client application translates data into a global format when the message is received for transmission. The gateway of the server application translates data from the global format into the format required by the target application when the message is delivered.
- Security: The ADI gateways for each application must perform security validation upon receiving a message. This validation will not reference the logon identifiers of any users of the source application.
- ADI provides facilities for health check processing, for example, checking if a queue is empty.

ADI Benefits

The benefits to the Bank are directly related to the objectives of the architecture:

- Reduced risk, cost and time to market of new /changed application systems.
- Reduced duplication of functions and better utilization of existing system components.
- Simplified introduction of new system components.
- Reduced complexity of end to end systems testing.
- Reduced complexity of the overall application systems configuration of the Bank by having a considerably more homogenous set of applications over time.

Discussion

Implementing ADI proved to be far more difficult than conceptualizing ADI for the following reasons:

- Infrastructure of this nature, which needs to be pervasive in order to be effective, may only be introduced in conjunction with major functionality changes and, on such occasions, the organization focuses on the new functionality to the exclusion of the infrastructure.
- Message-oriented middleware has matured considerably over the period and many candidate components have come on the market resulting in purchasing confusion.
- Since ADI does not address the problem of data integration, as might be done with a data warehouse, it failed to gain the organizational commitment necessary for its prompt and overt implementation.
- Expecting individual initiatives to bear the entire cost of introducing a pervasive infrastructure is a psychologically flawed approach because the individual initiatives will each reject the cost burden in turn.

10.5 Commentary

In this chapter, we have used terminology used at the Bank and in the ADI project, to describe the ADI concepts. It is clear though that the main issue before the Bank is tight coupling between applications, and its consequences. Coupling in terms of one application maintaining knowledge about the internals of another, specifically related to data formats and processing (especially the processing for balancing and control). The consequences of tight coupling are well known (and discussed elsewhere in this book), and the Bank's experience documented at the beginning of this Chapter accords with what we can expect.

The ADI solution quarantines application knowledge within applications, and imposes a defined interface between the application and the ADI gateway, in effect the application's window to the outside world. In its aims, concept, and form, the ADI structure – of domains interacting with other domains via an inter-domain router (Figure 10.8) – is very similar to the Federation presented in Chapter 8.

There was recognition in the Bank that the integration of applications into the Bank's environment was not likely to be achieved by forcing all elements to work in the same way through rigid compliance with an overall model based on data and process. Rather, the way forward was by the imposition of some simple interoperability, delivery, and compartmentalization rules or standards. This is very much the philosophy behind the Federated architecture, where domains are partitioned (or constructed) such that one domain need not know about the internals of another; all that is required is for a domain to adhere to its set standard for interacting with the Federal Highway (through the Gatekeeper). Figure 10.12 maps the ADI concepts to the equivalent Federation ones.

Indeed, the only significant divergence between the two is that in the Federation, it is advocated that domain boundaries be restricted to information dependencies. In ADI though, both informational and processing dependencies are admitted. Although it is recognized that purely messaging interactions reduce coupling (and increase isolation) to the greatest extent, because of the existing distribution of functions among applications the bank (and the desire to reuse these functions) some processing or client/server type interactions between domains was found to be a necessity.

Federation Concept	ADI Concept
Domain	Domain
Gatekeeper	Intelligent Gateway
Federal Highway	Router
Directory	ADI directory

Figure 10.12: Federation and ADI – mapping of concepts

11. *Pulling it all Together*

11.1 Application Software and the Enterprise

We commenced Part 4 following a discussion of coupling extended to distributed systems. As we progressed, we gradually moved into the realm of applications in general, and the use of distributed computing middleware technologies to improve the interaction between them.

Computer-based applications in an enterprise have grown to their current form typically over many years. It is very unlikely that these applications followed a single blueprint of enterprise-wide scope; neither would they have been constructed in a totally standalone fashion. Rather, they would have grown as tactical responses to successive organizational problems, requirements or business opportunities. They would have grown by adding on to or changing existing systems, building new applications that nevertheless had to interoperate with other systems in some fashion to preserve overall business integrity. The divisional structure and loci of management power within the enterprise is also a significant determinant of the manner in which applications have evolved in an enterprise: relatively autonomous business units can make their own development decisions, often resulting in applications where functionality is duplicated (or replicated). Alternatively, decisions have been taken that have resulted in incompatible infrastructure and platforms being purchased and used by these business units. These circumstances have created a number of problems that enterprises with large and mature IT infrastructures and application systems typically experience. These issues were illustrated in the Bank example and the hypothetical example of Chapter 7. To recap and summarize:

1. Custom interfaces. Applications that communicate with other applications via persistent structures, typically files: application A writes to a file, asynchronously application B reads from it. This leads to customized interfaces – the file that A and B use is purpose-built for the communication between A and B. Hence, this type of communication between an application P and each of the other applications potentially requires a purpose-built file interface.
2. Data and data representation. Incompatibilities arise in several ways.
   - The individual platforms where A and B are run have different low-level representations for data.

- There are application-level incompatibilities and problem spots with formatting. Some typical examples are:
  - The field length for the same data item differs from application A to application B.
  - Where compound keys are used, application A represents the key information in a different order from application B.
  - Especially in banking and financial systems, application A may encrypt a certain information item, while application B may not.
  - Application A uses the same field in a file for different purposes (typically based on the value of some other parameter or condition)
  - The file that links application A and B contain not only data, but also control information: for example, a flag whose value determines the type of processing B undertakes under certain circumstances.

3. Functions, their location and distribution: an application contains functions that are either duplicated or better implemented elsewhere or in another fashion. Typical examples are:

   - Application A has validation functions that are also duplicated in application B and application C.
   - Application A creates transactions that are also created by application C. For example, A, an order entry application, creates invoices. The invoicing system also creates invoices. Thus a substantial proportion of validation, processing, and database access logic is duplicated.
   - Application A has a function that executes a number of other functions that, in the light of the requirements of the business process, do not have processing dependencies with that function. For example, (as described in Chapter 7), the order entry component executing invoice, stock allocation, stock reorder and accounting functions, as part of the order entry activity.

As we observed in Chapters 7 and 10, these conditions have created linkages – or in our parlance levels of coupling – between applications, coupling levels that are incompatible with the requirements. These result in a massive integration burden for the enterprise. Especially in the Bank example we observed the effect of the burden of integration on large, mature IT environments. To reinforce this point, the let us walk through some scenarios again.

1. A new application F becomes an additional data entry point for stock items. Inventory items are also found in applications G, H and J, each of which has its own format for product code. With custom interfaces, F needs to write to a customized file each for applications G, H and J. Each of G, H and J need to be enhanced to read from this file. Furthermore, format conversions need to be written for each of G, H and J for converting the product code from F's format to that required for each of G, H and J. Hence the development activity is of course developing F; the associated integration activities include creating functionality in G, H and J for reading the relevant file and format conversion. In addition, we need to test the enhancements to applications G, H and J, and regression test G, H and J to ensure that their new functions have not disturbed their existing capabilities.

2. New "created by" and "on behalf of" fields need to be associated with every order (allowing one customer, under appropriate circumstances, to create an order on behalf of another) and the order validation logic changes. Both the new fields will contain (after validation) existing customer IDs.

Program A, which creates orders, need to be changed. So does program B which also creates orders under some circumstances. Program A interacts with programs K, L and M each with a custom file structure, mainly containing the order information. K, L and M each have to be modified to accommodate the new fields. L and M have different formats for customer; therefore, the format translation logic needs to be built into L and M. Orders are validated again in program M, which needs its validation logic to change…And so it goes on.

We notice the effects of change, enhancement and testing effort rippling through to many related applications. This results in the "rounds of spending" associated with each enhancement that we observed in the Bank example. There are many sources of coupling here:

- coupling associated with custom file interfaces, which grow geometrically with application numbers;
- coupling associated with early binding that knowledge of formats of one application in another engenders;
- coupling associated with early binding that replicated code engenders;
- coupling associated with unnecessary processing dependencies.

We have put forward an approach, based upon coupling and dependency, to analyse and address these problems. Taking a further step, we have applied these principles to advocate several remedies:

- Under appropriate business circumstances, loosening transactional dependencies typically to simple processing plus informational dependencies.
- Under appropriate business circumstances, loosening simple processing dependencies informational dependencies.
- Managing informational dependencies as follows: Converting custom file interfaces to standardized MOM interfaces. To have a single interface to a MOM to be used by several consumers, rather than one file interface per consumer. To agree on standard (directory-based or self-defining) formats for MOM-based traffic, and to insulate the outside world from your own formats.
- Where processing dependencies exist (as discussed in the three-tier architecture), making maximum use of reuse potential. In other words, minimizing early binding caused by function replication by having the relevant function in a single place, to be used by sharing at runtime.
- Using the concepts of processing and administrative independence to further quarantine the scope of effect of applications or groups of applications, so that a large unwieldy whole can be partitioned into smaller, more manageable components.

How do we put these remedies together in a fashion that is useful, as well as feasible to implement? Any scheme for rationalization faces several obstacles.

- The complexity of the problem. The linkages or the coupling between systems is typically very close. This is compounded by the fact that close coupling is often found among applications supporting the main business processes of the enterprise.
- The ownership of the cost. As we observed in the Bank example, this type of integration cost usually finds no ready sponsor in the enterprise. It is an internal plumbing issue, and much more difficult to sell to the business units that say a business system enhancement.
- Politics. The structure and relationships between systems can reflect some of the politics and power in the enterprise, and loss of control issues brought about by a rationalization may engender resistance. Furthermore, often those championing this type of change, an internal consulting function such as an architecture or planning group, have no direct authority to effect the changes.

Many attempts at rationalization have failed because the demands for conformity have been too stringent. For example, some enterprise-wide studies have produced deliverables of the ilk of data models, information models, and process models. Where some desired goal has been chartered in this manner, conformance has usually been loose at best, since the extent of change and compliance required of the existing systems have been impracticably high. What we require is not a straitjacket into which all programs and data need to be squeezed, a very rigidly defined framework with which every system should conform. *On the contrary, we want some mechanism that preserves (or even enhances) the autonomy of individual systems, and defines some consistent rules for their interaction.*

Taking a still further step, we have offered an architectural framework, the Federation, that aims to satisfy this objective. The domains are relatively autonomous, enjoying *processing and administrative isolation*, which enhances their autonomy. They process their own information, and have the freedom (the extent to which they exercise this freedom being an organizational matter to be negotiated) to grow, evolve, make decisions about their internal platforms, organization and management, *so long as certain commitments to the rest of the Federation are met.* These commitments are about messages: their content, formats, frequency; and also agreements about the behaviour under abnormal circumstances.

In keeping with the properties of an architectural style, a Federation conforms to a set of design principles. In building a Federation, you would construct superstructure components, which provide the backbone for the application-level components of the Federation. The Federal directory service is a good example of a superstructure component (an implementation of one is discussed in Chapter 9); the Gatekeeper is another. There would be a single such directory per Federation, but there would be a Gatekeeper for each domain. However, since each Gatekeeper will have very similar function, at the very least we should be able to work off a single initial specification, and compatibility issues permitting, we should be able to achieve a good deal of reuse.

We believe that the Federation has the best potential of clearing the hurdles we outlined above: it has the potential to match software interactions with business dependencies and to satisfy political considerations; it offers the least degree of intervention (compared to other solutions) thus providing a cost effective solution; and it allows the possibility of gradual or phased implementation thus providing the flexibility to adjust to the schedule and budgeting needs of the particular instance. So we present the Federation as an architectural style suitable for managing the applications that support the enterprise, or a group of cooperating enterprises.

11.2 Organizational Requirements

We introduced a theme at the outset, in Chapter 2. Essentially, we maintained that one set of criteria for "good" applications stem from the enterprise: the application forms or architectures we consider should be capable of satisfying certain generic requirements posed by current organizational realities. We have touched upon this theme subsequently. Let us now consider this issue in some detail.

Changeability

One of the main benefits of loosening the coupling between applications and application components is that you then make the systems easier to maintain. This alone makes the approaches better able to withstand, and respond to, pressures for change.

Specifically in three-tier applications certain types of changes, those whose effect is confined to the UI, can be tackled particularly easily. Changes affecting the internals of CS and DAS components too can be easily handled. The difficulty is in handling changes to the service interfaces, since their change can have an effect upon the components that use them. However, mechanisms such as method overloading can be used to contain these effects.

The ability to weather change, to make the cost of maintenance lower, is a driving force behind the Federated architecture as well. With the Federation, we possess the means of dividing and conquering a large, unwieldy environment. We confine closer coupling to domains, based on the business need for such coupling, and have a looser, freer interaction between the domains. Some may argue that this structure is vulnerable to changes in the way business is done: should there be a radical change in the business processes, then the shape of the Federation may be affected significantly. However, regardless of existing structure, such a change will require a great deal of change from the enterprise applications, and because of its modularity, the Federation will be in a position to respond better to this challenge than most other structures.

Formal and Informal Communication

Although we have not considered this aspect explicitly, the distributed computing technologies contain many capabilities to address communication within the enterprise milieu – for example, mail and groupware products. In addition, the architectural forms we presented are capable of accommodating various forms of communication: for example, Email (both the capabilities to send and receive Email) may be incorporated in a client application software module – indeed, mailing could well be an integral part of the user's task.

Variation from a Standard

The standardization inherent in centralized systems need not plague applications designed with distributed computing technologies. The three-tier architecture contains the capacity for software with a good deal of localisation. At the enterprise level, the Federation can provide domains with a great deal of local autonomy. They are free to manage their local operations and evolve to a considerable degree, without having an effect on the Federation.

Visibility and Interoperability

Let us revisit what we said about this requirement:

> "The extent to which the organizational form (the structure and relationships between organizational units) is significant in the organization. These arrangements often have considerable undertones of politics and power, and therefore, systems and applications that do not respect these demarcations often face strong opposition. These considerations have a great deal of impact on decisions on information system and application boundaries, visibility of data and processes out side of particular organizational domains, extent of cooperation between applications serving different domains."

This area is fundamental to the issues we explored in the second half of this book.

The communication capabilities of different types of distributed computing middleware illustrate that we can have different types of interactions between application software modules. Equally, there are different dependencies between the activities of a business process or between different business processes. We reasoned that the optimum benefit for the enterprise is achieved if we provide an appropriate mapping between the dependencies among the business elements and the interactions among software modules. As we saw with the Federation, this type of design is well placed to reflect the form and structure of the business. The isolation that a domain is capable of, the negotiation elements associated with the formation of the Federation, the well-defined nature of communication between domains, the absence of claims of one domain on the resources of another, all point to the potential of the Federation to respond to these issues. Indeed, the authors know of no other structural form that comes remotely close to the Federation in the potential to heed these needs.

11.3 Conclusion

Our focus in this book has been about "good" applications – specifically, about architecting and designing "good" applications with distributed computing technologies. At the outset we recognized that historically, principles of good design has lagged behind the introduction of technology, and that this trend persists with the technology of the "modern" IT era. In the quest for "good" design, the main themes we presented revolve around the following:

- The three-tier client/server application form is a suitable architecture for a single application or a related group of applications. Although the three-tier concept has received a good deal of publicity, the details of the architecture, at least in the public domain, have been sketchy. We presented a set of principles for use in designing client/server applications.
- Different types of distributed computing middleware enable different types of interactions between application components. These have different implications for application development/maintenance effort and cost. By extending the notion of coupling to the distributed environment, we have formulated a basis to analyze these implications. These principles can be used in the realm of the distributed client/server application, in designing or reviewing the designs of applications, or in assessing the potential effects of using different middleware in feasibility/preliminary design. They can also be applied when using middleware to better manage maintainability and interoperability in complex application environments.
- The consideration of different interaction models results in different structural and behavioural forms for applications. These architectural forms – generic structures for applications – serve as solution frameworks that address certain generic needs and reflect certain structural, behavioural, and communication patterns in the enterprise. These solution frameworks can be used to base individual designs.
- Using the capabilities of distributed computing technology to develop "good" software (a) in the sense of satisfying traditional software engineering criteria such as maintainability, robustness, performance, scalability, security, and cost, and (b) in the sense of supporting a more sophisticated model of the enterprise containing features such as the division and allocation of work, the different business interactions that exist in the enterprise, power and politics, and so on.

We have presented this material as a collection of related concepts, principles, techniques and experiences. We have avoided packaging of these components into a "methodology". We have developed certain styles or forms of houses you can build, and some techniques you employ in their design and construction. We have not presented a cookbook (to mix metaphors) of step-by-step instruction. Feel free, you the reader, to take on board all or some of what we have advocated here. Good luck!

Appendix 1

A Survey of Products

We provide here a brief survey of products, based on the classification provided in Chapter 2 in the topic "Technology Architecture". We focus on middleware, and "go out" into development environments where applicable. Then we look at systems management. Components of the technology architecture that are not specific to the distributed application are mentioned in passing.

Middleware

SQL-based Middleware

Standards
Provides the transport for SQL calls and calls to stored procedures from the client. There are two basic approaches:

- Embedded SQL (ESQL). ISO standard for embedding SQL in programming languages. Needs a precompiler; needs to know the target database at development time.
- Call-level interfaces: API (Application Programming Interface). Calling program executes SQL at run time; no precompiler needed.
  De jure standard: SQL Access Group (SAG) CLI.
  De facto standard:
  - Microsoft ODBC (Open Database Connectivity): SAG CLI with extensions;
  - JDBC (Java Database Connectivity) is an emerging contender.

Product Examples
Call-level interfaces: ODBC, JDBC
- ODBC: a Microsoft product, it enables access to different databases. Provides a call-level interface to the application (client). Supports a number of the popular databases (provides standard SQL plus specific extensions). However, support for some advanced features such as event triggering, coordination between different databases and switching between different access methods is questionable.

- JDBC: a set of Java classes that allows the connection of Java code to relational databases. It includes support to connect to databases, and provides SQL operations on the data and metadata. There are four types of JDBC drivers:
  - Type 1: JDBC-ODBC bridge, translates JDBC to ODBC calls
  - Type 2: Java to native API, converts JDBC calls into client API calls for a given database
  - Type 3: net protocol – all Java driver:
  - Type 4: native protocol – all Java driver

Gateways: EDA/SQL, Open Client + Omni SQL Gateway
- EDA/SQL: A product from Information Builders; provides an integrated data model comprising of different physical databases, in addition to ODBC type capabilities. Part of a suite of products that also offer transaction and messaging services.
- Open Client + Omni SQL Gateway: from Sybase; similar to EDA/SQL; it offers vendor and location transparency. Translates Transact SQL to the relevant SQL dialect.

Other: DRDA
- DRDA: an IBM product; designed for data transfers between different "heavy duty" databases at the back end. Complementary to others.

Pros and Cons of SQL-based Middleware

- Essentially SQL, so it ties calling programs to the particular SQL dialect.
- It presents a two-tier image, since the calls are built and passed on to the server. With procedural SQL, however, it is possible to include some application capabilities at the server side.

Product Sets Using SQL-based Middleware

Oracle Cooperative Development Environment 2

Product	Arch Comp	Comments
Oracle CASE	Application development	Upper CASE (data and process modelling) plus code generation (Forms, Reports, SQL)
Oracle Forms	Application development	Main application development tool; both client and server. Blocks of code "triggered" by events and forms events
PL/SQL	Application development	Procedural Language (Ada-like); it packages SQL statements. Execution of a statement block: the stored procedure (at server) may be called, packaged and submitted across the network, or executed locally at the client sending a DB call over the wire.
SQL*Net V2	Integration service	Supports TCP/IP, DECNet, LU6.2, SPX/IPX, etc. Mechanism that supports communication between client and server application components.

Oracle Transparent Gateways	Integration service	Access to other databases
Oracle Call-level Interfaces and precompilers	Integration Service	Allows access to 3GLs, DCE tools, etc.
Objects for OLE	Integration service	New interfacing technology, supporting multithreading and access of multiple databases. Supports OLE, Active X
Oracle 7 Oracle 8	Information management	See databases

Sybase System 10

Product	Arch Comp	Comments
Client development	Application development	No specific product. Through Open Client API, enables access to a variety of client development tools
Transact-SQL	Application development	Sybase's language for DB access and stored procedures (e.g. of Oracle's PL/SQL)
Open client	Integration service	Provides an API for a number of client development tools/environments
Omni SQL Gateway + Open server	Integration service	Gateways to a variety of relational DBs; converts Transact SQL to SQL of target DB. Through Open server, provides access to non-relational M/F sources (CICS/IMS applications)
Connection Manager	Systems management	Management of the administration and security of the DB gateways
SQL Server 10	Information management	See databases

Informix New Era

Product	Arch Comp	Comments
Window Painter, New Era language, Application Builder	Application development	Offers an object-oriented component-based application development environment. It uses a database application OO language. Web enabled, it supports OLE, Active X and Java code generation
Informix-Net	Integration service	Similar to SQL* Net; connects to Informix database Connections to other DBs possible through ODBC or EDA/SQL
Informix Dynamic On-Line Server	Information management	See databases

RPC-Type Middleware

Standards

DCE (Distributed Computing Environment): Developed by OSF, a consortium of vendors, it has been implemented on a major vendor environment – HP, DEC, IBM, etc. DCE is a standard, as well as a product.

Product Examples
DCE consists of a set of services, some or all of which can be used:

- communication service: RPC;
- naming service;
- directory service;
- security service;
- time service;
- distributed file service.

DCE is open, standards-based, robust, suitable for complex, mission-critical applications. However, it has not had the anticipated take-up, arguably because its API contains approximately 600 calls and is difficult to learn and use. Native DCE does not support transactions. If transaction processing is needed, it is necessary to use a distributed transaction processing monitor, e.g. Encina, on top of DCE. Increasingly, other distributed computing products are using DCE services in their infrastructure, e.g., IBM's OLTP (On Line Transaction Processing) system CICS/6000 and DFS Web (DCE-based WWW security).

DTP Monitors

Like other middleware, DTP monitors provide the "glue" for communication between clients and servers in a distributed environment; in addition, they provide transactional integrity, server optimization and balancing. Therefore, they are useful for heavy operational processing systems that need to operate in a distributed fashion.

Standards
X/Open's XT (between application and transaction monitor) and distributed transaction coordination XA (between transaction monitor and database)

Product Examples
- AT & T's Top End: AT & T (NCR) transaction processing for UNIX environments;
- IBM CICS/6000: DTP in all IBM, plus HP-UX and Digital Unix environments;
- Tuxedo: Developed by AT&T, now marketed by BEA. In addition to Tuxedo, BEA provides a suite of different types of middleware products;
- Encina: DTP environment; flexible and feature rich. It is also complex; runs on top of DCE;
- ACMSxp: from Digital. An evolution from ACMS TP, it runs on top of DCE. It provides COBOL and C development platforms.

DTP Monitors: Pros and Cons
- Except perhaps for Encina, they offer an easier alternative to DCE for communication between distributed clients and servers.
- Ensure transactional integrity, and offer access, location, and concurrency transparency.

- Support transactions in heterogeneous databases and two-phase commit protocol.
- Offer program-to-program services, such as access and location, data representation, RPC, client/server connections.
- Require APIs to client and server environments. Therefore, they usually work with a limited number platforms and products.
- Good choice for heavy Transaction Processing environments and where transaction integrity and recovery are paramount.

Object Brokers

Standards
- OMG (Object Management Group) CORBA: CORBA (Common Object Request Broker Architecture) is a standards specification by OMG, that specifies how distributed objects can work together. Unlike OSF's DCE, OMG did not develop technology, but left the implementation to vendors adhering to the standard.
- CORBA 1.1 (1991): IDL and APIs for client and server objects within a specific ORB (Object Request Broker) implementation. Also, provision of static and dynamic invocation of remote methods.
- CORBA 2.0 (1995): The CORBA 2.0 specification includes a mandatory protocol, Internet Inter-ORB Protocol (IIOP), which is designed to enable objects and applications to interoperate over a network with other OMG CORBA 2.0 applications. It also includes support for languages other than C, asynchronous messaging, transactions, and interfaces to products such as Tuxedo, Encina, etc.

Product Examples
- Forte: Forte is an object-oriented development environment that automates the deployment of an application into a specific distributed environment. In the process, Forte partitions the application into desktop components and a set of server components, each of which can be re used by multiple applications. It is possible to manually override the default partitioning. Forte has transaction processing capability, and also offers facilities to manage the deployed application: it can monitor traffic, multiple copies of a service can be created for performance, to avoid bottlenecks and as a fail-safe mechanism.

  - Runs over TCP/IP and DECNet;
  - Oracle, Sybase, Rdb, DB2/6000, Informix, Microsoft SQL Server, and supports ODBC;
  - Digital OpenVMS (VAX and Alpha) and Alpha/Digital UNIX, Data General AViiON/DGUX, IBM/AIX, Sequent/DYNIX, Sun/Solaris, Hewlett-Packard/UX, Windows NT (Intel, Digital Alpha) platforms;
  - Windows, Macintosh, Motif, Windows NT, Web browsers;
  - Includes support for integration via DCE and CORBA, OLE and Java.

Forte is a complete product set consisting of the capability to develop application components, and to deploy and run them. Suitable for enterprise client/server computing.

- IBM – Component Broker: Component broker is IBM's infrastructure technology for developing, executing and managing object applications. The development environment enables the import of designs from object modelling tools (for example, Rational Rose) and supports several object-oriented languages (see below). The infrastructure is CORBA 2 compliant, supporting a range of CORBA 2 services such as the Internet Inter-ORB Protocol (IIOP) for inter-ORB communication, transaction services, concurrency, security, etc. The Component Broker's systems management capability enables installation, deployment, monitoring and control of object applications. Supported languages include IBM's VisualAge family of products.

- Sun Microsystems – NEO and JOE
  - Solaris NEO 2.0: SUN's ORB, it supports OMG's CORBA 2.0, enabling NEO objects to interoperate with objects from other vendors" CORBA 2.0 environments. It supports NEO Connectivity for Microsoft Windows desktops, and provides Solstice NEO (bundled with NEO), a set of graphical tools to manage and administer distributed objects.
  - Joe 2.0: Java + NEO, it connects Java programs running in standard Web browsers with Intranet and Internet applications by establishing and managing connections between local Java objects and remote CORBA objects. Joe 2.0 supports CORBA 2.0 IIOP, enabling Java applets to connect to other similar CORBA environments.

Message-Oriented Middleware

As opposed to the other classes of middleware, these products offer most of the following capabilities:

- persistent data;
- guaranteed delivery;
- application view: connectionless;
- non blocking (asynchronous) operation;
- communicating partner does not need to be available.

It provides a relatively simple way of communication between distributed processes. Typically, knowledge of only a handful of API calls is needed. MOM has a relatively lower profile in the computing media, probably because possibilities and potential are not well understood. Proper application partitioning and design becomes very important. MOM is good for loosely coupled applications. Of all product types discussed, MOM has the best tolerance for legacy applications.

Standards

The Message-Oriented Middleware Association (MOMA) was established to promote message-oriented middleware, and to develop standards. Its members are: Applied Communications, Digital Equipment Corporation, IBM, Momentum Software, NCR Corporation, PeerLogic, and Sun Microsystems, among others.

Product Examples
- TIB: From TIBCO. Supports publish/subscribe, asynchronous request/reply, and broadcast request/reply type interactions.
- PeerLogic PIPES Based on the PIPES kernel to isolate the programmer from the underlying network protocol. Applications interact with the PIPES Platform system through PAPI, the PIPES API. It currently supports development in C, COBOL (CICS/MVS), and Visual Basic.
- Momentum Message Express: supports one-way guaranteed delivery, and asynchronous request/response type of interactions
- IBM MQSeries: supports asynchronous messaging, plus synchronizing point or transactional messaging (one synchronized unit of work, or multiple asynchronous units of work coordinated by a synchronizing point manager)
- DECmessageQ (now BEA MessageQ): Middleware for application connectivity in high-volume, high-performance multi-vendor environments. DECmessageQ enables guaranteed application to application messages via an asynchronous, queued message bus. It also supports publish and subscribe capability.
- Piccolo: Cornerstone's functionally rich, flexible, provides a protocol and platform independent environment that symmetrical for both client and server. Provides "NO-Waited" and "Non-blocking" protocols, and runs on many workstation and server platforms such as IBM AIX, HP 9000, SCO UNIX, Solaris 2.x - SPARC (UNIX), (Windows 95, NT), IBM OS/2.

Other Products

- BEA markets a good example of a composite suite of middleware:
  - BEA TUXEDO, the distributed transaction processing monitor, allows flexible mapping between clients and servers and manages their relationships. Tuxedo complies with The Open Group's X/Open standards and supports XA-compliant databases, including CA/Ingres, DB2, Informix, ISAM-XA, Microsoft SQL Server, Oracle and Sybase. Its high-level API, ATMI (Application-to-Transaction Manager Interface) has been adopted by The Open Group as a standard X/Open API. It includes application management, and an event communication and brokering system.
  - BEA ObjectBroker: Provides an OMG CORBA-standard interface across platforms, and offers PC integration (DDE, Visual Basic, and OLE), CORBA compliant C++ language bindings and request brokering via the CORBA Dynamic Invocation Interface. BEA ObjectBroker is especially suited to PC-to-mainframe integration and legacy wrapping technology.
  - BEA MessageQ: a MOM that supports synchronous and asynchronous messaging, and publish and subscribe mechanisms. BEA MessageQ runs on all major UNIX operating systems, OpenVMS, Windows NT, OS/2, Windows, MS-DOS, selected IBM environments via LU6.2, and on the various Digital Alpha platforms.

- BEA Jolt: BEA Jolt provides BEA TUXEDO applications with turn-key access to the Internet. Together BEA Jolt and BEA TUXEDO provide an application framework suited to building distributed Internet/intranet applications running on the middleware infrastructure. A set of software components allows Java code to make TUXEDO service requests from Java-enabled World Wide Web browsers. BEA Jolt clients can run in any Java-enabled browser including Netscape and MS-Internet Explorer. BEA Jolt also integrates with environments compatible with the Java Software Development Kit version 1.02 or 1.1.
- BEA Builder for TUXEDO Active Expert provides a base development kit, with tools to build TUXEDO client applications. It presents services as methods inside of ActiveX/OLE objects on Windows 95 and NT clients. It provides a graphical tool, the Application Builder, to help programmers build BEA TUXEDO-enabled clients, and supports rapid prototyping with popular tools such as Visual Basic, PowerBuilder, and Visual C++ 5.0.

- Sterling Software's COOL:Gen (Composer) (formerly Texas Instruments' IEF): CASE-based, can generate client and server components; also deployment platforms can be specified. Uses PIPES as underlying communications mechanism.
- Seer Technology's SEER*HPS: can generate client and server components. Originally for IBM environments, there is now a wider choice of client and server options such as Windows NT and OS/2. It provides communications services such as RPCs, and publish and subscribe functionality.
- Uniface International's UNIFACE: generates distributed logic applications. It has its own proprietary API for client and server communications. UNIFACE supports all the client Microsoft platforms, as well as Windows NT as a server platform. UNIFACE includes support for OLE controls and OLE Automation.
- Magna Software Incorporated's Magna X: Provides DTP middleware with good support of popular databases. It has its own client development environment, but also provides builds for Encina servers. Clients can be developed using C, C++, Java, Visual Basic and PowerBuilder.
- SilverStream: a Java based development environment to develop and deploy client/server WWW enabled applications. It includes a comprehensive development environment, and supports browser based clients, relational database access and Email communication.
- There are products that originated as client development products, and have undergone a good deal of evolution, to either provide both client and server development capabilities or interact with server-based components via middleware. Some provide their own middleware (e.g. VisualBasic and Activex) as well as API access to other middleware products. Examples are:

  - Microsoft Visual Basic;
  - Borland Delphi;
  - Powersoft PowerBuilder;
  - Open Software Associates Open UI.

Systems Management

The term "systems management" covers the mechanisms for managing and controlling the various physically distributed components in a distributed (possibly multi-vendor) environment. These mechanisms include the capabilities to remotely configure and manage servers and workstations, the management of these components, and the management of software distribution. The elements to be managed are:

- computers: PCs, multi user systems, file servers, print servers;
- software: business applications, databases, networking software, Email, etc.;
- peripherals: printers, disk drives etc.;
- network elements: routers, bridges, PBXs etc.

Standards

- SNMP (Simple Network Management Protocol): TCP/IP Internet community;
- CMIP (Common Management Information Protocol): OSI community;
- DME (Distributed Management Environment): an OSF architectural model, supports SNMP and CMIP protocols.

Product Examples

- Tivoli TME 10: it manages mainframes, client/server systems, workgroups, enterprises and Internet/intranets, software distribution and network resources, in an automatic or manual fashion.
- Tivoli NetView: network management, tightly integrated with other Tivoli's management applications. Provides the ability to display network topologies, monitor networks, gather performance data and effect changes on many devices.
- HP OpenView: a fully integrated suite of tools to manage IT resources, including service level planning, desktop and software management, and operations and availability.
- DEC Polycenter: Polycenter DECnet Manager provides management capabilities for all Digital networking environments, including DECnet Phase IV, DECnet/OSI, and Digital's legacy terminal servers and LAN bridges. It provides capabilities for configuration, fault, and performance management-for DECnet networks. Available on Digital UNIX and Windows NT.
- BMC Software Patrol and PatrolLink: supported on Data General AViiON systems running DG/UX and other UNIx platforms. An event-driven management tool that enables the integrated management of databases, networks, operating systems, and user-defined application executables. Late versions include management of Internet servers such as Web, FTP, Proxy, News and Mail.
- CA-Unicenter TNG: Computer Associates" management framework. It includes an object oriented GUI, an Object Repository and Distributed

Services: The CA Event Notification Facility (ENF) and Common Communication Interface (CCI) provide a messaging infrastructure.

Information Management Services: Databases

The main players here are the relational database products such as Oracle, Sybase, Informix, Ingress, and IBM's DB2. All major relational database products support procedural and non-procedural capabilities in their language (usually a dialect of SQL – for example, Oracle and PL/SQL, Sybase and Transact SQL, Informix and SPL), as well as support for stored procedures and triggers. Typically, they also support database transactions and database replication capabilities. Some support distributed transactions.

Network Services

These are the networking hardware and software that support distributed applications. Typically, there is no direct interface to the application, rather these capabilities provide interfaces to integration services, information management services and to the platforms.

Appendix 2

Queue Organization

Introduction

The MQSeries middleware uses queues to make possible the communication between running applications. The protocols discussed in Chapter 9 have been implemented on a prototype Federation. This section gives details of the domains' and Directory's queue managers, and the queues under their control.

All domains have at least a fixed set of queues that are specific for their interaction with the Directory. There is also a set of queues under subscribers control where publishing domains place their messages. When a publisher intends to broadcast a publication, its Gatekeeper checks an internal list of domains subscribed to the message and places the message on all the subscribers' queues. Therefore, in each domain there are two kinds of queues:

- queues to support the interaction of the domain with the Directory;
- queues to support the interaction of the domain with other domains when broadcasting or retrieving publications.

As shown in Figure A2.1 the Gatekeeper application is in charge of collecting incoming publishers messages from the local queues and delivering them to the appropriate application. Although the choice in this implementation has been to define a new queue for each application within the domain, there are other acceptable alternatives to setting up these queues. These can range from one single queue where all the incoming messages should be placed, to a case where there is a queue for each different subscription. It is also possible to have more than one queue manager serving a domain. To decide on a particular strategy, the designer must consider the number of applications serviced by the Gatekeeper and the number, length and frequency of the incoming messages, and make sure that the queue organization that the Gatekeeper manages is appropriate for the volume and characteristics of the traffic. Although it is not necessary to make this decision at the level of the Federation since the place and timing of message collection is really a matter for the subscriber to decide, a poorly designed queue scheme can clearly have a negative impact in the overall performance of the Federal Highway since messages will not reach their destination as promptly as intended.

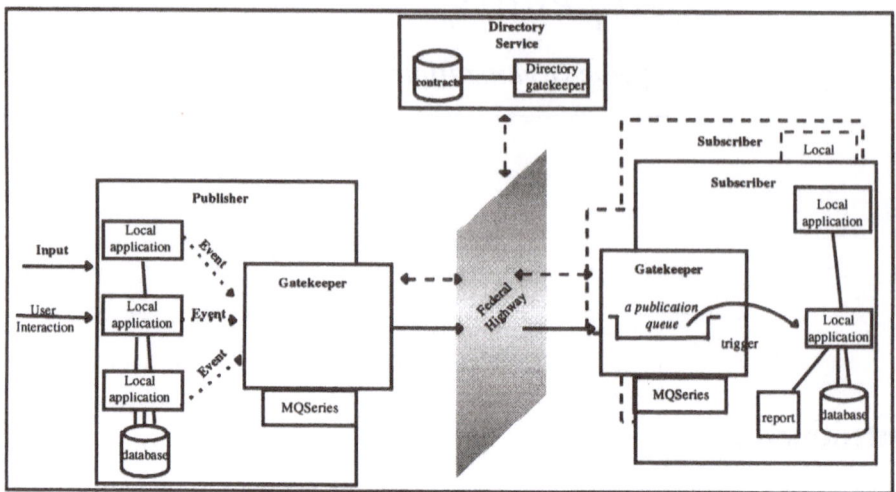

Figure A2.1: A publisher broadcasts a message

A subscriber should include the necessary queue information as part of the message requesting a new subscription. If the Federation publishes information as soon as the triggering event occurs rather than batching messages and sending them according to agreed frequencies, subscribers can then instruct their Gatekeepers to read messages from the queues at specified frequencies. Although there is no difference between approaches from the functionality point of view, there could be differences from the efficiency and network traffic standpoint.

Special queues also have to be created in the Directory to allow its interactions, as described above, with the domains. These standard queues need to be created, in the Directory and in each of the participating domains, before they can be used:

- Directory queues are created when the Federation is established;
- Domain queues are created when a domain joins the Federation. In addition, subscribers have specific queues to receive their subscribed publications which are decided upon every time a new subscription is established.

In our implementation, we have called the Directory's queue manager dirsermgr, whereas the domains' queue managers – publisher or subscriber – are named according to their role in a given interaction. In terms of queue names the combination <queue manager, queue name> must be unique. Consequently, while queues administered by different queue managers can share names, queues administered by the same queue manager must have different names. As mentioned before, a domain can have more than one queue manager.

The following sections describe the organization of queues and the specific commands such as MQPut and MQGet that have been used for implementation.

MQSeries queues

extpub queue

Queue manager: dirsermgr

(This section relates to Figure 9.5)

1. Subscriber identification.
2. Required information.
3. Subscriber's queue manager corresponding to the publication.
4. Queue name where the required information must be placed by the eventual publisher.

Figure A2.2 shows how a subscriber sends a message to the Directory requesting a publication by placing a message in the Directory's queue extpub.

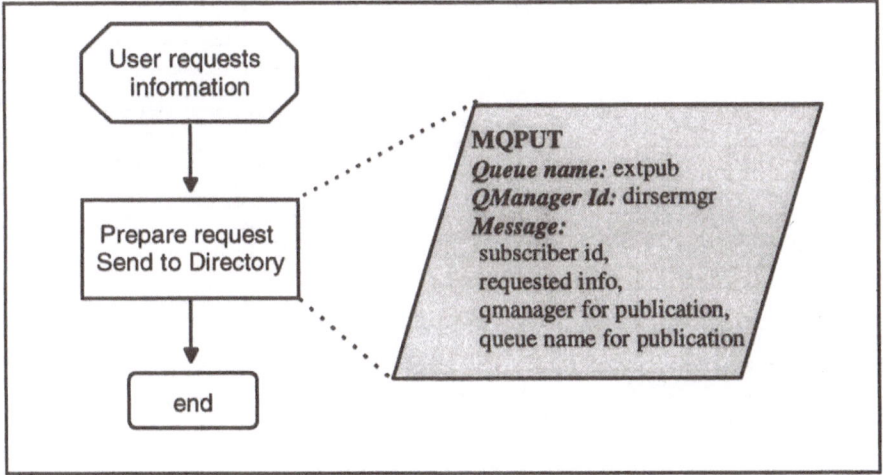

Figure A2.2: Subscriber requests a new publication

Figure A2.3 shows how the Directory retrieves the information from the queue and proceeds with the steps to publish the new information.

rep-to-extpub queue

Queue manager: dirsermgr

(This section relates to Figure 9.5)

This queue receives (affirmative) reply messages from domains that were consulted about the publication of new information. The content of the message is:

1. Subscriber identification.
2. Required information.
3. Answer for Yes, No or Already published.
4. Description or name of item.

Figure A2.4 shows how the consulted domains reply to the Directory by placing a message in this queue. Figure A2.3 shows how the Directory retrieves the reply from the queue and proceeds accordingly.

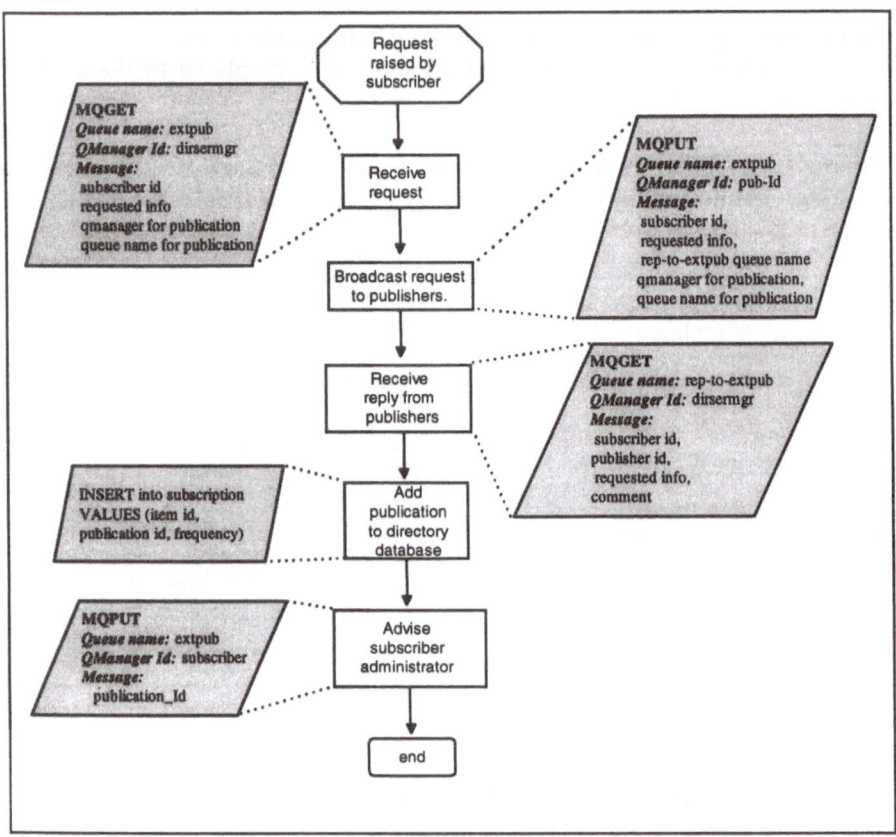

Figure A2.3: Directory manages a request for new publication

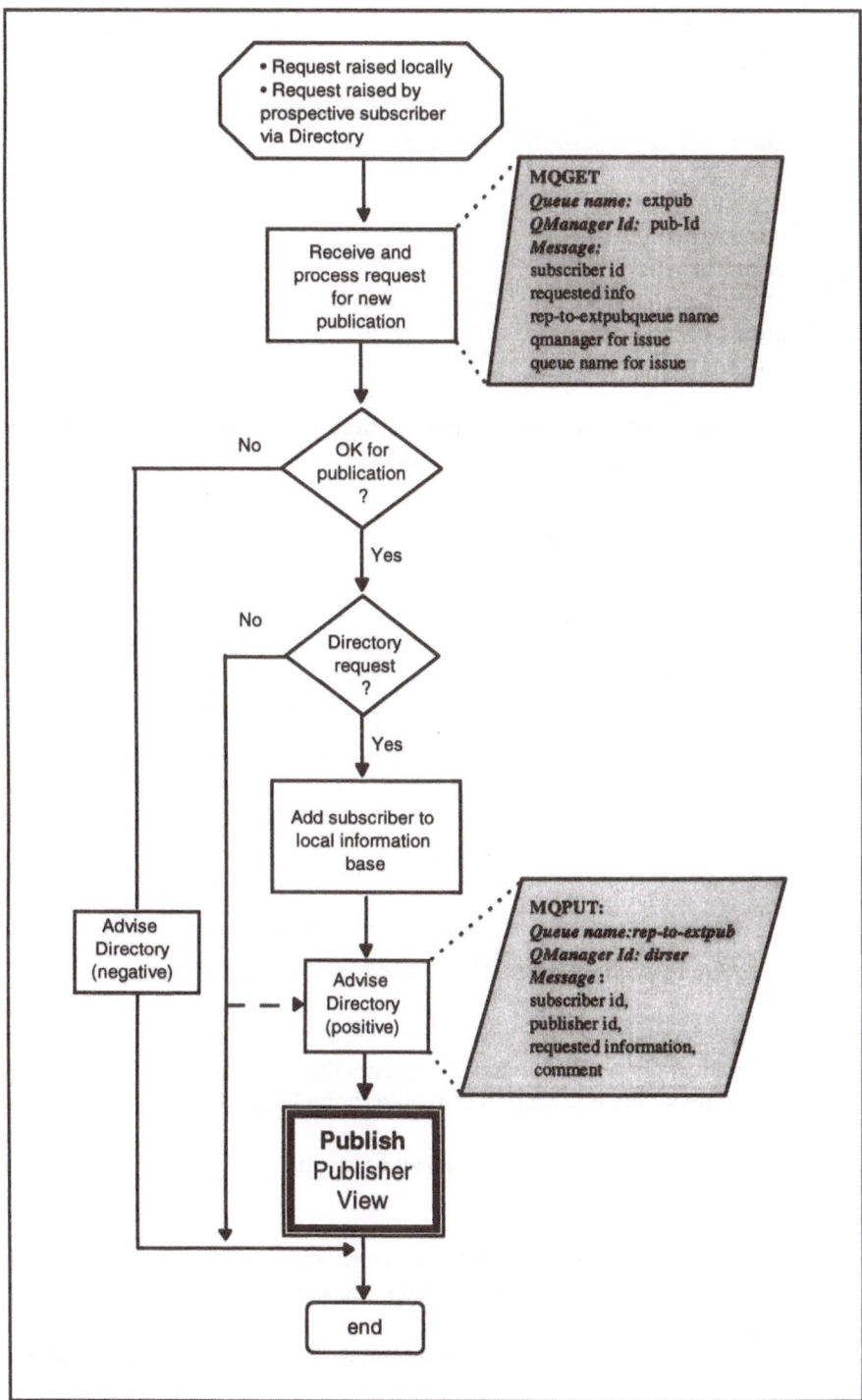

Figure A2.4: Publisher domain manages a new publication

newpub queue

Queue manager: dirsermgr

This queue receives messages from domains that want to make an item available for publication. The content of the message is:

1. Publisher identification.
2. Publication identification.
3. Publication format.
4. Publication size.
5. Publication description.
6. Frequency of publication.

Figure A2.5 shows how a publisher sends a message to the Directory to propose a publication by placing a message in this queue.

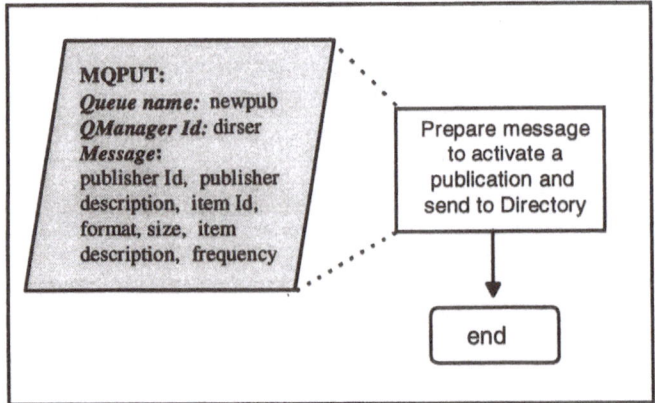

Figure A2.5: Publisher offers publication to the Federation

Figure A2.6 shows how the Directory retrieves the information from the queue and proceeds to make the publication available to the Federation.

Note: Although the queues rep-to-extpub and newpub play similar roles, they in fact reflect two different situations:

- rep-to-expub is used when a request has come via the Directory requesting a new publication, and the domain accepts the contract and starts publishing immediately.
- newpub: the publisher offers the publication, with no subscribers at this stage.

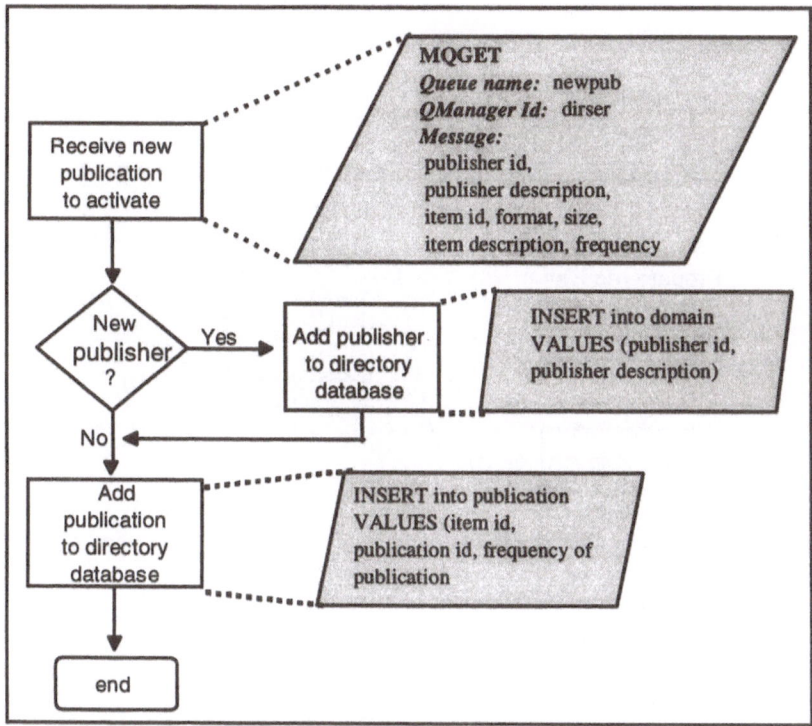

Figure A2.6: Directory activates publication

newsubs queue

Queue manager: dirsermgr

(This section relates to Figure 9.6)

This queue receives messages from domains that want to subscribe to existing publications. The content of the message is:

1. Item identification;
2. Publisher identification;
3. Subscriber identification;
4. Queue manager name;
5. Queue name.

The queue manager and the queue names specify where the published information is to be delivered by the publisher. Figure A2.7 shows how a subscriber sends the message into this queue to incorporate a new subscription. Figure A2.8 shows how the Directory retrieves the information from the queue and proceeds with the creation of a new subscription.

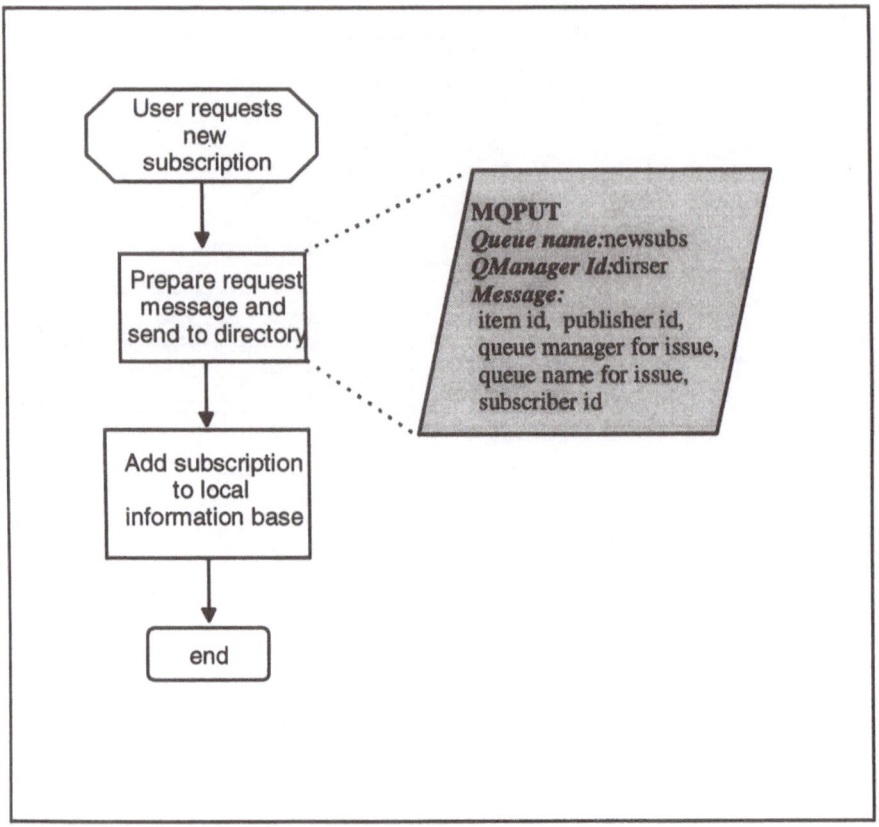

Figure A2.7: Subscriber initiates a new subscription

delsubs queue

Queue manager: dirsermgr

(This section relates to Figure 9.9)

This queue receives messages from subscribers that want to stop their subscription to an item. The content of the message is:

1. Item identification;
2. Publication identification;
3. Subscriber identification.

Figure A2.9 shows how the subscriber sends a message to the Directory to stop the subscription to an item.

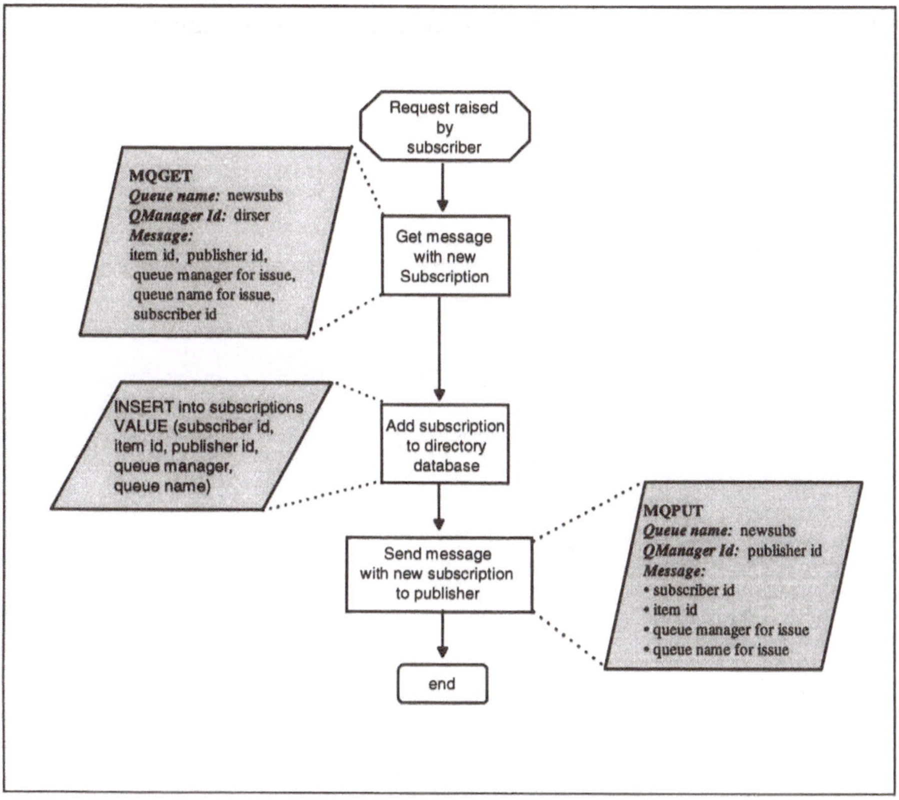

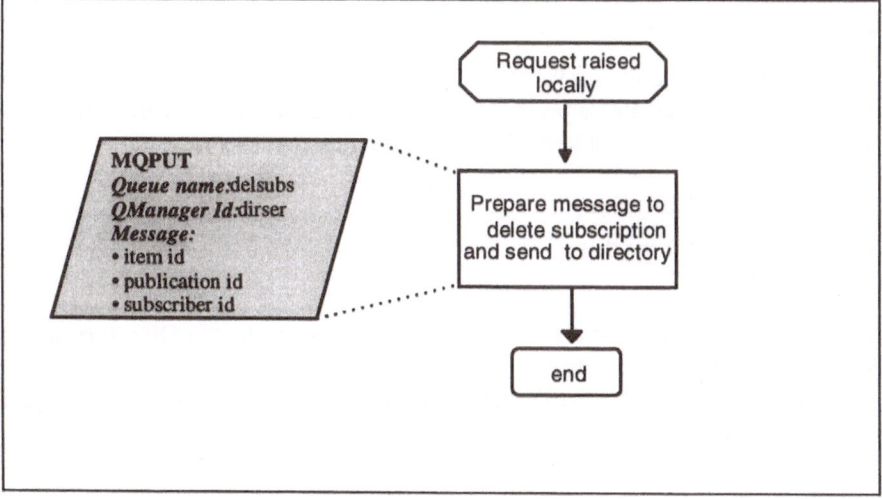

Figure A2.8: Directory activates new subscription

Figure A2.9: Subscriber stops subscription to an item

Figure A2.10 shows how the directory retrieves the message and processes it.

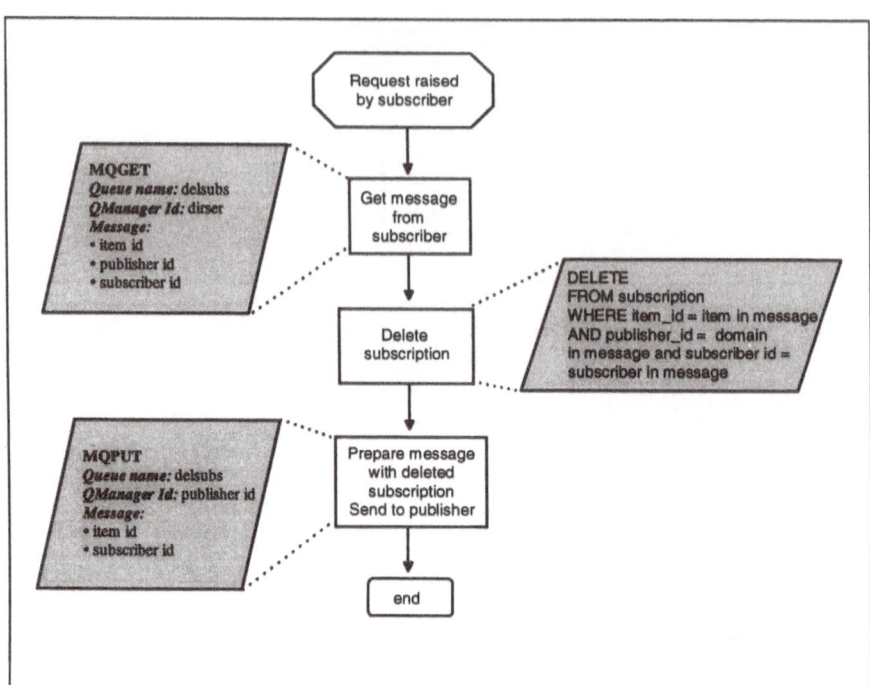

Figure A2.10: Directory manages stopping subscription to an item

delpub queue

Queue manager: dirsermgr

(This section relates to Figure 9.10)

This queue receives messages from publisher domains that have been requested to stop the publication of an item. The content of the message is:

1. Publication identification;
2. Publisher identification;
3. Reply queue name.

Figure A2.11 shows how a publisher sends a message to the Directory to stop the publication of information.

Figure A2.12 shows how the Directory retrieves the information from the queue and manages the deletion process.

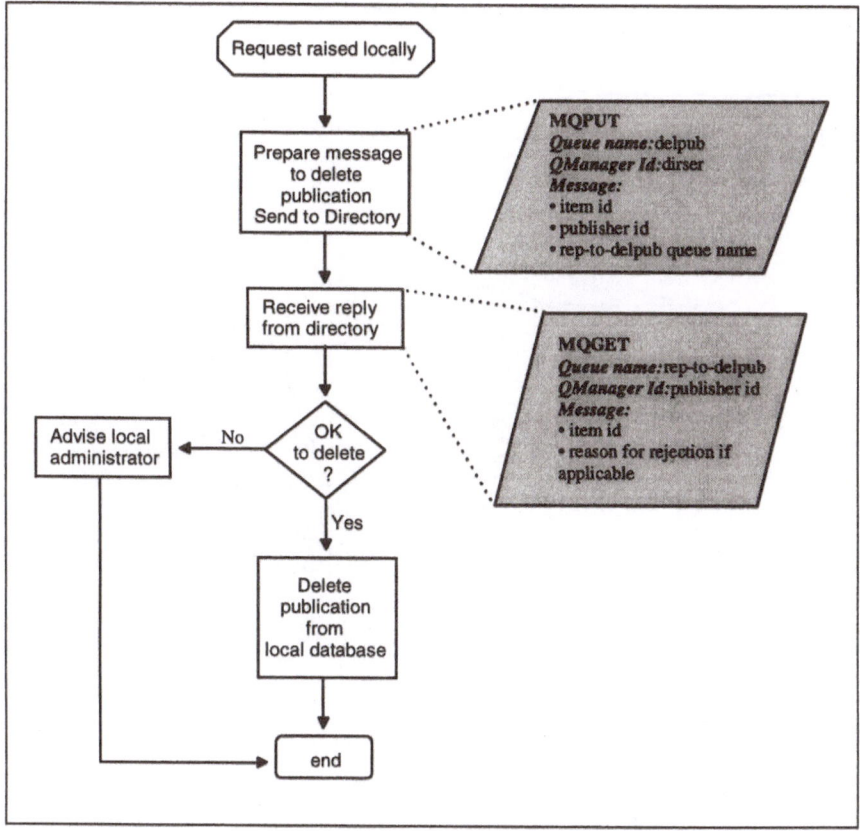

Figure A2.11: Publisher proceeds with the deletion of a publication

rep-to-stopsubs queue

Queue manager: dirsermgr

(This section relates to Figure 9.10)

This queue receives reply messages from subscribers when a publisher does not want to continue publishing a certain item to which they are subscribed. The content of the message is:

1. Item identification;
2. Publisher identification;
3. Subscriber identification;
4. Answer for Yes or No;
5. Comment.

Figure A2.13 shows how the subscriber replies to the Directory by placing a message in this queue. Figure A2.12 shows how the Directory retrieves the information from the queue and proceeds.

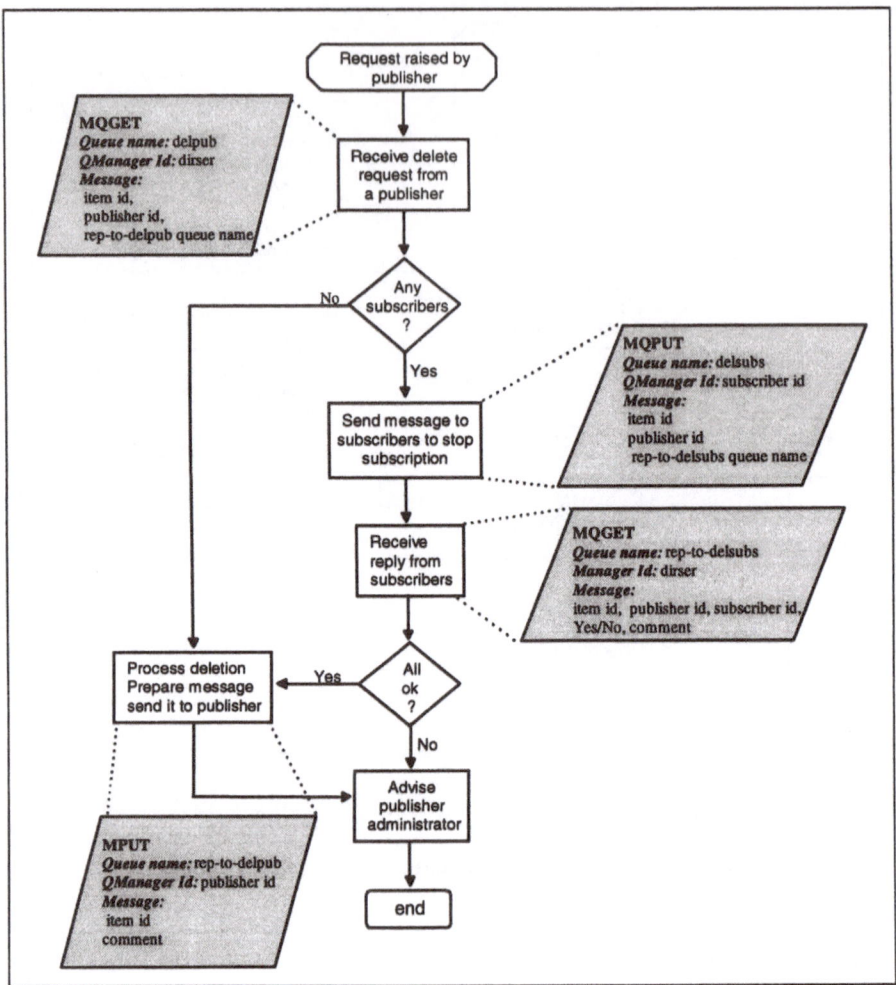

Figure A2.12: Directory processes the deletion of a publication

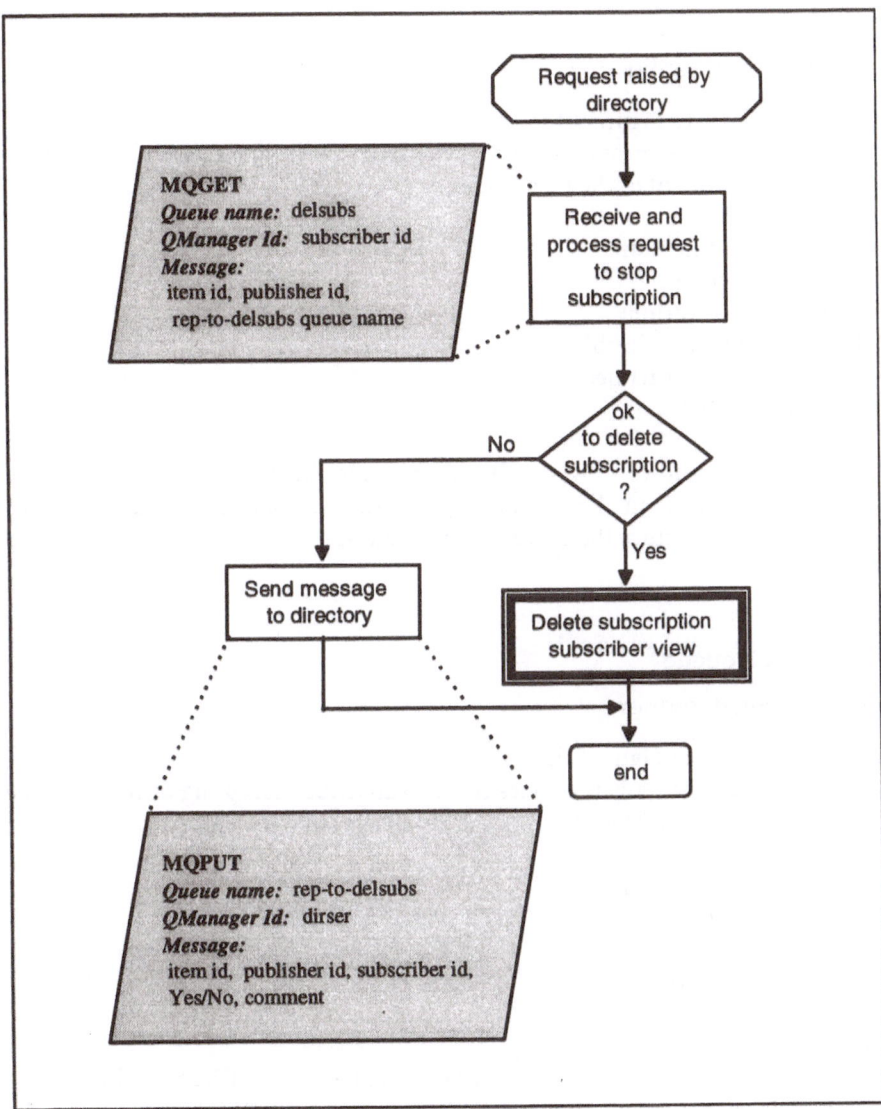

Figure A2.13: Subscriber processes stop to publication

reqmod queue

Queue manager: dirsermgr

(This section relates to Figure 9.12)

This queue receives messages from subscribers that want a modification to a publication. The content of the message is:

1. Subscriber identification;
2. Item identification;
3. Publisher identification;
4. Required frequency of publication;
5. New queue manager name;
6. New queue name.

Figure A2.14(a) shows how a subscriber sends the request message to the Directory by placing it in this queue. Figure A2.14(b) shows how a subscriber receives from the Directory the modification request message and how it replies to the Directory.

rep-to-modpub queue

Queue manager: dirsermgr

(This section relates to Figure 9.12)

This queue receives reply messages from a subscriber accepting or rejecting the modification to an item. The content of the message is:

1. Subscriber identification;
2. Publisher identification;
3. Item identification;
4. Answer of Yes or No;
5. Comment.

Figure A2.14(b) shows how the subscriber replies to the Directory by placing the message into this queue. Figure A2.15 shows how the Directory retrieves the reply and proceeds accordingly.

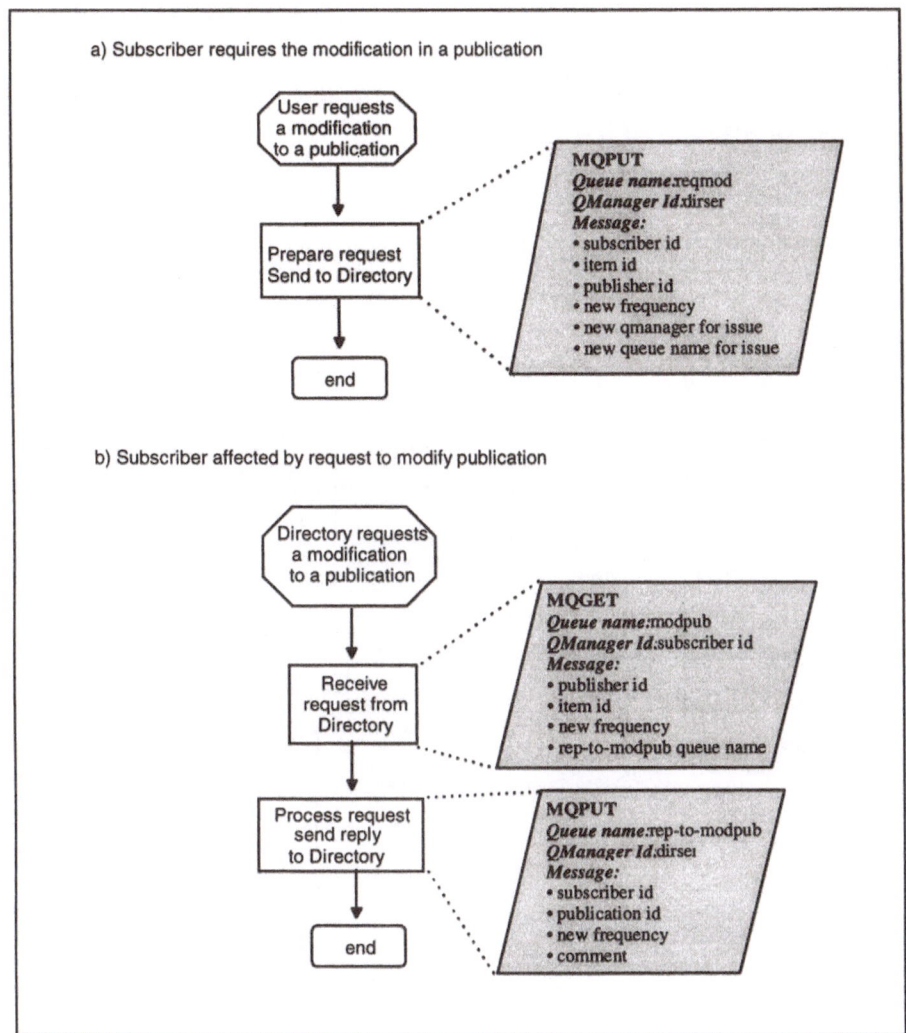

Figure A2.14: (a) Subscriber requests the modification of a publication; (b) Subscriber is requested to modify a publication

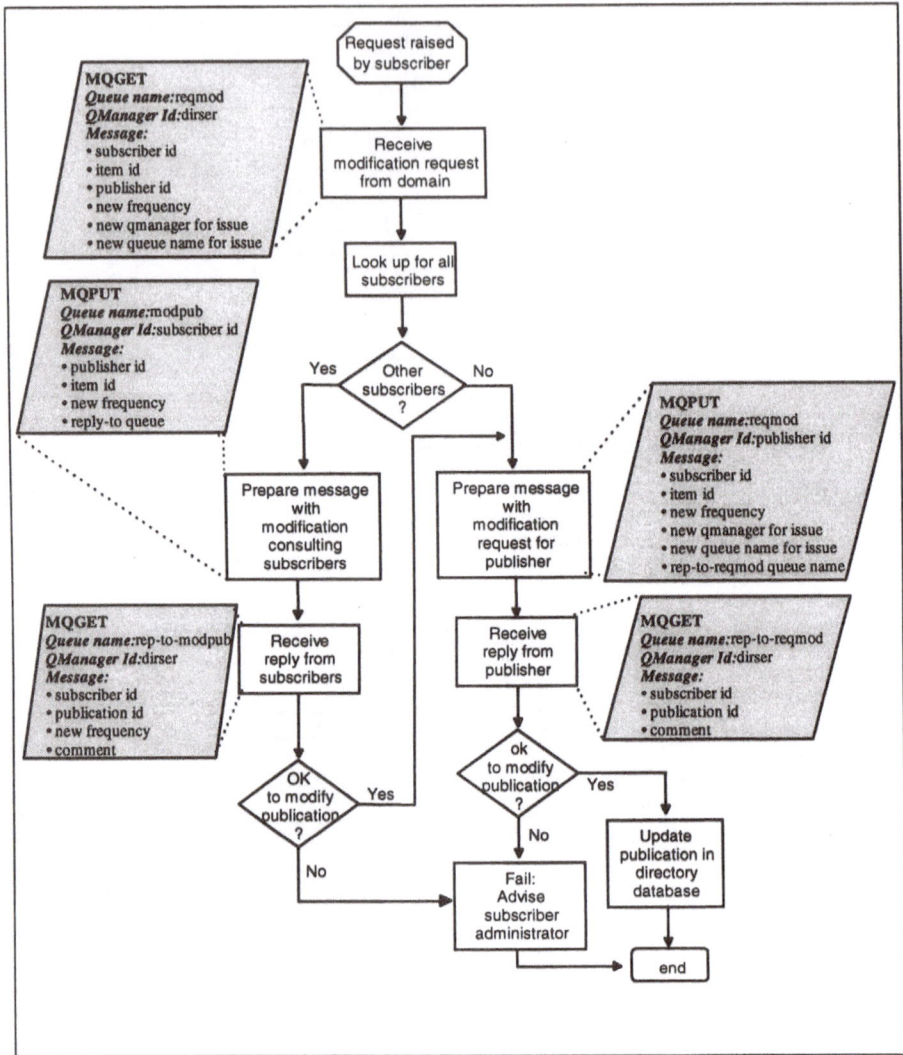

Figure A2.15: Directory processes reply to publication modification from a domain

deldom queue

Queue manager: dirsermgr

(This relates to Figure 9.11)

This queue receives messages from domains wanting to leave the Federation. The content of the message is:

1. Domain identification;
2. Reply queue name.

Figure A2.16 shows how a domain (publisher or subscriber) intending to leave the Federation, places a message in this queue. Figure A2.17 shows how the Directory retrieves the message from this queue and processes the request accordingly.

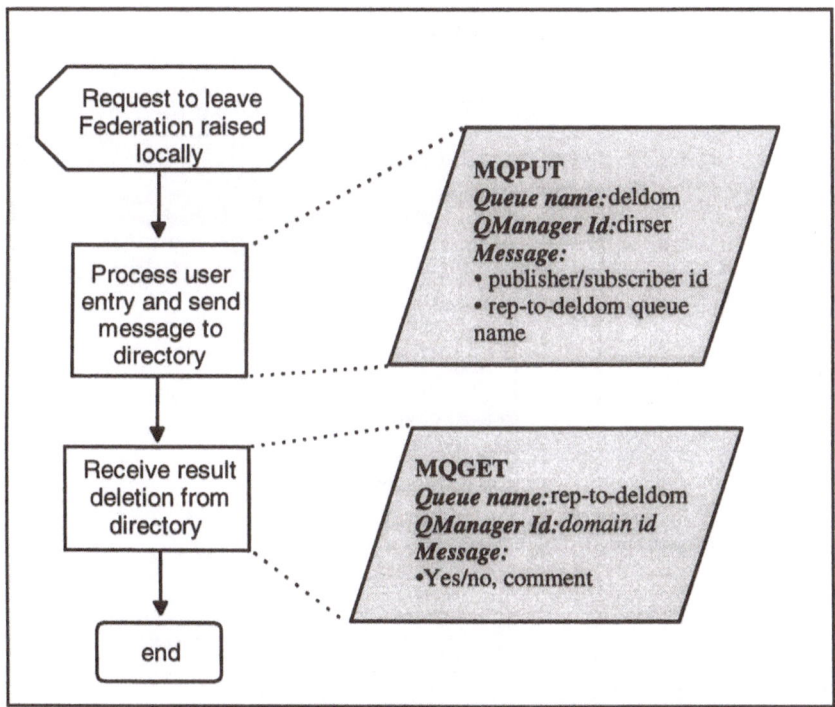

Figure A2.16: Domain intends to leave the Federation

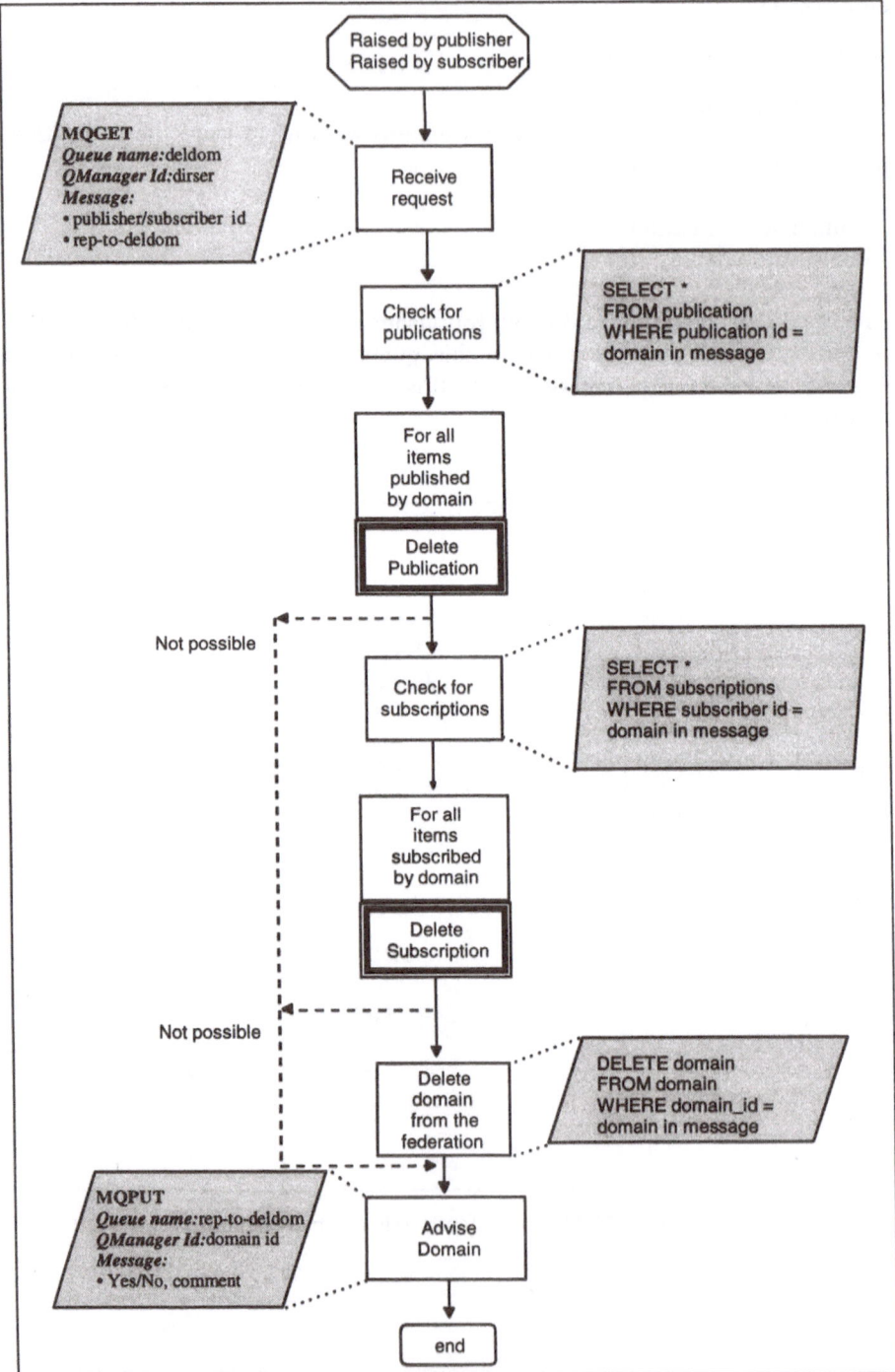

Figure A2.17: Directory processes a domain's request to leave the Federation

rep-to-reqmod queue

Queue manager: dirsermgr

(This section relates to Figure 9.12)

This queue receives reply messages from the publisher of the item. The publisher accepts or rejects the modification. The content of the message is:

1. Subscriber identification;
2. Publisher identification;
3. Existing publication identification;
4. Comment.

Figure A2.18 shows how the publisher sends the reply message to the directory by placing it into this queue. Figure A2.19 shows how the Directory retrieves the message from here and proceeds accordingly.

extpub queue

Queue manager: publisher

(This section relates to Figure 9.5)

This queue receives Directory's broadcasts asking about the availability of a new publication.

1. Subscriber identification;
2. Required information;
3. Queue manager name that will receive published information;
4. Queue name where the published information will be placed;
5. Rep-to-extpub reply queue name: each consulted domain will indicate on this queue whether or not it is able to publish the required information, and the name of the item, if already published.

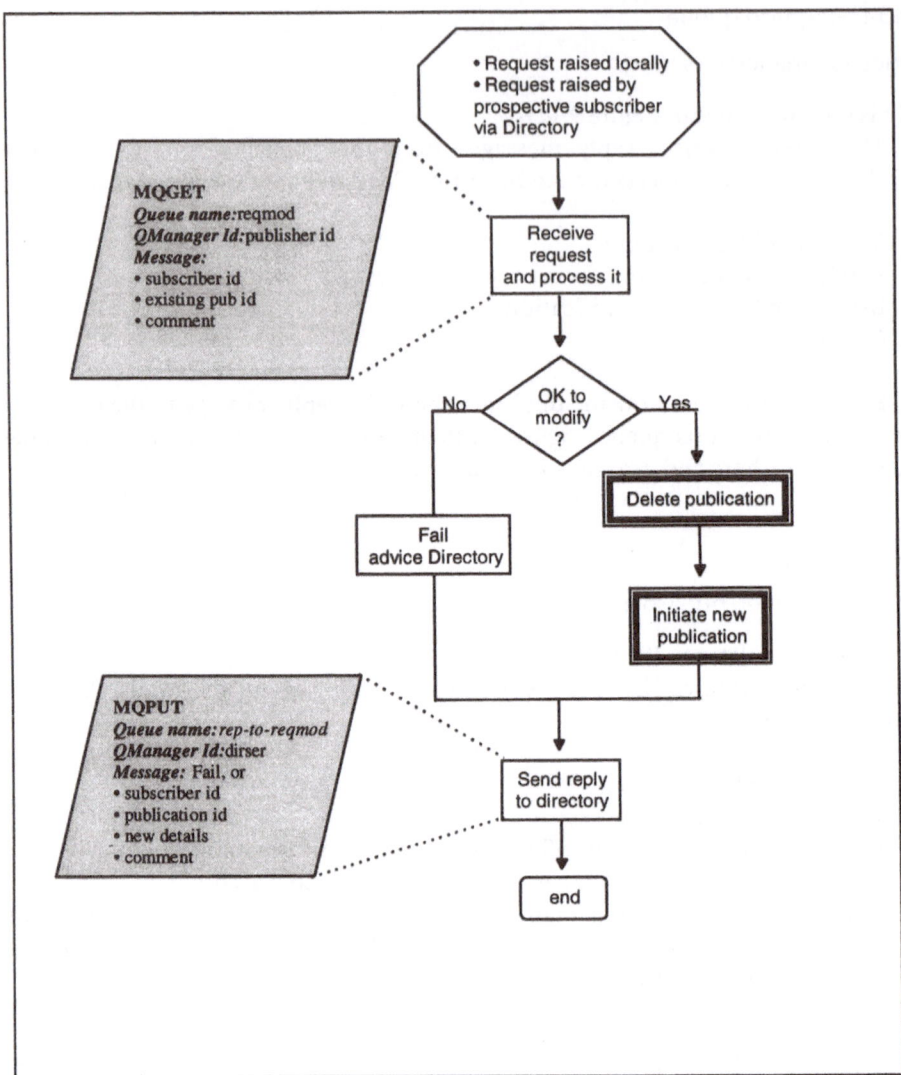

Figure A2.18: Publisher processes the request to modify a publication

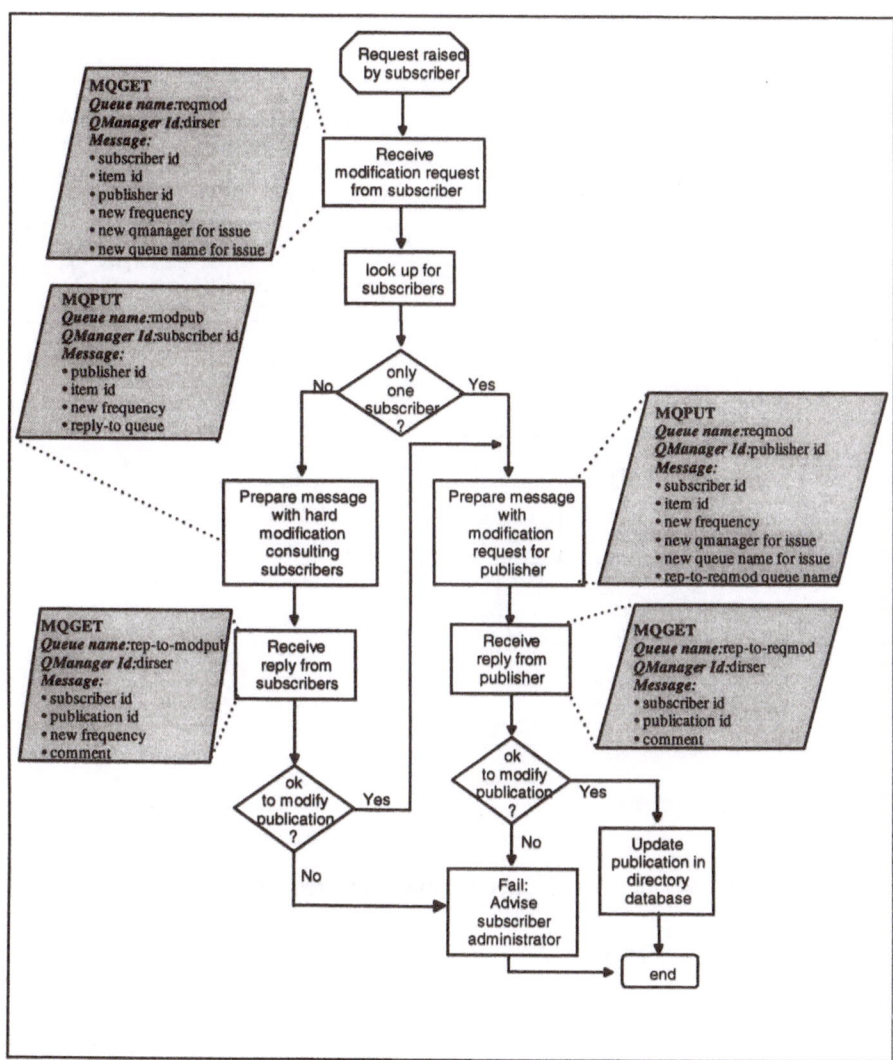

Figure A2.19: Directory processes the modification to a publication

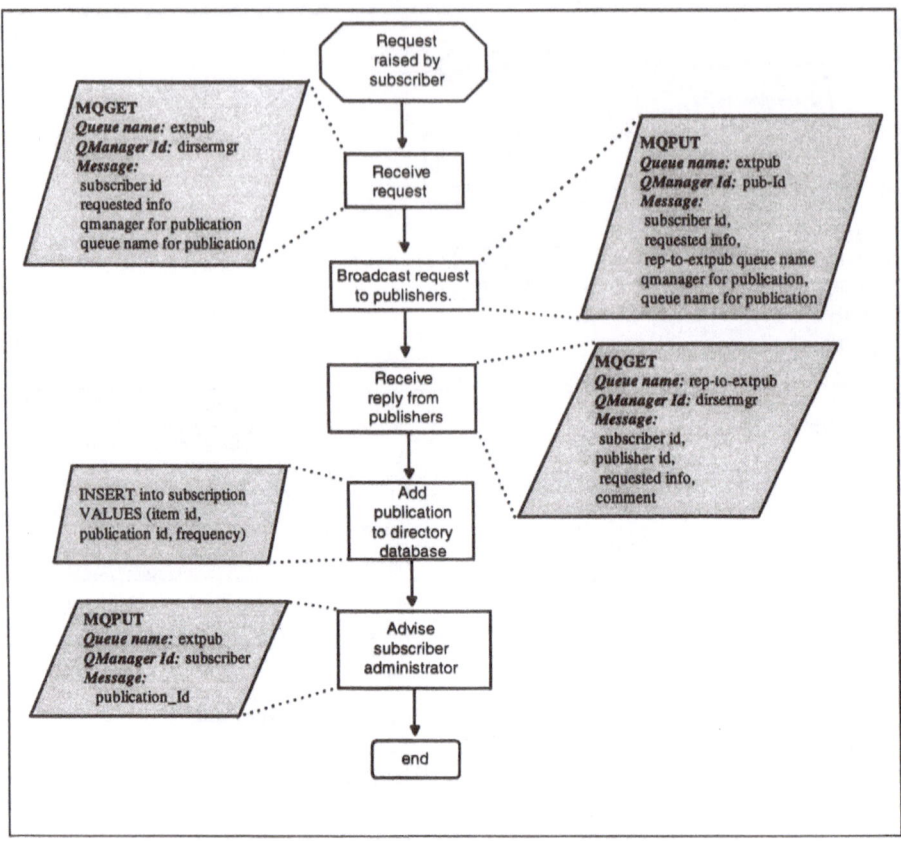

Figure A2.20 (also Figure A2.3): Directory manages a request for new publication

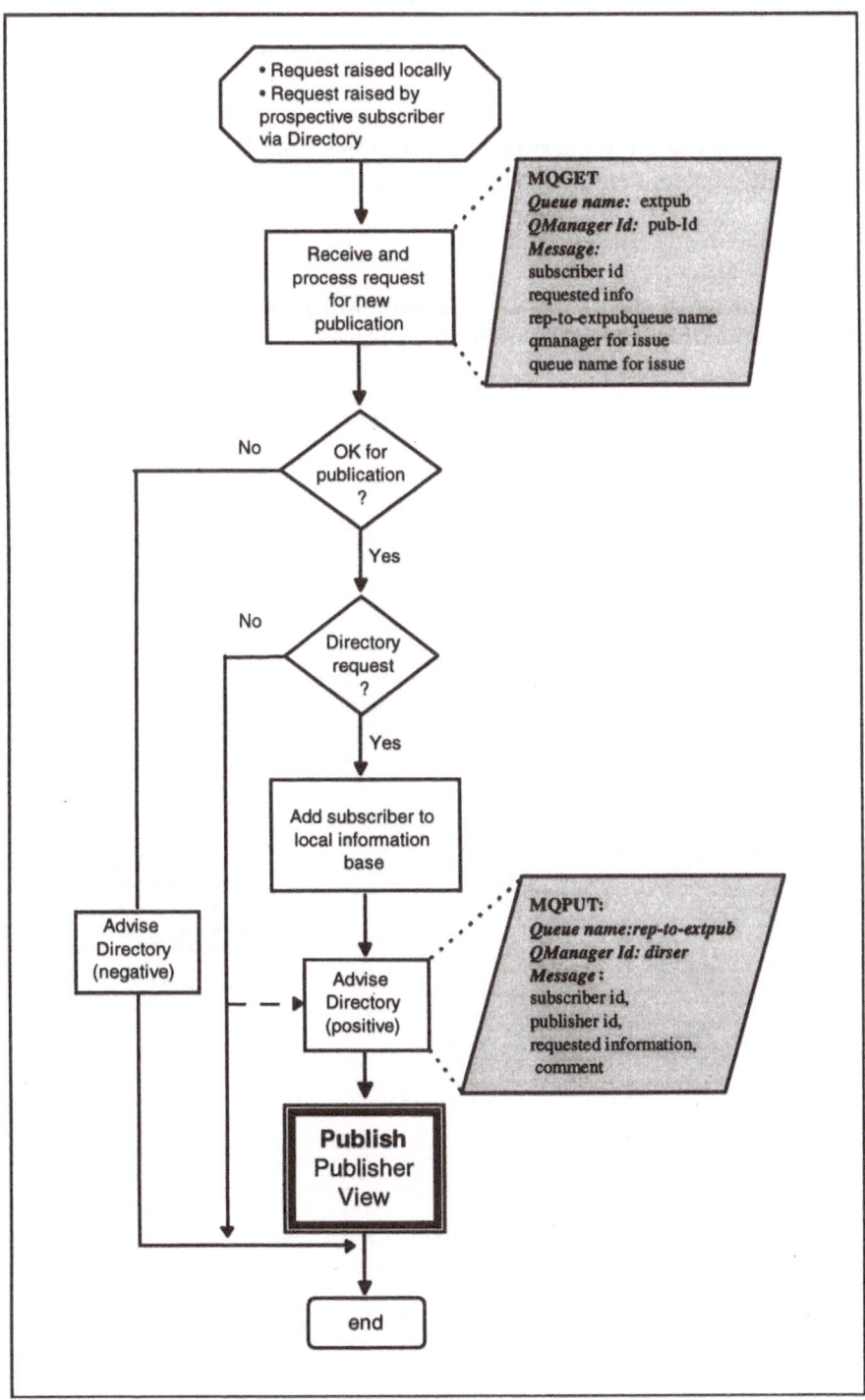

Figure A2.21 (also Figure A2.4): Publisher domain manages a new publication request

newsubs queue

Queue manager: publisher

(This section relates to Figure 9.6)

This queue is used to request new subscriptions from the publisher. Since the publisher must accept the request there is no need for acknowledgement.

1. Subscriber identification;
2. Item identification;
3. Queue manager name where the publication will be sent;
4. Queue name where the publication will be placed.

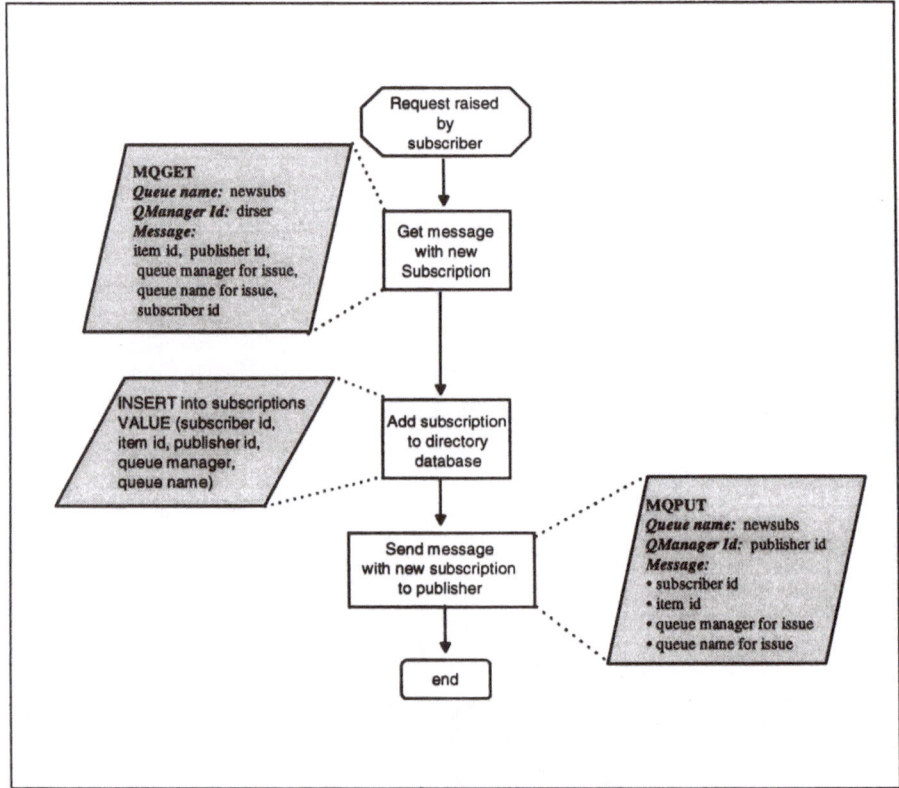

Figure A2.22 (also Figure A2.8): Directory activates new subscription

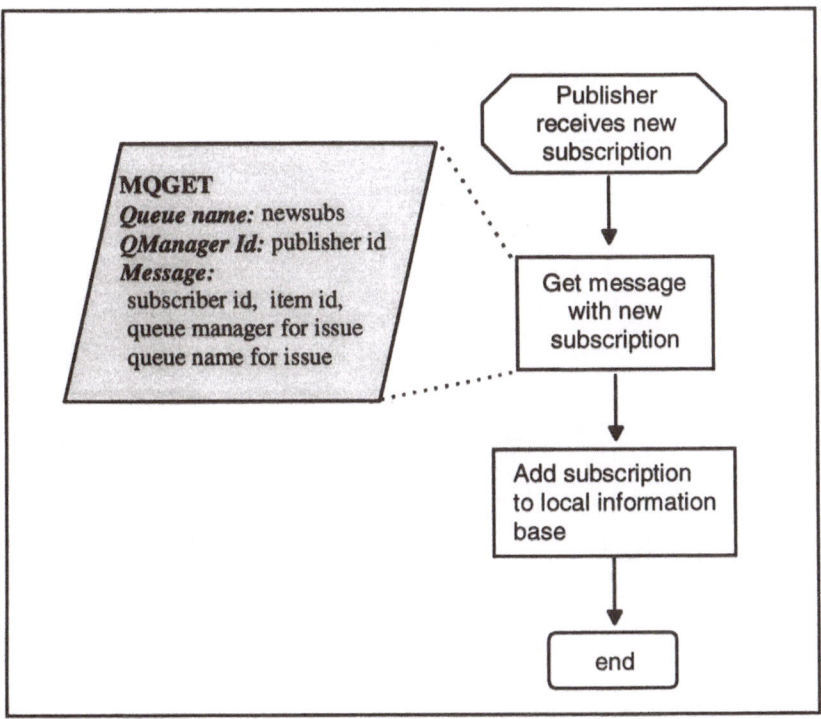

Figure A2.23: Publisher activates new subscription

delsubs queue

Queue Manager: publisher

(This section relates to Figure 9.9)

The delsubs queue is used to put messages to delete a subscription. Since the decision is taken by the subscriber unilaterally, there is no need for acknowledgement. The contents of the message are:

1. Item identification;
2. Subscriber identification.

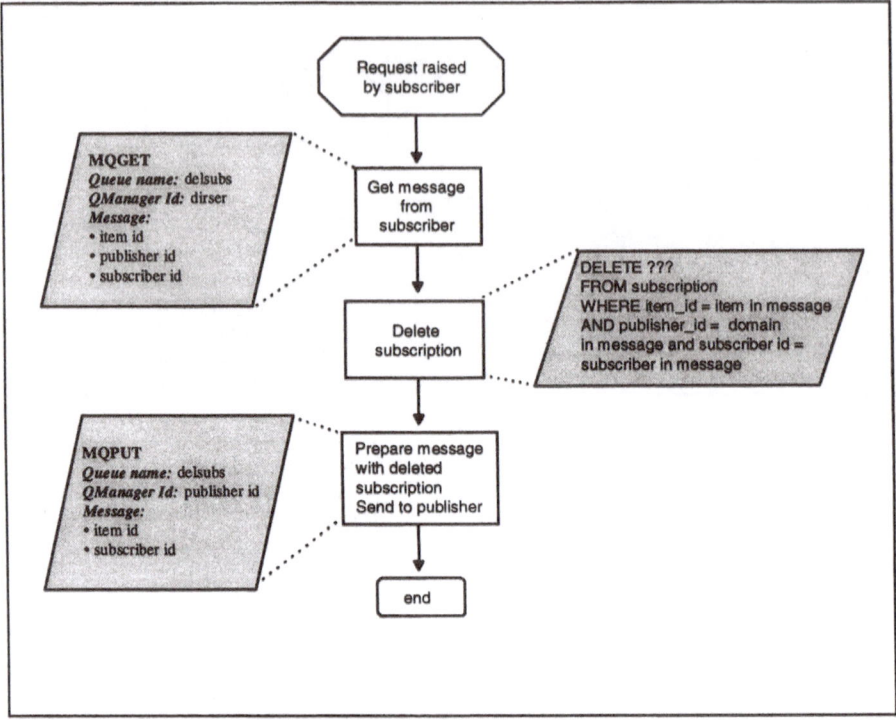

Figure A2.24: Directory processes stopping a subscription

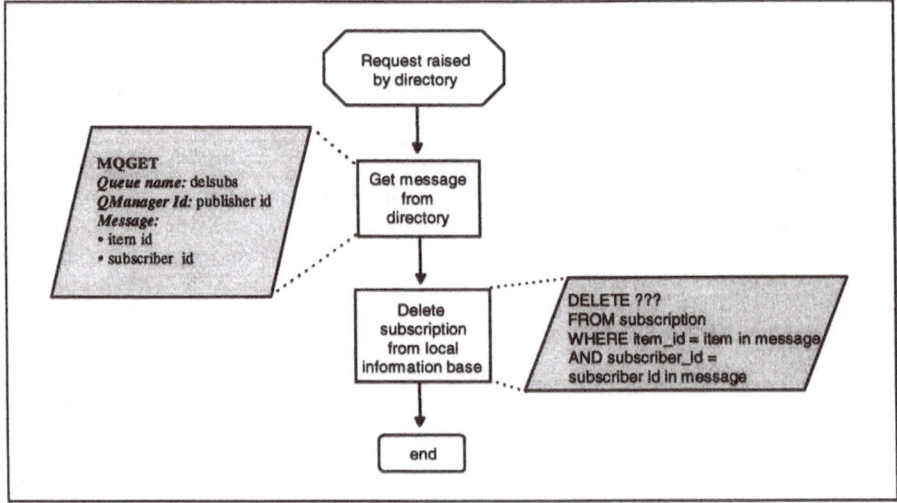

Figure A2.25: Publisher processes stopping a subscription

rep-to-delpub queue

Queue manager: publisher

(This section relates to Figure 9.10)

This queue receives the reply from the Directory to delete a publication. The messages contain:

1. Item identification;
2. Answer for Yes or No;
3. Comment.

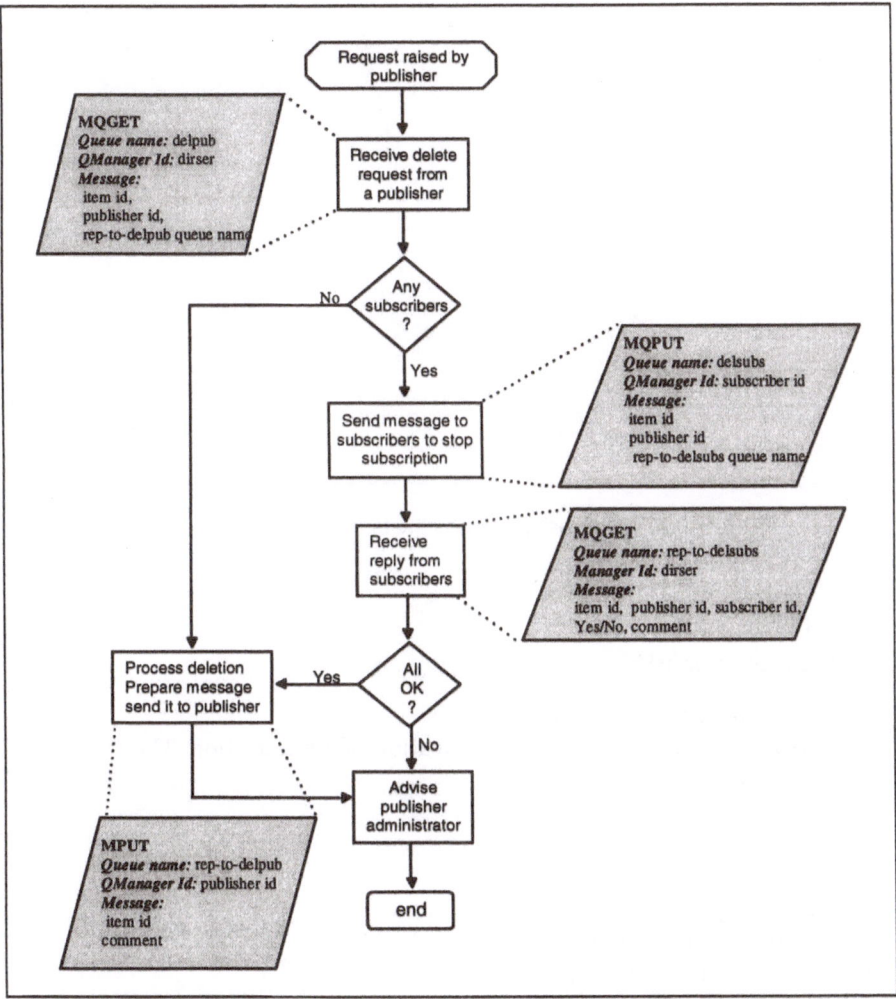

Figure A2.26: Directory processes the deletion of a publication

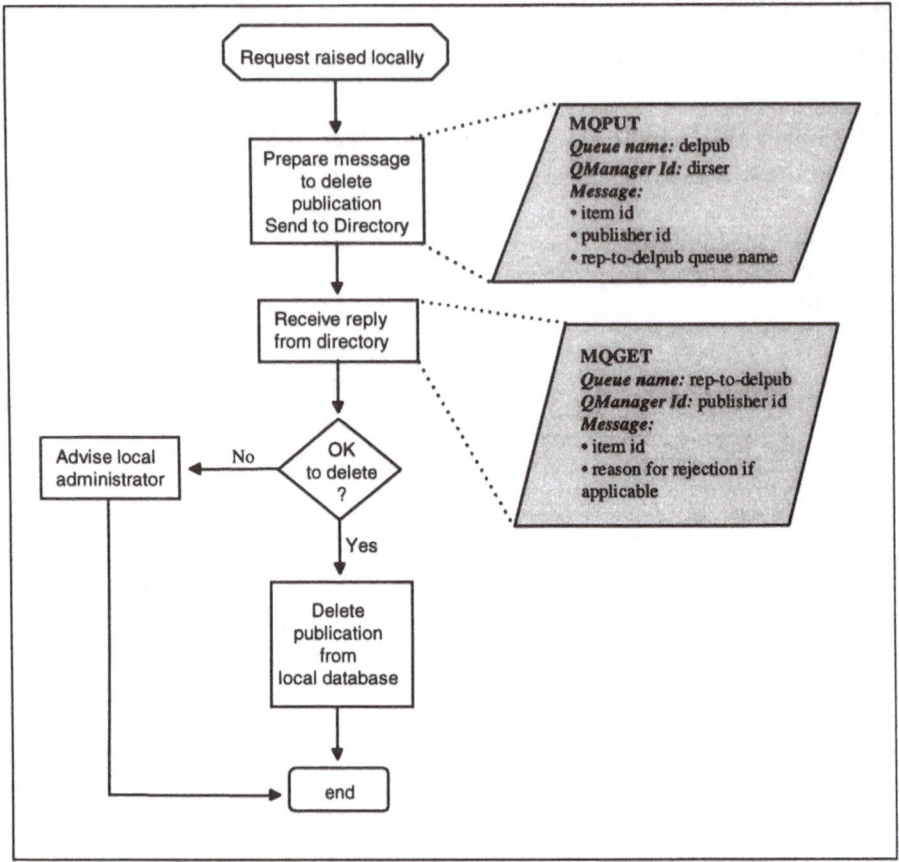

Figure A2.27: Publisher processes the deletion of a publication

reqmod queue

Queue manager: publisher

(This section relates to Figure 9.12)

This queue receives requests for modification of a publication. The contents of the messages are:

1. Subscriber identification;
2. Item identification;
3. New frequency;
4. New queue manager name;
5. New queue name;
6. Rep-to-reqmod reply queue name.

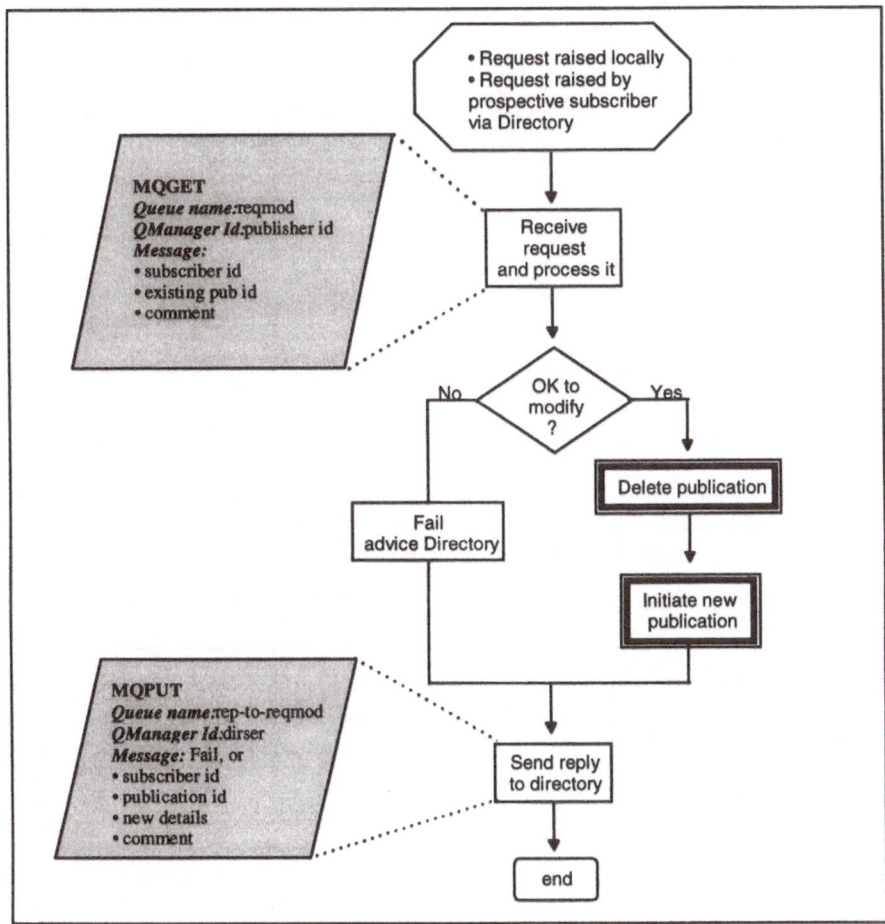

Figure A2.28: Publisher processes request to modify a publication

publication queue

Queue manager: subscriber

(This section relates to Figure 9.8)

These are the local queues that receive publication messages from publishers. The message contents vary with the subscription, but could include:

1. Format, e.g. "integer";
2. Size, e.g. "12";
3. Item, e.g. "000003000000".

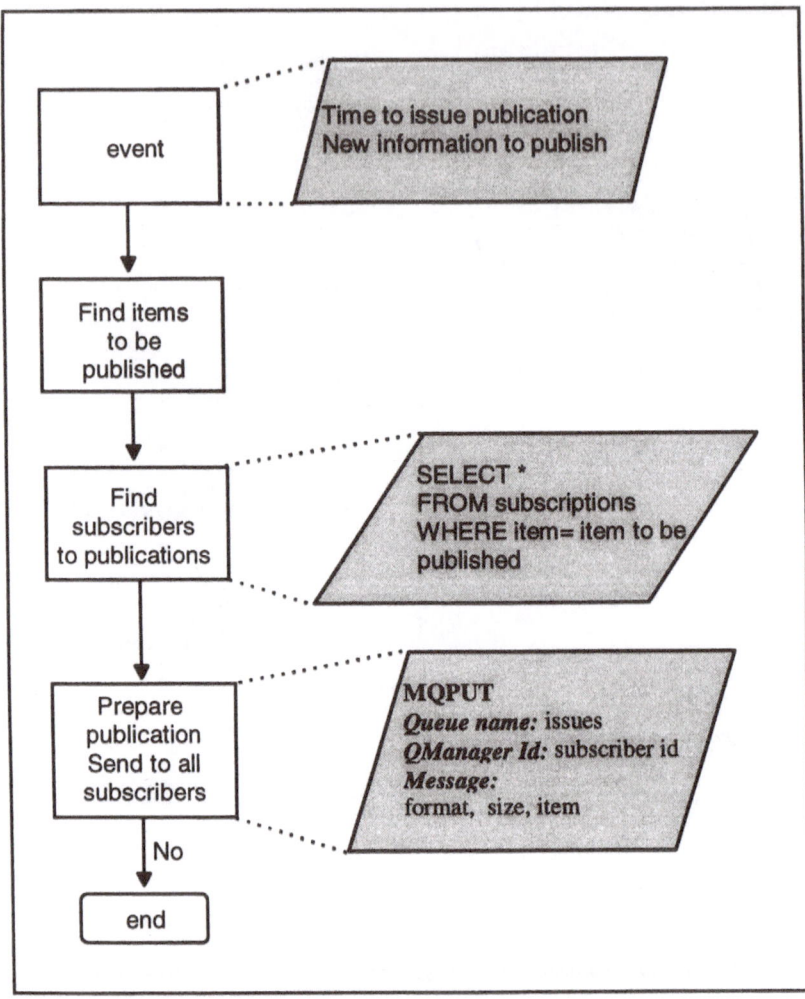

Figure A2.29: Publisher distributes subscribed information

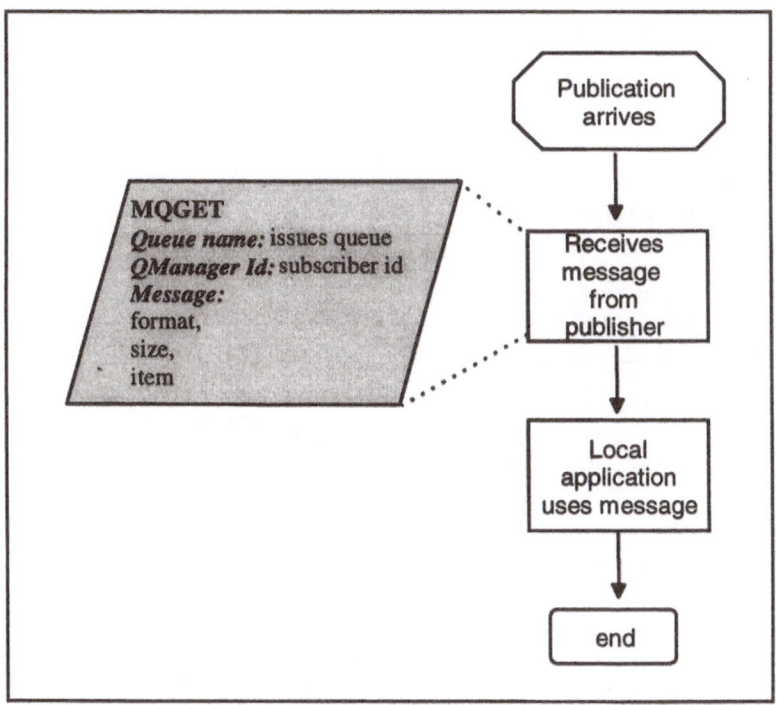

Figure A2.30: Subscriber retrieves a publication

stopsubs queue

Queue manager: subscriber

(This section relates to Figure 9.10)

1. Item identification;
2. Publisher identification;
3. Rep-to-stopsubs reply queue name.

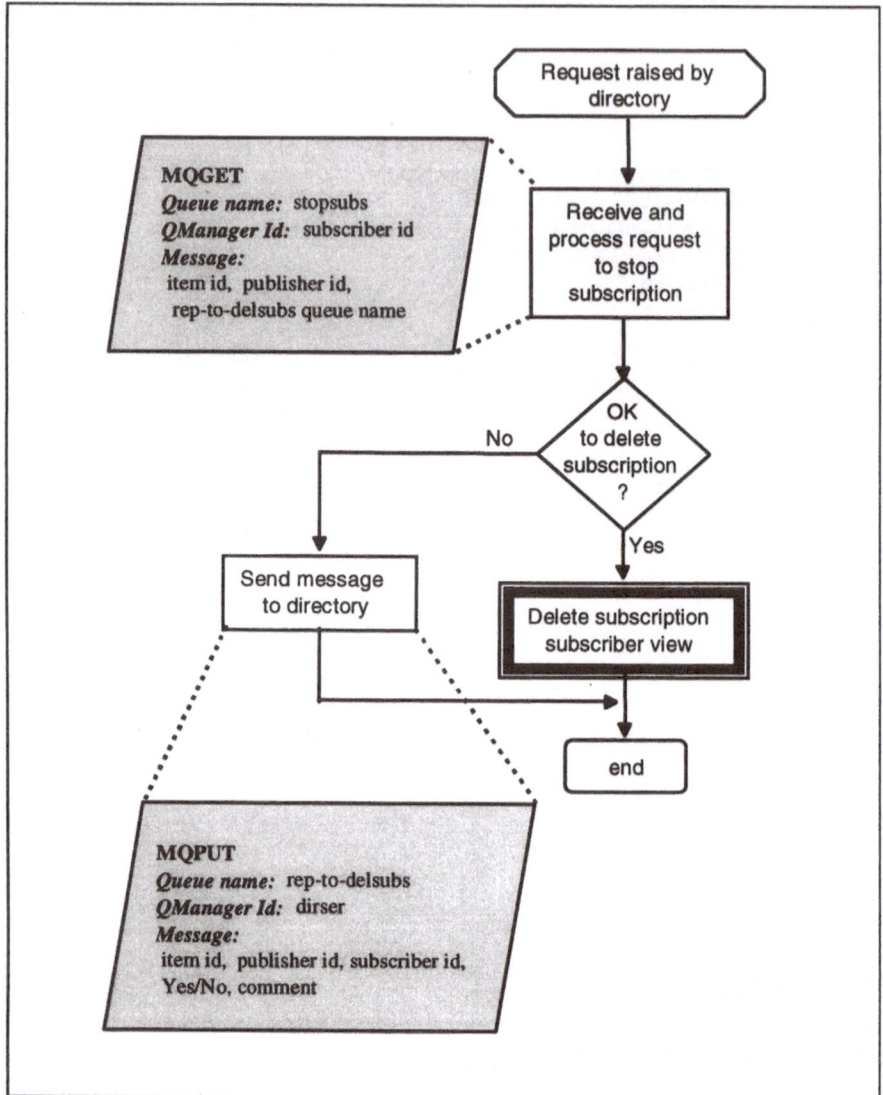

Figure A2.31: Subscriber process request to stop a subscription

modpub queue

Queue manager: subscriber

(This section relates to Figure 9.12)

This queue is used to receive requests via the Directory for modification of publications. The message consists of:

1. Publisher identification;
2. Publication identification;

3. New required publication;
4. New queue manager name (if applicable);
5. New queue name (if applicable).

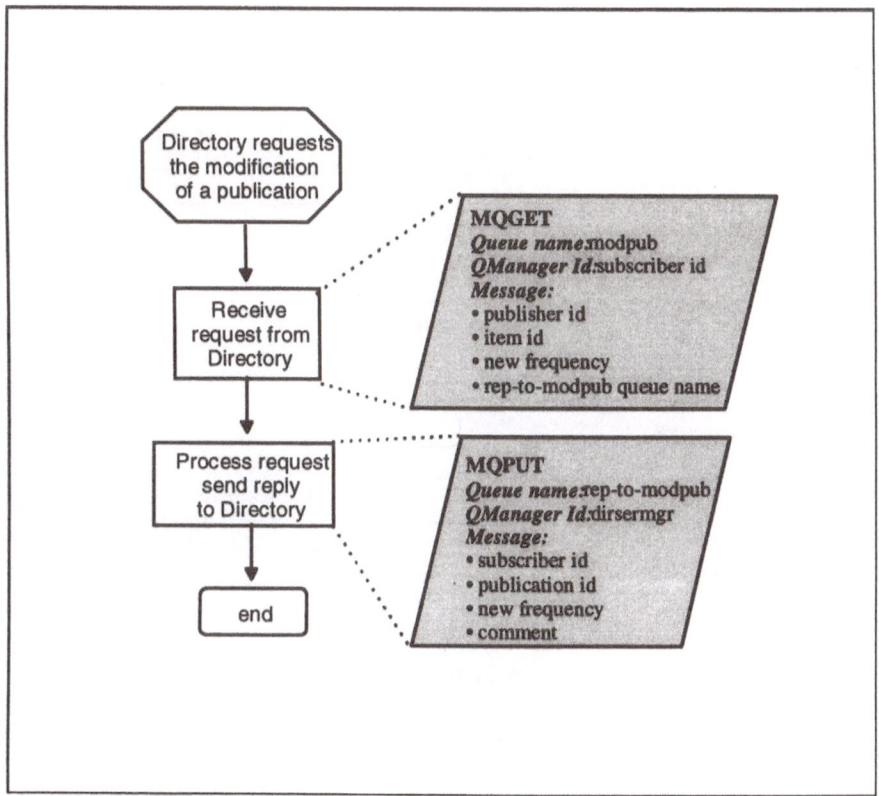

Figure A2.32: Subscriber processes the modification to a publication

rep-to-deldom queue

Queue manager: publisher or subscriber

(This section relates to Figure 9.11)

This queue receives reply messages from the Directory to a domain intending to leave the Federation. Figure A2.33 shows how the Directory manages the deletion of a domain from the Federation. Figure A 2.34 shows the domain's view.

1. Answer for Yes or No.

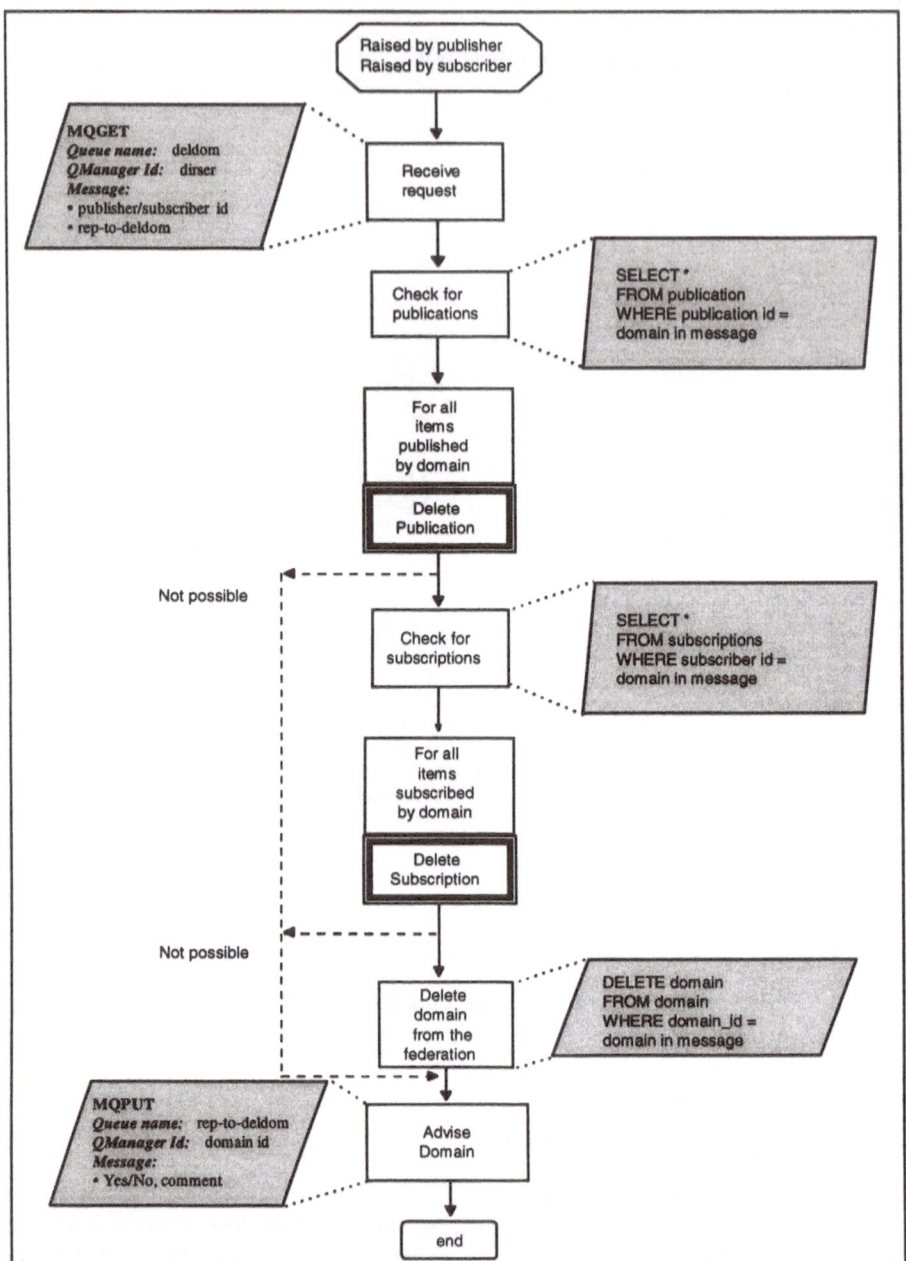

Figure A2.33: Directory processes a domain request to leave the Federation

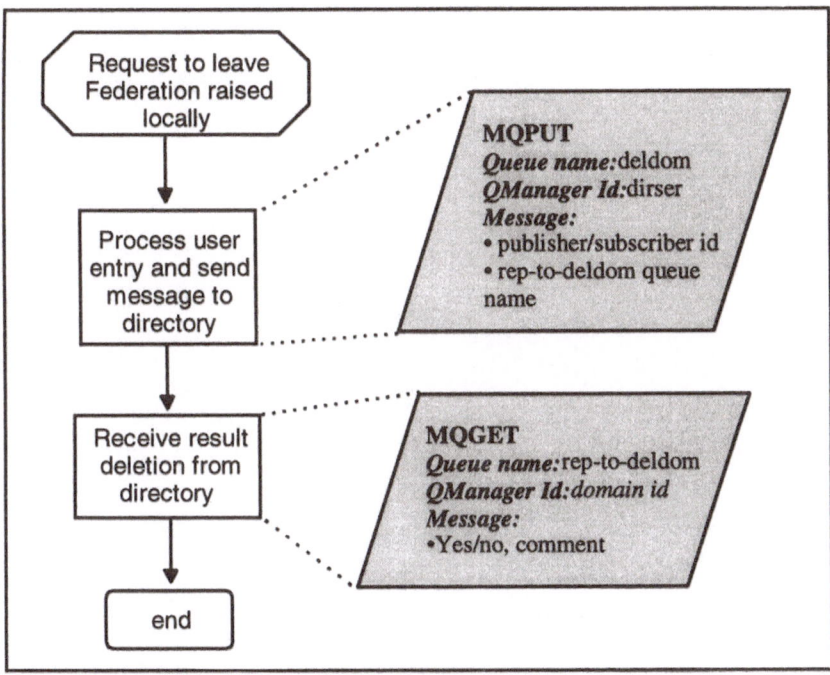

Figure A2.34: Domain requests to leave the Federation

References

Abwod, G., Allen, R. and Garlan, D. (1993) "Using Style to Understand Descriptions of Software Architecture", *ACM Software Engineering Notes*, December.

ANSA (1993) *The ANSA Naming Model*, ANSA, February.

Birrell, A.D. and Nelson, B.J. (1984) "Implementing Remote Procedure Calls", *ACM Transactions on Computer Systems*, pp. 39-59, February.

Boasson, M. (1995) "The Artistry of Software Architecture", *IEEE Software*, November 1995.

Booch, G. (1994) *Object–oriented Design with Applications*, Second Edition, Addison-Wesley, Reading MA.

Breslin, J. and Tashenberg, C.B. (1978) *Distributed Processing Systems End of the Mainframe Era*, Amacom.

Butler Group (1994) *Client/Server Strategies and Technology Vols 1 and 2*, Butler Group, UK.

Coulouris, G. Dollimore, J. and Kindberg, T. (1994) *Distributed* Systems, Second Edition, Addison-Wesley, Reading, MA.

Cyert, R. and March, J. (1963) *A Behavioural Theory of the Firm*, Prentice-Hall, Englewood Cliffs, NJ.

Davenport, T.H. (1993) *Process Innovation*, HBS Press/McGraw-Hill, New York.

Davenport, T.H., Eccles, R.G, Prusak, L. (1992) "Information Politics", *Sloan Management Review*, Fall.

Davenport, T.H. and Short, J.E. (1990) "The New Industrial Engineering: Information Technology and Business Process Redesign", *Sloan Management Review*, Summer.

Drucker, P. (1988) "The Coming of the New Organization", *Harvard Business Review*, January-February.

Duchessi, P., Chengalur-Smith, I. (1998) "Client/Server Benefits, Problems, Best Practices", *Communications of the ACM*, Vol. 41, No. 5, May.

El-Riwini, H. and Hamilton, S. (1995) "Object Technology, A Virtual Roundtable", *Computer*, October.

Enslow, P.H. (1991) "What is a Distributed Data Processing System?" in Ananda, A.L. and Sirinivasan, B. (eds.) *Distributed Computing Systems: Concepts and Structures*, IEEE Computer Society Press.

Fenton, N. (1991) *Software Metrics: A Rigorous Approach*, Chapman & Hall, London.

Finkelstein, C. (1989) *An Introduction to Information Engineering: From Strategic Planning to Information Systems*, Addison-Wesley, Reading, MA.

Gamma, E., Helm, R., Johnson, R. and Vlissides, J. (1994) *Design Patterns: Elements of Reusable Object-Oriented Software Architecture*, Addison-Wesley.

Garlan, D., Allen, R. and Ockerbloom, J. (1995) "Architectural Mismatch: Why Reuse is so Hard", *IEEE Software*, November.

Garlan D. and Perry, D.E. (1995) "Introduction to the Special Issue on Software Architecture", *IEEE Transactions on Software Engineering*, April.

Gerloff, E. A. (1985) *Organizational Theory and Design: A Strategic Approach to Management*, McGraw-Hill, New York.

Giddens, A. (1984) *The Constitution of Society: Outline of the Theory of Structuration*, University of California Press, Berkeley.

Goldner, F. (1970) "The Division of Labour, Process and Power", in Zald, M. (ed.) *Power in Organizations*, Vanderbilt University Press.

Greiner, L.E. (1979) "A Recent History of Organizational Behavior" in Kerr, S. (ed.) *Organizational Behaviour*, Grid Publishing, Inc., Columbus, OH.

Hammer, M. (1990) "Re-engineering Work: Don't Automate, Obliterate", *Harvard Business Review*, July-August.

Hammer, M. and Champy, J. (1993) *Re-engineering the Corporation*, HarperBusiness, a division of Harper-Collins Publishers, New York.

Hammer, M. and Mangurian, G.E. (1987) "The Changing Value of Communications Technology", *Sloan Management Review*, Winter.

Hesselgrave (1990) "Considerations for Building Distributed TP Systems on UNIX System V", *1990 UniForum Conference Proceedings*.

Hill, C.W.L. (1984) "Organizational Structure, the Development of the Firm and Business Behaviour", in Pickering, J.F. and Cockerill, A.J. (eds.) *Economic Management of the Firm*, Phillip Allen, Oxford.

Jacobson, I. *et al.* (1992) *Object Oriented Software Engineering – A Use Case Driven Approach*, Addison-Wesley.

Jacobson, I. *et al.* (1994) *The Object Advantage – Re-engineering the Organisation with Objects*, Addison-Wesley.

Johansson, H.J., McHugh, P., Pendlebury, A.J. and Wheeler, W.A. (1993) *Business Process Re-Engineering, Break Point Strategies for Market Dominance*, John Wiley & Sons, New York.

Johnson, R. and Foote, B. (1988) "Designing Reusable Classes", *Journal of Object-Oriented Programming*, vol. 1(2).

Keen, P. (1991) *Shaping the Future: Business Design through Information Technology*, Harvard Business School Press, Boston.

Lewis, T.G. (1995) "Where is Client/Server Software Headed?" *Computer*, April.

Lorin, H. (1988) *Aspects of Distributed Computer Systems*, Second Edition, John Wiley & Sons, New York.

Malik, N.A. (1996) "The Three-Tier Client/Server Model", in Bettone, G. *et al.* (eds.) *Tricks of the Visual Basic 4 Gurus*, SAMS Publishing, Indiana.

Martin, J. (1981) *Design and Strategy for Distributed Data Processing*, Prentice-Hall, Englewood Cliffs, NJ.

Mintzberg, H. (1983): *Power in and around Organizations*, Prentice-Hall, Englewood Cliffs, NJ.

Orfali, R. and Harkey, D. (1995) "Client/Server with Distributed Objects", *BYTE*, April.

Orfali, R. Harkey, D. and Edwards, J. (1994) *Essential Client/Server Guide*, Van Nostrand Reinhold, New York.

Orfali, R. Harkey, D. and Edwards, J. (1996) *The Essential Distributed Objects Survival Guide*, J. Wiley & Sons, New York.

Perrow, C. (1973) *Complex Organizations: A Critical Essay*, Scott, Freeman, and Company, Glenview, IL.

Perry, D. and Wolf, A. (1992) "Foundations for the Study of Software Architecture", *Software Engineering Notes*, October.

Pfeffer, J. (1986) *Power in Organizations*, HarperBusiness, New York.

Pressman, R. (1994) (adapted by Ince, D.) *Software Engineering, A Practitioner's Approach*, Third Edition, McGraw-Hill, New York.

Rockart, J. and Short, J. (1991) in Scott-Morton, M. (1991) *The Corporation of the 1990s: Information Technology and Organisational Transformation*, Oxford University Press, Oxford.

Rumbaugh, J. (1991) "Object-Oriented Modeling and Design", Prentice-Hall, Englewood Cliffs, NJ.

Scott-Morton, M. (1991) *The Corporation of the 1990s: Information Technology and Organisational Transformation*, Oxford University Press, Oxford.

Shaw, M. (1995) "Comparing Architectural Design Styles", *IEEE Software*, November.

Silverman, D. (1970) *The Theory of Organizations*, Heinemann, London.

Silverman, D. and Jones, J. (1976) *Organizational Work: The Language of Grading*, Collier McMillan.

Sinha, A. (1992) "Client-Server Computing", *Communications of the ACM*, Vol. 35, No. 7.

UML (1997) "Unified Modelling Language Version 1.1", UML Partners, Santa Clara, CA.

Wijegunaratne, I. Socic, M. and Chow, B. (1994) "An Architecture for Client/Server Application Software", *Australian Computer Society Journal*, Vol. 26, No. 2, May.

Wirfs-Brock, R., Wilkerson, B. and Wiener, L. (1990) "Designing Object-Oriented Software", Prentice-Hall, Englewood Cliffs, NJ.

Yourdon, E. and Constantine, L. (1979) *Structured Design*, Prentice-Hall, Englewood Cliffs, NJ.

Zand, D. (1981) *Information, Organization, and Power*, McGraw-Hill, New York.

Index